Smarter Than Their Machines

JIM,
GET WELL
AND LETS PLAY
SOME GOLF.

BEST

ACM Books

Editor in Chief

M. Tamer Özsu, *University of Waterloo*

ACM Books is a new series of high-quality books for the computer science community, published by ACM in collaboration with Morgan & Claypool Publishers. ACM Books publications are widely distributed in both print and digital formats through booksellers and to libraries (and library consortia) and individual ACM members via the ACM Digital Library platform.

Smarter than Their Machines: Oral Histories of Pioneers in Interactive Computing
John Cullinane, *Northeastern University; Mossavar-Rahmani Center for Business and Government, John F. Kennedy School of Government, Harvard University*
2015

A Framework for Scientific Discovery through Video Games
Seth Cooper, *University of Washington*
2014

Trust Extension as a Mechanism for Secure Code Execution on Commodity Computers
Bryan Jeffrey Parno, *Microsoft Research*
2014

Embracing Interference in Wireless Systems
Shyamnath Gollakota, *University of Washington*
2014

Smarter Than Their Machines

Oral Histories of Pioneers in Interactive Computing

John Cullinane

Northeastern University

Mossavar-Rahmani Center for Business and Government,
John F. Kennedy School of Government,
Harvard University

ACM Books #4

Smarter Than Their Machines: Oral Histories of Pioneers in Interactive Computing

John Cullinane

books.acm.org
www.morganclaypool.com

ISBN: 978-1-62705-553-6   hardcover
ISBN: 978-1-62705-550-5   paperback
ISBN: 978-1-62705-551-2   ebook
ISBN: 978-1-62705-552-9   ePub
Series ISSN: (to come)

DOIs: 10.1145/2663015 Book
        10.1145/2663015.2663016/ Preface
        10.1145/2663015.2663017/ Introduction
        10.1145/2663015.2663018/ Chapter 1
        10.1145/2663015.2663019/ Chapter 2
        10.1145/2663015.2663020/ Chapter 3
        10.1145/2663015.2663021/ Chapter 4
        10.1145/2663015.2663022/ Chapter 5
        10.1145/2663015.2663023/ Chapter 6
        10.1145/2663015.2663024/ Chapter 7
        10.1145/2663015.2663025/ Chapter 8

A publication in the ACM Books series, #4
Editor in Chief: M. Tamer Özsu, *University of Waterloo*

First Edition

10 9 8 7 6 5 4 3 2 1

To, my wife, Diddy, who, when I mentioned the idea of forming a company to specialize in software, responded with, "Go ahead and do it. If it doesn't work out, I can always get a job."

Contents

Preface **xi**

Introduction **1**

Chapter 1 **Two Entrepreneurs with the Same Idea 9**
> Dr. Herbert W. Robinson (CEIR)
> Sam Wyly (University Computing Company)

Chapter 2 **Two Computer Designers Who Thought Big 31**
> Richard Bloch (Honeywell 800, 400, 200)
> Gene Amdahl (IBM System/360)

Chapter 3 **Timesharing in Academia and ARPA 53**
> J.C.R. Licklider
> Ivan Sutherland

Chapter 4 **Packet Switching and ARPANET 87**
> Lawrence G. Roberts
> Robert Kahn

Photographs **121**

Chapter 5 **Artificial Intelligence and Changes at MIT and DARPA 137**
> Marvin L. Minsky
> Michael Dertouzos

Chapter 6 **Creating Something Great in Unusual Places 171**
> Joseph F. Traub (Carnegie Mellon, Columbia University)

Chapter 7   **Creating the Industry's First Successful Software Products Company**   **187**
John Cullinane

Chapter 8   **Summary**   **201**

Author's Biography   **203**

Preface

I was quite astounded to come across the oral histories of so many computer industry pioneers at the Charles Babbage Institute (CBI), University of Minnesota. They included the oral histories of people I had worked for long ago, such as Dr. Herbert W. Robinson and George Dick at CEIR, Inc. I even discovered my own recorded oral history there! Consequently, I began reading them and found them fascinating. What many of them showed was how government, academia, and industry worked together to create the computer industry. Initially, it was to save America in World War II with new weapons, such as the atom bomb. New machines were needed and they had to be programmed to do the necessary computations. This is where my friend, Richard Bloch, comes in. He was the first programmer of the first programmable machine, the Mark I at Harvard, but he had the whole machine to himself. What was needed was interactive computing where many people could use a computer for a wide range of applications. I wouldn't get involved with computers until much later when they began to migrate from academia to industry.

The more I read these oral histories, the more convinced I became that these pioneers had much to offer today's leaders in industry, academia, and government on how to get difficult things done. As a Fellow at the Center for Business and Government at Harvard University, I got a good sense of how our government operates. It often starts with an idea that makes its way into a paper or book that then finds its way into a political campaign. If the candidate wins, it can become the law of the land. This book contains such an idea.

The history of computing shows that it took government, industry, and academia working together in an effective way to create computing as we know it today. America's democracy is now the oldest in the world, so repeating this idea is very important. That's where the oral histories of the pioneers that led to interactive computing come in. Some once helped save our democracy and, in the process, created the computer industry, which led to the Internet—both unanticipated results. It's possible to read in their oral histories how they did it and how the cooperation between government, industry, and academia actually worked. This book is a personal "walk" because my company, which was the industry's first successful software products company, provided the database foundation for many interactive computer systems for industry, government, and academia.

Acknowledgments

I would like to thank Tom Misa, Director of CBI, for his great support and help with this book. Also, I would like to thank Jeffrey Yost for his suggestions, as well as the excellent oral history he did of my own experiences with Cullinane Corporation. Of course, Martha Burnham, my long-time assistant, was very helpful in many ways, as usual.

Introduction

This book has its origins in an Internet search I did on Richard Bloch, a true computer industry pioneer, and a good friend. I was surprised at the results. There wasn't much information about him until I came across his oral history located in the archives at the Charles Babbage Institute (CBI), University of Minnesota. It was fascinating to read because I realized how little I really knew of his background as a computer industry pioneer. Maybe that's because he was never into discussing what he did yesterday. Richard was really an entrepreneur, as well as a brilliant renaissance man, who was interested in the big ideas of tomorrow. In the process of accessing his oral history I discovered that there were about 300 others at CBI, including my own. Some were individuals from my distant corporate past.

When I read some of these oral histories, I was struck by the fact that they were much more than interesting personal histories that occasionally brought up names of people or companies that I knew something about. They contained important messages that are as pertinent today as they were then because they were all about getting things done against great odds. They could even help save our democracy, as they did then. Thus, the reason for the book is two-fold. One is to pay homage to a few great pioneers, such as Richard Bloch, who may otherwise be forgotten but, better still, to replay their messages that so resonated with me, and therefore will hopefully resonate with the reader as well. Some of these messages are as follows:

- One imaginative person can create something great in the most unlikely of places.
- One person can succeed with exactly the same idea when another fails.
- Most new ideas require getting around a "system" to succeed.
- Individuals can do remarkable things no matter how young, or experienced, they may be.

- Government, industry, and academia working together can do great things, such as create the computer industry.

- There are always unanticipated results to any action.

In essence, this book is a personal "walk" through the history of the computer industry as I participated in and witnessed it. To me, the industry has been comprised of three eras. The first was the "computation" era. This is illustrated by what Richard Bloch was doing at Harvard on the Mark I computer and what was happening at other universities. He was using a new machine to do the necessary computations for John von Neumann as part of the Manhattan Project in order to make an atom bomb in World War II, hence the name "computers." They were, in essence, saving our democracy. The next era is what I call the "data processing" era. This is when computer manufacturers began selling computers to industry primarily for data processing, which, initially, they were not well suited to do. Richard Bloch and Gene Amdahl were major contributors in designing these computers. The third era is what I call the "interactive computing" era, which we are currently in. There have been many tools and/or names involved in it over the years such as timesharing, on-line query, client/server, data mining, search engines, email, word processors, spreadsheets, social media, Big Data, mobile phones, etc. Everyone has always wanted more access to computerized data, whether they were in industry, government, or academia, and also to be able to communicate with peers about their work more effectively. In other words, it was all about interacting with the computer to make this possible.

In the process I learned what some of the great computer industry pioneers had to say in their own words about what they did, and how they did it, that led to the computer industry as we know it today. The reason I found this so remarkable was because there were so many parallels between what they had to cope with and what I had to do in order to succeed. In fact, in many ways I operated just as they did: find the best people you can, people that you can really trust—regardless of age or experience—give them lots of responsibility, and then help them to succeed in every way you can. Like many of the pioneers, I had to figure out what to do because there was no one to ask, as no one before had ever done what I was trying to do.

I also learned that it often takes the full cooperation of industry, academia, and government to solve the major problems of the day facing our country. The pioneers took this for granted. Where else were they going to get the money? Most importantly, they learned how to cope with the great inhibiter of new ideas, namely, the "system," just as I had to. The system is made up of barriers of entrenched interests, sometimes well intentioned, that almost always stand in the way of undertaking new approaches necessary to solve problems at any level, from the President of the United States on down to the lowest on the management food chain.

This is what makes the oral histories of the computer industry pioneers so compelling to read from the perspective of an entrepreneur. Amazingly, some pioneers are still at it today. For example, Ivan Sutherland, the father of computer graphics, and his wife, Marly, are working at Portland State University to get around the computer chip industry with their new asynchronous chips. Others are taking different approaches to solving problems such as "crossing the valley of death," a huge challenge for healthcare technology startups. Crossing the valley of death means generating enough business to stay alive.

Tom Misa, Director of CBI, took a keen interest in this work and has been very helpful with his encouragement and suggestions. Since he is an experienced author with numerous computer history titles, I have tried to implement his suggestions as best as I could. Jeffrey Yost, Associate Director, who actually conducted the interview for my oral history, was also very helpful with his encouragement and the suggestion regarding the dialog format of the book. Also, needless, to say, with no oral histories at CBI there would be no book.

My personal walk down the computer industry road began in the 1950's at Arthur D. Little, Inc. (ADL), the world's leading industrial research consulting firm of the time. I was a lowly co-op student from Northeastern University when ADL installed a Burroughs 205, the first commercially available computer in New England, right next to my office. Eventually, I would learn to run it and the experience would open many doors in the years to come because I was there at the beginning of the computer industry as it went mainstream. Yet, little did I know, I was in a microcosm of the great computing debate that many computer industry pioneers were engaged in at the time, namely, how to design a single computer that would solve both the data processing requirements of industry as well as the problems of engineers and scientists in academia. For example, ADL's computer ran its payroll and project billing systems mostly at night, which was traditional punched card data processing for industry. Yet, just upstairs, ADL's Operations Research Group wanted the computer for totally different applications, such as solving engineering and scientific problems for clients. Ironically, computer manufacturers would never succeed in designing the all-purpose computer. Regardless, all of them used the computer in a "batch" mode at the time, a horribly inefficient use of personal time. Everyone had to get in line. If there was a bug in the program, a programmer had to go to the end of the line and start all over again. Scientists and engineers in academia also wanted to share information with their colleagues. Batch processing was so onerous that some very bright and entrepreneurial academics set out to solve the problem with key financial help from the U.S. government. Again, these were all steps to interactive computing which led to the Internet and the remarkable mobile phone technology that we all use today. We have come a long way in interactive computing.

Eventually, I would play a role in the industry when I founded Cullinane Corporation. It would become the industry's first successful software products company specializing in database software, the foundation for many interactive computer systems for industry, government, and academia. Industry gurus at the time were skeptical: they said there was no future in software, it couldn't be done, that others had tried and failed, and they predicted that I would as well. This is the system at work. I came close to failing, but I learned how to get around the system and the "not invented here syndrome" of the time in order to survive and eventually prosper. In the process, we demonstrated to Wall Street, venture capitalists, investors, and entrepreneurs that a company could make money selling software as a product. The resulting IPO was so successful that many took notice, and, in my opinion, this was really the start of the software products industry.

When I was beginning to move on from the company in 1983, I changed the name from Cullinane Corporation to Cullinet Software, Inc., in recognition that all computers would work together in a network in the future. Ironically, the industry media considered it a controversial name change, and I took some "heat" for it at the time. However, it seemed obvious to me that, eventually, all computers would work together. In fact, we were already doing it. Recognizing the obvious before anyone else makes you a visionary. Of course, I had no idea about the coming of the Internet.

One challenge regarding this book was choosing which of the over 300 CBI oral histories to use, and how much of each history to actually include. I decided to abridge them when appropriate. Anyone wishing to read an entire oral history can visit the CBI website: www.cbi.umn.edu/oh. However, since this book is a personal walk through the history of the industry, I selected Dr. Herbert W. Robinson's oral history to present first because he had a large impact on my career. His company was the Corporation for Economic and Industrial Research, Inc. (CEIR), the first computer consulting and services firm to have a public offering as well as a "hot" stock on Wall Street. Dr. Robinson was a scientist and visionary but, unfortunately, not so successful with implementation. This is a classic syndrome in the computer industry. CEIR's high-flying shares, inevitably, crashed after rising from $6 to $96. New management was brought in by investors, but it did not work. Ironically, as a new employee, I was a beneficiary of much of the company's financial turmoil because I received all sorts of management experience at a very young age. I learned very quickly that no one in the company seemed to know what to do, so I just did what I thought would work, and it did. I would never have had access to such experience in a well-managed company. From it came the all-important confidence, which is always a big asset.

The second oral history is that of Sam Wyly, whom I paired with Dr. Robinson because Sam had exactly the same idea for a company as did Dr. Robinson. However, Sam brought it to life with the skills of a great entrepreneur. He would even buy one of CEIR's excess computers at a bargain price to help him do it. As a result, he had a successful business overnight, University Computing Company (UCC), which ultimately would make him a multi-billionaire. At the same time he promoted something called DATRAN, a data transmission system for industry which didn't work out well, even though it was a very important and much-needed service. In this case, he was the visionary looking to introduce interactive computing for his customer base so that they could avoid driving long distances across Texas to get to his data center. He invested a fortune in time and money, but couldn't get around the voice-dominated communications industry of the time, which, in this case, was the system. He learned, as all entrepreneurs eventually learn, bringing good ideas to life is the hard part.

My next choices for oral histories were Richard Bloch and Gene Amdahl. Both were great computer designers and enthusiastic entrepreneurs who thought big. Richard designed Honeywell's 800, 400, and 200 lines for industry, and Gene would design IBM's groundbreaking 360 line. Richard wanted to go head-to-head with IBM's very important 360 line with a whole new generation of computers, but he couldn't get any computer manufacturer to back his ideas with the necessary $500 million investment. Eventually, interactive computing would get a big boost with the introduction of the MVS (Multiple Virtual Storage) operating system by IBM.

Following these oral histories are those of J.C.R. Licklider and Ivan Sutherland, then Larry Roberts and Robert Kahn. Much of what they were focused on was interactive computing for academia vs. data processing for industry and getting the funds for it. They had to invent and implement new technology, such as packet switching, to get around the communications industry that had thwarted Sam Wyly. This would eventually lead to the Internet. They all had pretty much a common goal: to make computers easier to use, with more accessible data, and with the opportunity to share information across different platforms and different universities. To a remarkable degree, all this was taking place not far from my corporate offices—at MIT (Massachusetts Institute of Technology), Harvard, and BBN (Bolt, Beranek and Newman), a company that was referred to as the third university in Cambridge. Of course, DARPA (Defense Advanced Research Projects Agency) located in Washington, was the great source of the funds to make it all possible.

Michael Dertouzos came along later as very important changes were underway at MIT and DARPA that would have a big impact, one still felt to this very day. Also, he had an excellent sense of where the industry was headed. I paired him with Marvin Minsky, whose focus was on artificial intelligence. I think Michael Dertouzos' views of artificial intelligence, as well as the position of computer sciences at MIT, along with what DARPA was like at that time, are really important. Big changes were in the air, and he had a great ability for putting it into perspective. Space didn't allow me to include the oral histories of other major players such as Wes Clark, Vint Cerf, John McCarthy, Fernando Corbató, and numerous others, but they can be located on the CBI website: www.cbi.umn.edu/oh.

I realize that the histories I selected have a bias to the Cambridge–Washington axis and that there was great work going on at other universities, laboratories, and companies across the country and internationally. However, I was in Cambridge at the time and it was difficult not to have this sense of things from my perspective. I can't help but feel that those in Cambridge, including Harvard, MIT, and BBN, were the driving forces as they reached out to key players, or provided talent that migrated to various institutions across the country. Also, I did not include international oral histories, even though there are some very important ones. For example, when it came to packet switching, Donald Davies in England did major early work after becoming aware of the communications problem at MIT. However, he lacked the necessary government funding at the time. Larry Roberts of DARPA would take advantage of his work. Louis Pouzin of France was another who was involved in the problem in a very significant way. The beauty of reading the CBI oral histories is that they provide connections to other key contributors, such as these that I didn't know, because the computer industry at the time was a pretty small community where everyone knew each other and "social capital" was paramount.

I included Joseph Traub's oral history because I have always been fascinated with how good things can emerge in not so obvious locations. I saw this happen many times as my company's database software would be installed in what I thought were unusual places. I would learn that there was usually one person there who was making it happen. On the other hand, often, nothing was happening in places that seemed like it should. I was always curious as to why Carnegie Mellon University was ranked with the great institutions in computer sciences, such as MIT and Stanford. After all, Pittsburgh at the time wasn't Cambridge, Chicago, Michigan, or California. However, pioneering work done by others in artificial intelligence, such as Allen Newell and Herbert Simon, certainly provided an outstanding foundation for Joseph Traub to build on at Carnegie. He took over from some excellent people and made it happen. It's another classic example of how one good person can make great things happen in unexpected places, and we have his oral history to explain how he did it. I think it serves as an inspiration for anyone trying to get something done despite obstacles.

There are always obstacles, whether one is in Cambridge, Palo Alto, or Pittsburgh. But, it can be done. My company was a perfect example. With some trepidation, I concluded with my own oral history. As background, I don't think of myself as an industry pioneer in the same sense as some of these academically brilliant scientists and engineers. I didn't invent any breakthrough technology, such as packet switching. Yet, I did create the industry's first successful software products company when it was said it couldn't be done. In fact, as a member of various panels at industry shows, I would be on the receiving end of much ridicule from other panel members for attempting it. That's because the computer industry had a hardware focus at the time. They sold "boxes." They even claimed that all software would be built into microcode in the future and would just go away. What I had to prove was that a company could make money selling software as a product. It wasn't easy, but I did it when others had failed. Today, people would marvel at such an industry mindset because since then, with few exceptions, the industry has been all about software.

Ironically, some of the software problems associated with major system implementations, such as health care, have reappeared of late and are worse than ever. Incredibly, government agencies are back to re-inventing the software wheel. Only the well-paid consultants benefit. Not re-inventing the software wheel is where my company came in. In the introduction to my oral history, I focus on some of the technical accomplishments of the company which, in retrospect, were remarkable. What makes them pertinent is that packet switching technology implemented by Robert Kahn, Larry Roberts, and others at DARPA, would be key. It would have a big influence on the design of our database/data communications products and would be very important in helping us compete with IBM, and other strong companies in the business, to become the technology and business leader in database software.

Usually, technology companies are either good at technology or good at sales. We were unique in that we were very good at both. In fact, when asked by a Wall Street analyst what our greatest strength was, my answer was that we had no weaknesses. Of course in time this would change, but there was a moment when we really had it all together, and it was fun to be a part of. In fact, one competitor said our customer base was a "cult." It was because we genuinely cared about them, and they knew it.

In Chapter 8, the summary, the major purpose of this book is to remind people in high places, and others at all levels of the chain of command, that they will always have to find ways to get around the system to implement new ideas, just as the computer industry pioneers did, and I did. However, I also discuss how ideas often become the law of the land and include one possibility to address our country's problems—a "Domestic DARPA." If, in the process, I can recognize some very important computer industry pioneers, and point to many others via CBI's oral histories, then that's a major bonus.

Two Entrepreneurs with the Same Idea

Dr. Herbert W. Robinson (CEIR)
Sam Wyly (University Computing Company)

Introduction

Dr. Herbert W. Robinson was a visionary. His idea in the 1950's was to provide large-scale computers and software-related consulting services to industry in major cities around the United States and England. CEIR expanded very fast, irrespective of demand. This wasn't the 1990's and the e-commerce boom when venture capitalists were very enamored with this "first in" strategy. Demand was something that was going to take time to create.

"Computer services" became the hot new term on Wall Street in the 1950's and CEIR rode the wave with a public offering, the first such firm to do so. Its stock zoomed from $6 to $96, despite being unprofitable. When I joined the company in 1961 its shares were selling at $44 on their way to $4. Managerially, things were very frenzied in the company, but I was to be a major beneficiary of this chaos as I went from sales trainee, to salesman, to sales manager, and then (Acting) Center Director of the Boston computer center, all within not much more than a year. The center featured a large-scale IBM 7090 mainframe computer with a staff of about 75 consultants, programmers, sales people, etc. CEIR would be considered a batch operation where programs and data, in a punched card format, would be handed in and run on a first-come, first-served basis.

The company brought in a new management team, some of whom had spent 19 years with IBM, to turn things around. Unfortunately, they turned out to be a poor match for the problems at hand. For one thing, most IBM executives of the era were not trained or experienced in managing relatively small companies where cash flow is extremely important, particularly, in a turn-around situation. I would learn much about the computer industry and how technology companies often worked because CEIR would be the first computer company that I knew that had a fantastic takeoff on Wall Street and then crashed and burned. Many others would follow, always with the same story but different names. Without realizing it at the time, I learned just about everything, good and bad, about running a high-tech startup from my experiences at CEIR, all by 1964, and I wasn't even out of my 20's.

Sam Wyly appeared on the scene around this time. He saw an opportunity for a computer services company in the Control Data Corporation 1604 computer that CEIR was selling at a bargain price. He bought the machine and installed it at Southern Methodist University where the faculty and students could use it during the night shift and on weekends. They were more than pleased to get this powerful computer because they had no money to buy a new one. He then sold the remaining time to major oil exploration companies in the Dallas area for engineering applications. This is where Wyly's was different than most other service bureaus of the time. They were business application focused, but he focused on engineering clients using the FORTRAN (FORmula TRANslation) language, which was much easier to sell and support. However, it was still a batch-oriented, punch card-driven center. Nevertheless, he had a successful business, literally overnight, using a computer that at the time CEIR couldn't give away. This would be the start of University Computing Company (UCC), which would take him down the road to being a multi-billionaire. Of special interest is his promotion of the DATRAN data transmission system for industry as a major step forward for the time in interactive computing. It's a perfect illustration of trying to get around the voice-focused communications industry of the day. He spent an enormous amount of time and money trying to do it, but failed. This critical problem will show up again in Larry Roberts' oral history.

CEIR's troubles seemed to have a way of helping others, such as Sam Wyly, succeed. For example, Project MAC (Project on Mathematics and Computation), MIT's major time-sharing initiative, needed office space and a computer room for its large-scale GE computer in Cambridge. CEIR had two floors at 545 Technology Square, a big new development right behind MIT. One floor was designed to accommodate a large-scale computer; the other floor would be offices. CEIR wanted to get rid of the space, just as they wanted to get rid of the CDC 1604 computer. Professor Robert Fano, head of Project MAC, jumped at this incredible opportunity to solve Project MAC's space problem.

Dr. Robinson's and Sam Wyly's oral histories provide the reader who is not familiar with corporate startups with a perfect example of how two people can address the same opportunity and have dramatically different results. In a few words, Sam Wyly was a brilliant entrepreneur and Dr. Robinson wasn't. Or, said another way, good ideas are easy to come by, but bringing them to life is very difficult. However, both companies demonstrate the need for interactive computing that academia was working on at the time with DARPA's support.

AN INTERVIEW WITH

Herbert W. Robinson

Conducted by
Bruce H. Bruemmer
July 13, 1988
Bethesda, Maryland

purl.umn.edu/107609

Photo courtesy of Charles Babbage
Institute (CBI 50 154)

Bruemmer: I'd like to get some background information from you. Are you a British national?

Robinson: No, I am a U.S. citizen, but I was born in England and took a London degree in economics with a special subject of mathematical statistics, and first-class honors degree, got a fellowship to London School of Economics and took a Ph.D. Then I was the senior researcher of the Oxford Institute of Statistics. I also got an Oxford Ph.D., and the war broke out just as I finished the second Ph.D. It turned out that a physicist from Oxford was a personal friend of Churchill—Professor Lindeman of Christ Church. He was invited to set up a small brain trust of young people to help Churchill in the Admiralty. They thought of me because I was one of the very few people at that time that combined mathematics, economics, and mathematical statistics in one person. There were very few of us in those days. That was 1939. So I joined Lindeman and we ended up with about six or seven young people who were between 25 and 30 years old. When Churchill became Prime Minister, we went over to his private office. So I was there doing quick and dirty studies on the war effort and military activities and so on.

Then America got into the war in 1941, and I happened to be specializing in that area on lend-lease. That was before America got into the war, helping Britain with lending and leasing equipment, ships, and other things. So I happened to be quite knowledgeable about America. I studied its military potential and that sort of thing. In England they decided to combine all the separate production departments of the three services—army, navy, air force—into one, called the Ministry of Production. I was loaned as assistant to Lord Layton, who was the personal advisor to Lord Beaver-brook, the Minister. It turned out that a short time later everybody began to think it was desirable to coordinate world production and world distribution of scarce items. So an agency was set up in Washington called the Combined Production and Resources Board—British, Canadian, and U.S. I was sent over as a staff member of that organization.

That's how I came to America in 1943. I fell in love with America. I emigrated to America as soon as the war was over and I could be released from what was called the "control of engagements"—which meant you couldn't leave your job. After working as Chief, Economic Order Trends in the Veterans Administration, for a year I was in Poland as Economic Advisor to the UNRRA Mission to Poland—the relief organization. When I came back I was in the World Bank until about 1951. Then I joined the Defense Production Administration. In view of my background in the British war effort, I was appointed as Deputy Chief of Foreign Requirements. Of course, that ended at about the end of 1953. So I was at a loose end wondering what I would do next. In the course of looking around I went to the National Science Foundation and they had heard of a company that had a contract with the Air Force involving operations research, model building, and that type of thing. Somebody there gave my name to the people that were heading the company. So I got involved in that. It turned out that there were three major movers, one of which was Wassily Leontief, a Nobel prize winner, and . . . there were two other people from the Rand Corporation—that type of people.

• • •

Bruemmer: I think there was a [Air Force] contract moving you into the [CEIR] operation. Were there any competitors in this area at that time?

Robinson: Not at the beginning. Later, Computer Sciences was set up.

Bruemmer: Computer Sciences Corporation?

Robinson: Yes. That was the first real competitor. There were a few smaller ones, and we acquired some of those, as a lot of them were willing to be acquired once they had started up. I think some of our own people left. You see, it was a successful company, and our stock was a hot stock. I really shuddered every time I saw it go up, because I knew the price was ridiculous.

• • •

I had always been attracted to operations research and management science, maybe too much, because it was a very strong side of our business. I may say there were two equal pillars of the business—one was computers and software. The other was all the professional services—economics, statistics, operation research, management science, and their applications. We had a very big crew. We recruited top people. That was the policy right from the beginning, to be top-class. And we started one on our own in England, Corporation for Economic and Industrial Research (CEIR) U.K.

• • •

However, we expanded too fast and we had lost a lot of money. As it turned out, CEIR was a bold idea, but it came too soon. I felt that we needed a huge computer, because it was much more economical to operate. The number of computations per dollar was much higher, so I said, "We've got to have the biggest computers all the time." That was a policy. And we always ordered every new machine that came out. We ordered a raft of them from IBM on the understanding that we'd take them as we needed them. I figured that there would only be room for maybe one computer of that size in a city like Washington, one in New York, one in Los Angeles, and one in San Francisco. Obviously, the costs to set a computer operation up with the staff and everything were enormous. So, what I tried to do was find partners where possible. We got into New York with a partnership with Union Carbide Corporation. We took two floors of their New York building. It was with a [IBM] 709, I believe, and we had 50-50 sharing of cost. In San Francisco we went in with the Del Monte people. In Los Angeles and in Houston we went on our own.

I felt that we had to have the biggest computer; that there was only room for one and we'd better get there first. So we decided to have this big program of expansion. In one of the reports, you will see a chart showing when and where we'd installed the equipment. Anyway, in 18 months we multiplied the business five times. And it was just too fast. We were losing about 10% of sales volume. Obviously there was no way we could judge in advance how much business you'd get on that installation and that group of people. You couldn't predict. There was no experience to go on, really. We were, however, only just missing. That happened for two years; we lost $2 million a year. We were down to almost a negative net worth at the end of one fiscal year, but then we dug ourselves out.

Bruemmer: But the stock brokers seemed very entranced with the computer business, and thought this was going to take off.

Robinson: Yes, they were enchanted with the potential. They used to think of us as another IBM. Of course it was, really. [Ross] Perot really made a big success of the computer services side of it. You now have in this area American Management Systems. You've got Management Science, Incorporated. All of these things that have come into their own in the last 15 or 20 years, we were trying to sell to people that didn't really understand what we were doing and weren't willing to entrust things to. Today they will, and it's accepted. But we had to fight that difficult period of non-acceptance at the beginning.

• • •

Bruemmer: I think George Dick recalled that he was singularly insulted by the [initial] meeting with Control Data Corporation (CDC)?

Robinson: Yes. Well, I also think they were not impressed too much with George and Bob Holland, because they recognized them as kind of pure marketeers. They were wondering what the strength of the company was. I think if you look at Apple and all those companies, the guys that have succeeded have been somehow involved technically. You have to have the technical insight, or else you're really unable to judge. In my personal investment operations today, I will not go into something that is fifty times earnings because of some technically terrific advantage it's supposed to have. I can't judge that; there's no way I can judge it. I feel I'm not qualified to judge if that's good or bad. It could be the greatest thing in the world, but I can't tell. I think they were in that position too, that they just didn't grasp technically what they were doing. They were unable to grasp the basic businesses.

Robinson: Yes, that's another thing. George Dick and Bob Holland did recruit some people, but nearly all of them were not really highly professional people, but marketing people. One successful operation was suggested by a man called Meade; it was a really brilliant idea, and George Dick supported him. One of our biggest problems was the tremendous idleness of professional people. Between contracts, you'd have maybe 30% idle. That was a huge overhead. So, they developed the Institute of Advanced Technology idea. That was great, because it meant these people could go and give courses when they weren't busy. Meade spearheaded that, and he was very good, because he's a good salesman, you see—a good marketing man.

Bruemmer: Now, did CDC [after buying CEIR in 1967] keep you on in some capacity for a while?

Robinson: Yes. I was kept on first as an assistant to the head of marketing, Bob Schmidt. So I just did any odd jobs he wanted. They used me a lot for, you might say, public relations. For instance, they were asked to give a paper in Johannesburg, so I went and gave a paper on data storage and retrieval. So I was completely cut off from it, which I didn't mind. It was their company; they bought it.

Bruemmer: Had CDC not purchased you, where do you think your next move would have been? You mentioned that time-sharing, at least, became important for one center.

Robinson: The rest of that paper was a plan.

Bruemmer: And one other thing, I assume [CDC's Bill] Norris went looking for CEIR?

Robinson: Yes. He wanted to see me one day, and I took him to the Cosmos Club here. We had dinner and we kept talking, and he said he definitely wanted to acquire CEIR. What was my attitude? He felt that was important, whether I would go along with it. So I said, "Well, if the price is right, I would go along with it," because I thought there were some pluses to joining up with CDC. We agreed on a price.

· · ·

Robinson: Oh, I think I know an area, but I don't know how to promote it. You see, the computer and its capabilities has only begun to just touch the surface of the applications. I think a tremendous application will be in the home. It really isn't explored much today. You look at our house. There isn't one computer. I don't think there's a computer in the house, other than the one we use for investment. Yet I have a feeling that there are applications in the home where you could have computers attached to individual things. I tried to interest [CDC's William R. "Bill"] Keye, who was an engineering type, way back in about 1970. They were thinking of acquiring a machine company. I went to see him and I said, "What I have in mind is, can't you build into a machine tool a computer so that you can actually program what the tool will do, and isn't that a field where CDC and this other company could start new products altogether? Really, automation, I guess." But he didn't seem at all enthused about the idea.

AN INTERVIEW WITH

Photo courtesy of Charles Babbage
Institute (CBI subject file)

Sam Wyly

Conducted by
David Allison
December 6, 2002
Washington, DC

purl.umn.edu/107720

Allison: I am David Allison at the Smithsonian National Museum of American History on the sixth of December, 2002, conducting an interview with Mr. Sam Wyly on the history of software and his personal role in that industry. Sam, what we've been doing in these interviews is starting by asking people about their background and education. Now you grew up in a small town, and I wonder how that later came to affect your personal development and your going into the software industry.

Wyly: Growing up I certainly didn't have a vision that there would be a software industry.

Allison: Well, how about business more generally?

Wyly: I grew up in a small town based on agriculture. Our economy was cotton, soybeans and cows. Historically, my people had been a part of the cotton farming world, but were also educated people for a long time. At a time when most people didn't go to high school, my folks went to high school. At a time when maybe one in a couple of thousand went to college, they went to college; one of my grandparents was a doctor and another one was a lawyer. Going back through a line of Presbyterian ministers and educators, there was a Sam Wyly who graduated from Princeton in 1836. His granddad graduated from Princeton in 1763, which was a little ahead of James Madison and Aaron Burr. Going back further, coming from Scotland, Katherine

Cleeland landed in the Chesapeake area in 1657. So I heard tales of these folks who were part of the building of America.

• • •

Allison: So you got a lot of training in business just watching your family try to stay successful.

Wyly: Yes, the big businesses of the 1950's were cars and oil. I'd come out of the oil patch and the cotton patch. With IBM's approach, it looked like they could sell to any business in any industry. Pretty good thing to be, I thought. Gasoline engines power cars. What are you going to do if the car business slumps? If you make gasoline motors, you're out of a job. I was still somewhat affected by the fact that the price of cotton had dropped. I just had all kinds of good impressions about this company called IBM, and what they seemed to be doing made sense to me. So that was my route into the world of computing and what later became software; it was through my impressions of IBM and the sharp people that worked for them.

In our senior year, when it came time to interview, another thing that impressed me was that IBM said, "We don't talk to anybody who doesn't have at least a B average." So they were selective. Any of us could go work for Shell Oil. IBM had the best interviewers. Omar Harvey was the Shreveport branch manager and another interviewer was his boss from Houston. They had this good guy/bad guy thing. One of them told you how tough it was to get an IBM offer. And the bad guy was telling you that you probably aren't good enough to work here. Then the good guy was telling you how great you were, how wonderful you were, you're a champion. So they did a good job of selling you. I wanted to work for IBM, and I actually accepted the job. But then I got a chance to get an MBA at the University of Michigan and I went there. So I applied for and got the scholarship and I was off to Michigan. It was more serendipity as opposed to any great, carefully planned process. Michigan was great for me because it gave me a different atmosphere and a different perspective.

Allison: There must have still been some sense of being a southerner in a northern school, even at the graduate level. Did you feel that?

Wyly: Oh yes, sure. In fact, I was constantly reminded by people from the Midwest that I didn't talk right. They all wanted to debate black/white issues, assuming that I must be prejudiced.

• • •

Allison: So you went straight to IBM when you came out of business school, is that right?

Wyly: First I went to Lackland Air Force Base for boot camp. Then I went to work in Dallas in February of 1958 for IBM in its Service Bureau Corporation.

Allison: How long did that last?

Wyly: It lasted about six months. I was soon able to work out a special arrangement with my manager. We had this oil royalty job that came in from West Texas, and it took about four or five days to run, but it was actually only about forty hours of continuous work. I went to my manager and said, "I will run that job continuously starting on Monday, but once I'm done, I want the rest of the week off to go back to Dallas." And he said, "Well, that's not legal because of wages and hours law; we have to pay you overtime for over eight hours a day." And I said, "I'll tell you what. I'll fill the card in, it'll be eight hours and you don't worry about it and I won't worry about it, and the customer will love the quick turnaround." So I was back in my apartment in Dallas for half of each week. At the end of the year, the oil recession was over and I got back my full time job as a sales rep in Dallas with my own accounts.

During the schooling part of this interview one of your questions was about Ross Perot. I think Ross was about a month ahead of me at the IBM school in Dallas. The first time I met Ross was when we had a 407 panel with about 400 red, blue and yellow wires plugged into its back. He came up to me and said, "Hi, I'm Ross Perot, Texarkana." He'd been four years in the Navy. He was training for the hardware division and I was training for the Service Bureau division.

• • •

Allison: Were you already thinking about maybe going out on your own? Seems like you would have been happy with IBM.

Wyly: I was not thinking of going on my own. Back then I thought that I would work for IBM forever. Maybe be president of IBM—that was my thought then. Actually, it was three years later when they hadn't even made me a branch manager. Then Honeywell came along. I had just one little piece of Dallas for my IBM territory and Honeywell said, "We'll give you two and a half states; we'll make you the area manager and you will get to hire the first sales people and hire the first programmers and you will be in charge." I asked, "Where will my boss be?" They told me that he would be in Chicago. I thought that was great, to have a boss who was not even in town, but I also thought that leaving IBM would be a little traumatic because I would have to change my belief system and stop thinking of the industry as IBM!

I had two good years at Honeywell in Dallas. We sold the first computers for Honeywell there, and we built the sales team up to five people. We had better sales than some big cities that had 39 man teams. We had a good record and it was fun, particularly because I realized how tough IBM was, and I was able to go back and beat them. One of my big wins was with Republic Insurance, which I loved, because it was just one block away from the IBM office where all the guys that I knew were located. There was one old friend of mine on the account, and I went to see him because back then IBM's practice was if you lose an account you're fired. So I went to this fellow and told him he had to get off the account because he was going to lose. He said you're crazy; nobody is going to buy Honeywell. It turned out that he was right for a while, because the computer committee met and voted four to two to turn down Honeywell and go with IBM. But I went to Russell Perry, who was the president, because I knew that IBM had screwed Perry earlier. I found out in earlier conversations with him that IBM had told him it was an eighteen-month delivery, but he had traded deliveries with another customer to get a sixty-day delivery. IBM had screamed bloody murder; he had ruined them and been a bad guy. It ticked Perry off that they would talk to a customer like that. So he voted one to nothing for the committee to take another vote. And Honeywell won.

Allison: A little lesson in executive management, too.

Wyly: Right, right.

Allison: Let's talk about going from Honeywell to starting your own business.

Wyly: Well, after being at Honeywell for a while, I realized that it was really going to be like IBM for me and I was not likely to be made president of Honeywell. I was more likely to be fired for insubordination. Part of the problem was that they kept changing my boss. The chain of command above me at Honeywell turned out to be just like IBM. I thought my first manager at IBM was a genius, but after that it went downhill. The second one was really fine, too, but by the third one it was not so good. Anyway, it became clear to me that if I really wanted to be independent and control my own destiny I couldn't be with any big organization, whether it was Honeywell or IBM. I really needed to have my own business, like a good cotton farmer does or a good newspaper publisher does.

Allison: Now remind me how old you were.

Wyly: I was 28. When people asked me if I started my own company to get rich, I tell them I didn't. I had a vague notion that you could acquire wealth, but that was not really my purpose. My purpose was freedom; my purpose was independence. I was already making far more money than I had ever thought possible when I was in college. In fact, I had figured that the most I would need to make was $10,000 a year and I was already making $30,000. So it wasn't about money. I began to shop around to see what you could do and was intrigued with these guys I'd heard about in Massachusetts who were coming up with something called a mini computer. This was the Digital Equipment Corporation.

Allison: Did you meet Ken Olsen or any of their people?

Wyly: I did not meet Olsen. I was just looking at their literature and the ads and the stories touting their $100,000 machine which could give you $1 million worth of computer speed. They were using manufacturer's reps so I looked at being a manufacturer's rep for marketing and servicing hardware. But I also had another notion from my Service Bureau experience with IBM. Somebody at IBM had studied the economics of creating a service center that was focused on the engineering market, as opposed to the business market in North Texas. There were a lot of business-oriented service bureaus then, but this would basically be a FORTRAN system using an IBM 7090 that cost $3 million. IBM concluded that the economics just simply didn't support it.

But I started poking at it intellectually. I thought that you don't have to do it with a $3 million 7090. Seymour Cray at Control Data had just created the CDC 1604 and it sold for $1.5 million. That's half the price of the 7090. My folks had started *The Delhi Dispatch* with a second-hand printing press because a new one cost too much. These 1604's were even sold second hand. Even though the [U.S. Justice Department's] 1956 Consent Decree had said that IBM equipment could be sold second-hand, that wasn't done much because IBM still controlled the second-hand market. Poking around, I found a company called CEIR, out of Washington, DC, which had gotten into this large computer stuff. They were doing body shop-type programming, and they were also in service centers. They had acquired 7090's and 1604's, but they had expanded too fast and were losing money. They had a 1604 that they had paid $1.5 million for and were selling it for $600,000. I saw that and realized I could get my cost down. If you cut your capital cost from $3 million to $600,000, you get your break-even point way down.

I looked around for some big customers and the biggest one that looked sellable was Sun Oil Company's research department. They used big FORTRAN machines for simulating oil reservoirs. They needed a lot of memory, and they needed a lot of speed. They were an engineering customer; they were not a business-oriented customer. They didn't have high speed telecommunications then; you got in a car in Richardson, Texas, and you drove out to Grand Prairie to use the big 7090 at Ling Temco Vought Aerospace. That's what the engineers did. I said to them, "How would you like a shorter drive, and how would you like to save some money? And, would you like to help out Southern Methodist University?" SMU had this ancient Univac 1103, an old vacuum tube computer, but the University didn't have any budget for new machines. SMU was interested in any transistorized machine. It didn't matter if it was IBM or Honeywell or Control Data. So I negotiated with SMU to put in a machine that they could use part-time. I would sell the prime time to Sun Oil, Texas Instruments, and other commercial customers. Students and professors would have to run nights and weekends. They thought that this was a great deal, so I got free space and free electricity and SMU shared the maintenance costs. Between those two contracts, the really big one was Sun Oil, but the next big one was SMU.

Allison: Who else was involved in getting you started?

Wyly: There were several people who were important—some were hugely important. Probably the biggest was Sun Oil Company's research group as the biggest customer. But the one with the biggest possible market was Texas Instruments. I had promises of business from engineers out of Texas Instruments, but no contracts that a banker could believe in to close the gap between my $10,000 and the $600,000 I needed. As I went through different iterations of this, I walked the streets of Dallas looking for a banker with imagination. I knew it was a tough sale from my own business school training, but I'm always an optimist. I started with the biggest bank in town and got a "no" and then went to the second biggest bank in town and got another "no."

Someone said to me, "Well, we have a leasing company and we can add a little credit to this deal and then you can pay off the bank loans to us; we will buy the equipment for you and take it for collateral but you still have to sell the bank." So I went back to the Sun Oil Company and said, "I can get the bankers in on this if you guys will prepay part of your five year contract." They agreed to pre-pay $250,000, and I could show a balance sheet with my $10,000 and their $250,000 even though I didn't have much net worth. The Sun Oil engineers were all for that arrangement because they were getting a great deal. They were getting computing at a third of the regular price, and it was more convenient. They even got to hang around the professors at SMU. This was all good stuff for the Sun Oil researchers.

However, the engineers had to deal with the beady-eyed controllers at Sun Oil downtown who said, "Well, what if Sam's business goes bust and we don't get what we bought, how do we get our cash back?" I was pondering this problem when a guy walked in. He heard that I was getting this big computer, and he wanted to sell me property insurance. I understood that because my parents used to be property insurance agents. I told him, "Yes I'm going to need insurance. However, I have to get into business first" and I explained the problem to him. He said, "Oh, this is easy. All you need is a performance bond. We sell those too." And I said, "What do you charge?" And he said, "We charge 2% of the original amount and then 1% of the declining balance as the risk goes down. It's just like a contract for construction bonding." I told him to bring me the bond because Sun Oil wanted a bond as insurance on the deal. They either wanted the computer service or their money back. This agent represented the New Hampshire Insurance Company that provided the bond. There was another company called Diversa that added a guarantee to the lease. By the end it wasn't a big risk, but Diversa still got half the business for the guarantee. So that's how we were able to get started.

Allison: That's how the deal got made. And it was basically you doing all this. I mean it wasn't a small group.

Wyly: Yes, it was basically me.

Allison: And how fast did your business start to grow then?

Wyly: We had a little revenue at the end of 1963 [$67,000], and then we had a good year, a profitable full year in 1964. We had about $700,000 in revenue and about $100,000 in profit the first full year. At first I was going to name the company Mustang Computing because we were doing it at SMU but then Rosemary, my wife, said, "You know, you could do the same thing in some other places." I agreed and decided to call it University Computing Company (UCC) so it wouldn't seem to be limited just to Dallas.

About a year later in Tulsa we made a deal with the Sunray Oil Company, basically in the same way as in Dallas. As I was putting that together, I came across a man named Ben Voth who had sold his company and retired from the insurance business. He owned an empty building across the street from Sunray, which would be a convenient location for us. He then brought up the idea of investing in my company. Later on, Ben wrote a book saying he invested $100,000 for 10% of my company, which turned into $20 million in five years. I invited him to come on as chairman of UCC. Ben was the first outside investor. After that we felt that if we could do this in Tulsa, we could do it in Houston or LA or London, if there was enough capital available. There was a public market interest in fast growing companies.

• • •

I think the big idea that we came to pretty quickly was to be right where the computer meets the telephone. We saw that if businesses could support customers over the phone lines, then they wouldn't have to get in their cars and drive to their customers and back. The input was not done as it is with today's PC; it was punch card input. We looked around to see who had a good tool for input. The one that looked like the best for engineering was the Univac 1107. Univac also had different terminals. They were jury-rigging their machine, which was competing with the IBM 1401, to create a cheap batch processing "terminal" to connect to an 1107. We were intrigued with that and were wondering how to get it, because the Univac had most of what the engineers needed. The 1107 wasn't like Control Data's 64-bit word machine, but it looked like something that you could market in both worlds. It didn't seem that IBM had anything like it. We had the opportunity to acquire an 1107 system in LA where we were already beginning to serve several of our customers in the petroleum and aerospace markets.

Then we decided that we needed to sell convenience. We needed to make it convenient for the corporate customer. We needed to make it convenient for the engineer to the degree that we could sell him anything, and the controller, too. The engineers were easier to sell because they wanted the machines, but the controllers decided who got to use them. The engineers had to stand in line. Therefore, our initial route to business was through selling the scientific and engineering side of the house. We could quickly see that we could sell them convenience and quick turnaround by serving them over the phone line instead of them having to go to the batch center. If we could do this, then we would be the leader.

Our tool was the Univac 1107 with its related batch processing devices for remote entry. So we were immediately faced with saying, "How do you get more through that phone line? How do you get the cost down? How do you make it more reliable?" We had a phone line that was set up for voice so it was analog. It was controlled by the AT&T monopoly, so it was priced at $2,000-$3,000 a month for a private line. But the computer was made for a digital world. It didn't fit well with the analog phone system. We had to have digital-to-analog and analog-to-digital conversion devices on both ends. We immediately questioned how could we get this faster, how could we get it cheaper? We needed to know who was making what, where we fit in, and how we could have something proprietary so that we could make a good margin. Something that later became a huge threat, but that we saw initially as a help, was what the Digital Equipment minicomputer people were doing. We found that these PDP-8s, and later the other PDP models, could be used as front-ends since they were very low cost even though we had to write our own software. We went from a $3 million IBM 7090 computer to a $1.5 million new CDC 1604 computer to a $600,000 second hand computer. But here was Ken Olsen making a $100,000 computer. That was a huge change. We didn't know that later the boys from Apple would bring out a $5,000 computer, which would go down to $500 today. We were already on the Moore's Law cost reduction curve.

Allison: Let me ask you a little bit about the business climate at your company. When you were analyzing the field and looking at the growth opportunities, was that a brain trust, or was that you doing your own study? I'm trying to get a sense of how the thinking in your company was progressing in this period because we are looking at a pioneer era of what the entrepreneur does. It sounds like you were as interested in the technical side as you were in the business side.

Wyly: The IBM System 360 was sheer genius. IBM said we are going to have top to bottom compatibility, and the system will work for both the engineers and the accountants, and it's going to solve all of these compatibility problems. I thought, "This is gorgeous; it's a great idea." But I'm watching all of the IT guys in the audience squirm, because everybody had some other machines, including more than one kind of IBM system. They had 1401's and 7070's; they had all these different computers. The high-level languages had promised that all you would have to do would be to plug in the new machine. But this idea never worked; it was a great theory but you always wrestled with the practical stuff. Our niche was at the confluence of the telephone world and the old data processing world, which we were beginning to call computers. Data processing was the interim world between punch card accounting and computing. When IBM was recruiting Charles and me at Louisiana Tech, they were hiring for EAM [electric accounting machines] and we "computer experts" were using EDP [electronic data processing]. Gradually the words changed. I believe Fletcher Jones [co-founder of Computer Sciences Corporation in 1959] was the first one to use the term computer science. Later many universities called their departments computer science.

Allison: And there's still a lot of debate over whether it really is or not.

Wyly: Yes. I've always been intrigued with the words people use and what they call things. I noticed that my doctor grandfather had his own jargon. The engineer who taught computers had his own jargon. Later, programmers developed their own jargon. So you have all these words and then you have some people who are trying to understand the whole business and they create their own category. For instance, we used the phrase "computer utility services" to describe delivering the integration of the computer and the phone line. We were doing things to work around the analog phone lines and the phone company monopolies. We could see that we as the computer folks were in a very much different timeframe from the phone folks who thought in terms of forty years to write off their equipment investment. They thought in terms that nobody had competitive choices: the customers had what AT&T told them was good for them. AT&T had a government granted monopoly for most local as well as long distance services. AT&T was regulated on revenues but they had a bookkeeping department to deal with that.

Allison: So this is getting up to when you started Datran.

Wyly: Yes, but long before we started Datran, there was the problem of how do people in the digital world, computer people, adapt to using telephone capability for computers. The computer "language" was totally alien to what was in place for people to talk to other people. We were wrestling with that problem all along. If we could have a phone line that cost only $300 a month instead of $3,000 a month, we would have a lot more market. We needed lines that were not full of errors, because we were trying to send digital signals through a system designed for analog signals. The quality of the analog system was not bad; it was good quality for phones, but it was bad quality for computers. Computer folks were trying to do something next week and the phone folks were trying to do something two years from now. It was a different way of thinking. The computer folks had to survive in the competitive marketplace, while the most important mission of the phone folks was to convince the lawmakers in fifty different state capitals not to bother them and to give them a 12% return on a government quality bond.

Allison: So how did you start working this problem? Is this something that you started to talk to other people and other companies about, or were you negotiating with the phone companies; what was the process you used to try to make progress?

Wyly: All of the above. Making an installation meant having to deal with the phone company folk. Actually, when I went to Italy and saw that it took two years to get a phone, I thought Southwestern Bell was not so bad if they took two months. But you know I'm a computer guy and, if my customer wants it next week, then two months is awfully long. But the phone company doesn't care, they have no penalty, they're not going to lose the customer. They have no price to pay for being slower or for having more errors except that somebody might write a letter to the Public Utilities Commission; it's just a different world. So, we did a lot of things before we started Datran. We spent some time building the Cope 45—short for Communications Oriented Processing Equipment—"the fastest terminal in the West." We engineered the product to push data through the lines faster, giving the customers faster turnaround and higher quality service at a lower cost. We were working on the cost of the line and the cost of the terminals. We were using whatever digital equipment and anyone came up with to provide a better answer than what we had.

We were more innovators than inventors because we weren't starting from scratch. We had to take what was there and figure out how to use it smarter, quicker, and better at low cost. We were wrestling with those problems. We had some smart people, guys like Gene Scott who came from the development world in Arizona with General Electric. Gene's technical team produced the GE operating system, and they were embedding communications in their 600 series and their 225 series. They were focused on what they called timesharing, a word that I never liked.

Allison: Why is that?

Wyly: It sounded like real estate. They named Ross Perot's business "facilities management"—that sounds boring and not very digital. It's just words, but mainly we were in the communications business. By just being in the computing business, we had to be in the communications business, and we were dealing with ways to handle digital traffic. The way we got into Datran was the same way we got into business in Dallas through FORTRAN. We used a trial and error process. Probably the first step toward what became Datran was my recruiting Sy (Seymour) Joffe, a great Univac salesman in Houston, to market what we were doing. Sy said that the smartest guy in Univac that he knew was Ed Berg, who had come out of the Navy. Ed was much of the brains behind what Univac had done with the 1107's and 1108's, particularly their front-ends. This was the part that married computing and communications. Datran was really Ed Berg's creative thought. He had the big idea that there wasn't any way to make the analog facilities from a telephone company provide effective communications for computers. What you needed was an all-digital network with a digital switch. It was out of all of his work that we said that we would make the first digital switch work. We said we would put in place a digital highway for computer folks, just for data. The phone folks can be the phone folks. We will be the data folks, we will do it all digital, and we will do it switched. It was really Ed Berg's engineering thought that created the idea of Datran.

Allison: This is late 1960's now?

Wyly: Yes, this is the late 1960's—around 1967 when we were starting. For competition we not only had Southwestern Bell, but we also had AT&T. There was both state regulation and federal regulation. You had two different markets, the local phone market and the long distance market. How did this happen? Did God give AT&T this monopoly? Of course not. First came the telegraph wires that went along the railroads' rights-of-way. Then Alexander Graham Bell said here's the phone, but Western Union didn't want to accept it. So the phone companies were created. These understandings were made to get around federal monopoly laws. Congress never passed a law; it just kind of became the way things were done. The first big idea we had was that even though AT&T controlled all the local phone companies and the long distance business, there was one avenue around their monopoly: the old telegraph routes, the old telegraph right-of-ways. In terms of the law, it wasn't just what was there physically, but what was there legally. The telegraph franchise was a legal loophole to the phone company monopoly. It was intriguing to see how the body of law built up. There was the telegraph law and the telephone law but, after reviewing it, it became clear that the guys who were sitting on what seemed to be a mother-lode of rights of way and a mother-lode of legal rights and copper wire connections was Western Union. So in April 1968 we made a tender offer for control of Western Union. But we were stopped by a New York State law that said that no one could buy control of a telegraph company in the state of New York without the approval of the legislature in Albany. And that stopped us.

Allison: How big was your company then? What you were trying to do was a pretty big idea.

Wyly: We were bidding for a company ten times bigger than we were and one that had been around for a long time.

Allison: But it wasn't doing all that well even then.

Wyly: It wasn't. It was not doing well in the 1960's. It had never adjusted to AT&T.

Allison: This is five years after every banker had turned you down in starting UCC.

Wyly: Yes. But we were a public company, we had public currency, and we could raise money in the ebullient 1960's, if we could only get the telegraph franchise. In 1968, our market capitalization was exceeded by only five companies in Texas.

Allison: You had done quite well in your market sector, but I'm trying to get a better sense of the scope of your business.

Wyly: We had already defined that we were a computer utilities services business. This meant that we needed a "telephone" company for computers.

Allison: The part of the story I don't understand is whether you were alone in doing this. Were there other service bureaus that were coming together with you? Did you go to the professional associations to try to bring people together, or was it just your individual initiative?

Wyly: It was just our initiative. We never had much luck with committees and the industry associations. We went to a few meetings but basically we viewed these as places where we recruited people. We weren't real big on our own people going to these, because they were going to be recruited there. We were getting together but the "we" was a bunch of competitive barracudas.

Allison: So what happened next as you tried to roll out this idea? Was it tough going?

Wyly: After we were stopped from merging with Western Union, we decided to try to get a franchise from the Federal Communications Commission. *Forbes* magazine described what we did at Western Union with these words: "Sam Wyly's motto is 'If you can't join 'em, lick 'em.' " That's so good I wish I'd actually said it! Basically I did, but they shortened it, made it punchier. We made our own filing; it was a huge thing. Congress can make the laws and the courts can judge the laws. But regulatory agencies are able to make rules and judge their own rules. We had a lot of receptivity from the people in the Common Carrier Bureau who had been wrestling with what to do with the phone monopoly for a long time. We had Ed Berg and Sy Joffe and a bright lawyer named Jack Scorse. Anyway, we had basically turned our engineering plans into the language of the law for the legal folks and the regulatory folks—they were really the ideas of Ed Berg. Pursuing this added up to something like $400,000 in 1967 dollars, which would be like $2 million to $3 million now.

In the 1960's we were having an earlier version of the 1990's irrational exuberance. But one week before we were going to do our public offering, the investment bankers said that they couldn't sell it. The offering will fail. So I called up four or five people to buy some stock and it turned out that the bankers were wrong. The stock doubled on the first day—the same stock that they couldn't sell a week earlier. Our University Computing Company stock doubled in 1965, the year it came out, from $4.50 to $9.00 per share. In 1966 it tripled to $27.00, but then dropped to half during the 1966 tight money squeeze. But the net for the year was that the price tripled. I'd actually taken a holiday to Europe when the stock dropped in half, and I thought somehow it was dropping in half because I'd gone to Europe and wasn't minding the store in Dallas, but it turned out that everybody else's stock was dropping in half, too. In 1967, we were up 7 times. That was about the time I wondered how we could possibly be worth this much. But other companies that are kind of like you are being bid up the same way.

Everything I learned in the investment course in Louisiana Tech about valuations and all of the old rules on multiples were being changed. People liked these little fast-growing companies. In fact, they didn't want the old Dow companies, the old smokestack guys. They wanted the fast growth companies. It was like the world of the 1990's when capital was available for telecom and Internet ventures—not just millions but billions of dollars. If we had had for Datran just 1% of all the money that the investors put into the various telecoms and Internet companies, we could have built the new Datran network. There was that kind of market in the 1960's, so if we had gotten our permissions, we could have raised the capital we needed. But we couldn't get capital because we had to wait for the Federal Communication Commission's permission.

Allison: So how long did that take? I know that Datran ended up not succeeding, but what was the time period?

Wyly: We started in 1967 and we didn't get permission until 1973. It was docket 18920, which permitted Bill McGowan at MCI to sell private voice line. At that time it wasn't phone calls; Bill got that later by just doing it, getting sued and winning the lawsuit. That is how he changed the law on selling phone calls one at a time. All he got was private voice line on docket 18920. What we got was the authority to build a data-only network with no phone calls; a data-only, all digital, switched network, which was really what the world needed.

Allison: And that was 1973?

Wyly: That didn't come till 1973.

Allison: The Carterphone decision—where does that fit in?

Wyly: Carterphone came earlier. The Carterphone decision was in 1968. We have Nokia because of Tom Carter, and there are multiple long distance phone companies because of MCI and Bill McGowan. The basic policy-making decisions that created what later came to be called the Internet, and what we call the cell phone world today, were Carterphone, MCI, and Datran.

Allison: They really paved the way.

Wyly: Yes, they really helped to change communications policies at all levels of government. The other huge part goes back to the 1956 IBM Consent Decree. In 1969 came IBM's unbundling of software and services from hardware. A good old Texas liberal named Ramsey Clark was Lyndon Johnson's Attorney General. On the last day of the Johnson administration in 1969, he filed an antitrust suit against IBM. IBM, trying to keep that from happening, had already announced that they were unbundling. But motivating them to unbundle was old Ramsey's boys poking at them. After the Democrats lost the election in 1968, they filed the antitrust suit. Once Nixon came in, the Republicans couldn't appear to be pro-business and reverse it so they had this suit going for twelve years. They paralyzed IBM.

• • •

Two Computer Designers Who Thought Big

Richard Bloch (Honeywell 800, 400, 200)
Gene Amdahl (IBM System/360)

Introduction

I first met Richard Bloch at an ice hockey rink at Noble & Greenough School in Dedham, Massachusetts. I knew who he was by reputation because I had been associated with Honeywell EDP for a short time, but I never expected to meet him in a hockey rink, not at his age. However, he had a son Richard, Jr., who was an outstanding goal tender; hence, we were just two hockey fathers standing in the cold with a common interest. I knew Richard to be the famed designer of the Honeywell 800, 400, and 200 machines, all elegant machines, at the Honeywell EDP offices in Wellesley, Massachusetts. He also designed the earlier Datamatic 1000, whose tapes were as big as tires and just as heavy. Ironically, he had just joined Auerbach Corporation, as I had to open its Boston office. So we had something else in common. Eventually I would ask him to join the Board of Directors of my company.

The Honeywell 200 was particularly successful because it came with an emulator that allowed a customer to run IBM 1401 programs without converting them, which was a big selling point in those days. Honeywell was one of the Seven Dwarfs whose computers were all incompatible with IBM systems, the de facto standard of the era. This made selling against IBM in the commercial market at the time an incredibly difficult task. It was almost impossible to dislodge IBM from one of its data processing customers. It's difficult for people today to appreciate how strong the relationship was between the IBM salesman and his customers. They were like gods in their accounts. They earned it by not only selling the account, but by making sure everything worked. They delivered on all their promises. However, it's important to note that IBM was really in the punched card business and computers and punched cards really didn't match very well. So, this is what both Dick and Gene were designing for, namely, a punch card, batch oriented industry market place that would be moving to on-line systems. They would definitely not be designing to meet academia's requirements, as much as they would have liked to, since they were both scientists and knew the requirements well.

Yet, Honeywell did pretty well in competition with IBM thanks to some very good sales people such as Sam Wyly. Much of their success was due to Richard Bloch's sophisticated computer line. Eventually, Bloch would be recruited to greatly expand General Electric's (GE) footprint in the computer space. At the time, GE was providing the computers to support the Multics (Multiplexed Information and Computing Service) timesharing system at Project MAC (the Project on Mathematics And Computation) at MIT. A meeting was arranged between GE and Honeywell's boards of directors to discuss the acquisition of Honeywell EDP as part of the effort. The conversation shifted from GE acquiring Honeywell EDP to Honeywell EDP acquiring GE's computer division, a most unusual development.

Gene Amdahl's IBM System/360 line had a huge impact on the industry and still does to this day. What customers wanted was upward compatibility with no conversions. IBM was providing it via an integrated line of computers from small to large. Customers hated conversions because they were very expensive, time consuming, and fraught with trouble—making them a total waste of money. Thus, this upward compatibility was very appealing from a marketing point of view. IBM pretty much killed the competition of the day with it. Of course, it wouldn't work out exactly as promised because there still would be many conversions, particularly from one operating system to another. Converting from DOS/360 (Disk Operating System/360) to OS/360 (Operating System/360), which many DOS/360 users did, was a major undertaking, but the IBM S/360 line was still a big step forward for industry. It would not be for academia because IBM didn't offer a competitive timesharing version of the IBM 360 that was successful. However, industry was looking beyond batch oriented, punch card systems to online, real time systems as they were called at the time. They were really interactive computing systems for industry, which is where my company's database software played an important role.

Richard always thought big as did Gene. Richard wanted to take on IBM, head to head, with a complete product line both at Honeywell and GE, but it wasn't to be. One reason is that computers were just divisions of Honeywell and GE, not their main businesses as was the case with IBM. Also, IBM was very entrenched in its industry accounts. This would be a very risky $500 million undertaking that few wanted to, or could afford to take on. Gene would eventually do it when he left IBM and formed Amdahl Corporation to compete head to head with IBM, a very audacious move.

AN INTERVIEW WITH

Richard Bloch

Conducted by
William Aspray
February 22, 1984
Newton, Massachusetts

purl.umn.edu/107123

Photo courtesy of Charles Babbage
Institute (CBI 50 52W)

Aspray: This interview is being conducted by William Aspray on the 22nd of February with Mr. Richard Bloch in his home in Newton, Massachusetts. Why don't we begin by having you tell me something about your early education and home life. Where were you born? Where did you grow up?

Bloch: I was born and brought up in Rochester, New York, and went through the public school system there. I expected to concentrate as time went on in my favorite subjects, which were science and mathematics. Just what profession I was going to go into, specifically, I didn't know; but that was my leaning. I went to Ben Franklin High School and entered into a competition in my senior year for a scholarship to Harvard offered by the Harvard Club of Rochester. I was fortunate enough to win that competition. So I was due to go to Harvard in September of '39 as a Harvard Club of Rochester scholarship recipient, which would hold for four years provided my grades were satisfactory. They had to be more than satisfactory. I might add that in my youth, before leaving Rochester for Harvard, my activities included quite a bit of music training; I studied at the Eastman School of Music as a flutist and I also played in various orchestras and bands in the city—high school orchestra and they had an inter-high school orchestra that I also played in. I was also pretty active athletically and I tended to take seriously anything I went into. I played table tennis to a point where I gave demonstrations in which I played against some Chinese experts that were making a tour, and I got to the point where I was considered to be one of the better table tennis players in the vicinity.

• • •

Aspray: Let's turn to your Harvard days. You planned on majoring in what area?

Bloch: I decided to major in mathematics with some minor emphasis in physics. However, I also was involved in courses in economics, philosophy, and psychology. But the concentration was in the science area. Since it was for a B.A. degree and Harvard had no engineering of any consequence, I never took any engineering courses.

• • •

Aspray: You graduated in 1943?

Bloch: That's right. Because World War II came upon us. In 1941, I joined what was then known as the V7 program, which was a program under which you committed yourself to go into officer training in the Navy immediately upon graduation. They would allow you to finish your undergraduate career.

Aspray: I see.

Bloch: I joined that and immediately upon graduation in June of '43 I was off, within a matter of weeks, to Notre Dame for midshipman training. It was a three-month course where you started as an apprentice seaman, became a midshipman, and then became an ensign all in 90 days. They used the term "90-day wonder." If it weren't for the war, I might never have gotten into the computer field. It was a strange situation because my abilities in mathematics were known to the extent that just before graduation, or just about at that time, I got an offer from the University of Pennsylvania to join their staff to teach mathematics, but obviously not with tenure. I think it was Klein at the University of Pennsylvania that headed up that department. I couldn't take that offer because I had to go off with the Navy. So I completed my stay at Notre Dame coming out as an ensign with the war boiling. We all wanted to do our thing and my idea was to get on the biggest ship possible. So I applied for duty as a navigator on a battleship. When Washington reviewed my background they said "nothing doing." I thought I was going to sea, but I was the only one that thought so. They sent me down to the Naval Research Laboratory to work in what was called the consultant section of the Radio Division. So I went there to do some mathematical work that related to the war activity in that division.

Aspray: Computational work?

Bloch: Analytic and computational work. Some work in antenna design and so on. It was chiefly the mathematics involved in this.

Aspray: Did you get experience at the time, say, using a desk calculator?

Bloch: No. They had some calculators there, which I used, but there was no real heavy use of the machine. I was only there from about September of 1943 to about January of 1944. A visit was set up for Howard Aiken to the lab, which was in Anacostia. He was visiting on some mission. As I recall, the head of the laboratory at the time was Admiral Van Curen. Aiken was to visit him, and I got a call from the top there at the laboratory to escort Aiken around. In the process of doing that, he was telling me about some of the work that was going on there. When he heard of my background at Harvard he asked me if I would like to get involved. He told me about this fabulous machine that he had designed and asked if I would like to spend my naval duty up at Harvard? Of course it sounded intriguing to me; so I jumped at it. I didn't understand completely what this was all about, other than there was a giant automatic calculator, as he called it, that he had been working on, and that he was looking for staff. So in March I was ordered to duty at Cambridge, to the computation laboratory, which at the time was in Cruft Laboratory basement. I remember it being next to the acoustic laboratory in which Leo Beranek was working at the time. When I got there, the machine wasn't there. It was just being delivered from IBM from Endicott at the time. I helped in an elementary fashion, helped get this thing put up in place, but in the process, of course, I was beginning to learn what this was all about. The only other officer that was there was Bob Campbell. I guess he had preceded me there by a couple of months.

Aspray: What were you asked to do when you got to Harvard?

Bloch: Well, the first thing that I did was to get to learn the machine. Of course there was no manual or anything of this sort; so I guess I just picked it up from discussions and basic blueprints of the circuits and so on. But there was very little, if anything, really written at the time. There were just piles of prints. I picked up this information from Aiken and to some extent Campbell. Then I was given the task of programming for the machine, and I ended up being probably the prime programmer. Eventually I also got involved in being responsible for the operation of the machine and the solution of problems, some of them being used in the war effort directly. I was involved in the programming side of the picture and also in the maintenance and debugging of the machine. I lived in bachelor officers' quarters next to the Commander Hotel which was within a half mile of the place.

· · ·

Aspray: Was there square root?

Bloch: No, no there was no square root function that I recall.

Aspray: That seems odd. That seems to come up so often. Though you can do it easily by an approximation method.

Bloch: Yes, but there was no root at the time and that's an interesting point. I do not remember there being any square root in that machine. The machine had the inverse functions so you had sine. I'm trying to recall. It did not have arc sine. This came in through the interpolator functions. But some of these functions would take as much as a minute to run on the machine. It was a very expensive operation. Addition and subtraction were implicit in the fact that the 72 storage registers did their own addition and subtraction literally using these IBM counter wheels. Inside of a multiplication there were cycle times that were not being used by the machine. The multiplication itself had its own sequence of operations within the multiplier unit of the machine. The way the buses were set up, you could easily perform additions to your heart's content without disturbing the multiplication—while the multiplication was going on.

Aspray: I see.

Bloch: We programmed a number of problems for the Navy and the Bureau of Ordnance. Next I got involved with John von Neumann in programming a partial differential equation of the second order, which dealt with spherical shock waves relating to the implosion occurring in an atomic explosion. At the time I didn't know that. It was a very complex problem and von Neumann was there for some time. He obviously knew what the problem was that he wanted to do and started setting up the formulas in mathematical fashion. I had to take that and move them into difference equations and eventually get to program the thing. One thing I do remember is that the first twenty pages of this report dealt with describing a problem, how it was going to be attacked, and so on. Von Neumann insisted that my name be put in front of his as the author, which embarrassed me a little bit because he was the great mathematician and mathematical physicist of the day. I really didn't feel I deserved that; but that's the way it came out, so I prize that.

Aspray: Could you tell from working that closely with von Neumann how much he knew about automatic computation?

Bloch: I would say this. He knew he had a mind that moved in rapid fashion on any subject relating to mathematics or physics. When he came, he did not know the design of the machine. He knew numerical computation, say the contents of Whitaker and Robinson which, let's face it, was well known before.

Aspray: Sure.

Bloch: You might have to do it with your hand or with a desk calculator; but the point is he knew how to apply numeric difference methods and things of this sort. Exactly how to do this on the machine was left to me. I would say in all fairness that he neither had the time or the desire to know the details of how the machine operated. I'm sure he picked up a fair idea of that and later on, of course, got himself involved in the area of machine design.

Aspray: Fair enough. Can you describe some of the other problems you worked on?

Bloch: Well, one of the major assignments I had involved the need for more exact tables of Bessel functions. I got involved in producing a gigantic series of books. Some of these volumes were issued later by the Harvard Press and stand to this day as a monument to the machine and to computation as used to put out tables of functions to accuracies never before really achieved. We put out Bessel functions, J0, J1, J2, and so on. The results were done to 23 decimal places. In order to achieve that accuracy we operated at 46 decimal places, which required chaining registers and working in double precision, you might say, in the machine. This was a huge project that was one of my babies and, interestingly enough, the printed results [i.e., photocopy ready] were not transcribed so we never lost anything in the process of it going from the machine, to paper, to transcription, to being printed.

• • •

Aspray: I'd like to turn to your post-Harvard days in just a moment, but I wanted to give you a chance, if there were any other things about the Harvard days that you'd like to get on tape for posterity's sake.

Bloch: Well, I would like to say that I think that Howard Aiken accomplished a great deal at a time when the tools were few and far between. He clearly came up with a machine, and probably the first machine really that could be called a computer today, one which was essentially automatically sequenced. He also should be given a great deal of credit for concentrating on what the machine did, for whom it did it, and the accuracy with which it did it. Certainly during my time, and I think even later, he was not involved in wanting to win any races in machine design. I think that's overlooked. His concentration was that he got a kick out of machine design at the early stages when it was really new to the world. He did some pioneering there. His concentration soon after that was on solving problems and he was a stickler for accuracy. Even though some very important inventions came out of Harvard, some of which are not generally recognized as coming out of Harvard and out of Aiken's group, he did not really want to engage in battles that subsequently came up involving who was the first to do what with which.

He certainly was, as far as I am concerned, a great pioneer, a tough task master. I remember that he'd come in at any hour of the morning or night and sometimes he'd show up at four in the morning. I might be there trying to get some bug out of the machine. And he'd show up having had, I don't know, three or four hours of sleep and his comment was "Are we making numbers?" That was a favorite expression, "Are we making numbers?" His big satisfaction, once the machine was designed, was to see this output coming forth. He was very nervous when the machine stopped. That to him was unacceptable. The reliability that he wanted to bring into the machine was there so that those results would be accurate.

By the way, as far as checking is concerned, there was no automatic checking at that time, it was done by program. The trick there was to arrive at the solution by two different methods, or by an inversion of the process. I remember we had been spending a great deal of time making certain that if it were done in two different ways that truly were different a particular bug could not possibly be in the machine and show up so as to create the same wrong answer in both cases. What we did was to compare the answers, the idea being that if they were correct, presumably everything was okay. I think the fact that the huge computational job, for example in those Bessel functions, stands to this day, is proof that this intricate checking that went on and filtered out just about anything that could have possibly occurred in the machine.

I knew Howard Aiken very well at that time, and then there was a period afterward when I didn't see much of him, and then I saw him before his death fairly frequently. He had interests in some new developments, interestingly enough in miniaturization of computers for home use and so on. He foresaw the advantages of having not only mini-circuits, but mini-input and mini-output devices. He was talking to me about even setting up some companies to probe this and move into this area at the time. So he kept his aggressive thinking in the field going all the way really to his death. He was a man that kept up with the field all the way through and to his last days was still conjuring up new ideas. I sometimes think that because of his rather brusk personality, as subsequent events turned out, he was perhaps not given the credit that was due him in many ways. He didn't seek it and he didn't seek to patent anything. He wasn't interested in monetary reward. He had a way about him which either endeared him to somebody or made him absolutely ferocious. I think to the extent that he was in the latter mode, it didn't help him at all in later days when people were trying to dole out credits for what had happened in the field. So I really think that it's a little bit unfortunate that he hasn't been given what I believe to be his due place in the field. I certainly know that at the time I was there we were putting out information from equipment when no one else was doing so. It clearly was the first practical application of the computer as we know it today.

• • •

Aspray: So after Harvard you went with the [Raytheon company division you'd joined in 1947] to Honeywell.

Bloch: Yes. It was my division that really was the inauguration of Honeywell into the [computing] field. Honeywell had made control devices previously.

Aspray: That's right.

Bloch: This group consisted of some of the best engineers in the field. In size the group was comparable, if not larger than, the number of engineers that were working at IBM in the mid-1950's. Certainly in the early days that may well have been true. It was quite a group that we had there, and they were responsible for some of the earliest and finest magnetic tape drives, magnetic tape heads and multiple heads. In fact we produced those for others and I remember the group at Princeton—Goldstine, von Neumann and so on—who were working on the MANIAC (Mathematical Analyzer Numerical Integrator and Computer) at the time. They wanted to use our tape mechanisms in that machine. Raytheon bowed out of the field in 1955 after certain government contracts were no longer available. Raytheon was heavily dependent upon government work and still is to a great extent. I had some moonlighting going on in my operation, looking for a commercial version of RAYDAC (Raytheon Digital Automatic Computer) which we dubbed privately "the RAYCOM." We did a fair amount of work on this in the attempt to get Raytheon to sponsor a commercial version of this machine with its own funds. We knew what was going on at the time with Eckert and Mauchly and Remington Rand.

Aspray: You could see Raytheon as a competitor to Eckert and Mauchly? Could they bid on the same contract, was it the U.S. Census?

Bloch: That's right, it was on the Census machine. Because we were binary, we ended up doing the Navy machine. The Census contract was given the Univac, presumably because it was a decimal machine.

Aspray: I see.

Bloch: We were dubbed the scientific version and they were the commercial version. By the way, that machine ran for many years and used mercury delay lines for storage. It had, as I recall, water cooling. It was quite a group. They became the Datamatic Corporation in 1955 and were jointly owned. Raytheon didn't let it go completely; they owned 40%, Honeywell owned 60%. The management at Raytheon did not believe that there was really a future in the commercial area of computers. Their evaluation was that there may be a market, but not to the extent that it was worth going into it. So they accepted what amounted to something like $4 million and turned over everything.

Aspray: Oh, I see.

Bloch: People, developments, and everything else went over to this Datamatic Corporation, which then became the Datamatic Division of Honeywell in 1957. Raytheon decided not even to keep its 40% interest in the field.

Aspray: I see.

Bloch: Thus Raytheon bowed out of the field. They came back since, but never to the degree of being a mainframe competitor, which they easily could have continued to be had that operation continued. So this was the beginning of Honeywell. But in the course of developing this Datamatic machine, I came up with orthotronic control which essentially enabled one, through redundancy, to have the machine correct its own errors. It certainly operated very well. It was a case of being able to spot a single bit error simply by having a two-dimensional array similar to horizontal and vertical checking, and if column 3 did not check and row 4 did not check, then the intersection of 4 and 3 represented your point of error. It turned out that this, when combined with the weighted count, was quite powerful because the weighted count was applied in both directions. Now you could actually get multiple errors literally picked up. In practice it worked out extremely well. I headed up the Raytheon operation, came over to Honeywell and directed the product development of the Honeywell line of equipment. I was director of product planning first and then became vice president for product development. We embarked on a series of machines that eventually was called the 800 series and the 400 series, and then came the 200 series. The 200 series machine really was a fabulous machine. It was multi-programmed and had all of the correction and detection features in it. In the previous machine, the Datamatic 1000, we had the ability to hold the results of the previous operation until the machine had checked them and then went on to the next operation. When that operation was finally checked, we could erase memory of the previous operation, move that back over so that at any time an error was detected, the machine automatically reverted to the previous operation as though the current operation had never occurred. Then it proceeded from there. It would give you some blinking lights saying, "Hey, I've caught an error. I know what to do about it. Don't worry about it." It might print out where the error occurred, but the machine never stopped. This was, in essence, the beginnings of the non-stop or fault-tolerant machines. It was some time, of course, before that came back into vogue.

It's curious how some of these things I mentioned in the Aiken days come back much later. There were many attributes there that have come up two or three decades later which were really foreseen at that time. So Honeywell became a very strong element in the 1960's, but it was based primarily on a 200 series machine. The 200 series, which we designed, had the capability of gear-shifting into an emulation mode of the 1400 series of IBM or into its own mode. In the emulation mode, it had actually performed the IBM instructions, and run them just about as fast or maybe even a little faster than the original IBM machine. If you went into the native mode, it went very much faster. This whole thing was called "the Liberator attack" which said "you don't have to throw your programs out, you just take them and put them on this machine." This was probably the first instance of the transportability of programs.

Well, IBM's [counter] attack was quite successful—as it always has been. They didn't really lose a great share of the market, although Honeywell did a substantial job of becoming a major element in the second tier of the market at about this time. There was only one in the first tier. Interestingly enough, more than a decade later, IBM came out with a self-correcting approach on tape. It was praised very highly. It's interesting to note that this has occurred many times. Something will pop back up under a different label or with a different code on it, people will look at it, and unless you have a perspective that goes across all of this time element—which very few people have—you won't recognize this apple popping up in the basket again. It's really quite amusing to see this sometimes. It's happened more than once.

So the Raytheon experience led to Honeywell. I was at Honeywell for some 11 years. We started at zero and, by the time I left, we were at about $500 million in annual sales. The company had it made at that time. I was anxious for Honeywell to not let its guard down. It made great inroads, but I was anxious to move up into IBM land a lot more quickly. I had some differences of opinion at this point with upper management, that is, between myself and those who felt that we really didn't have to go into some of the grand developments that I had been thinking about. It was clear they were going to be taking a more conservative posture, I always like an aggressive posture, and so I left in 1968.

• • •

Bloch: A decision was made at GE to get someone to join forces with them in the computer field. The plan that I set forth was going to require some $500 million dollars of investment in a five year period. GE, as large as it was, was being stung at the time by a huge strike which had cost them a couple of hundred million dollars to amend. The result was that GE exited from the field and, of all things, the buyer was Honeywell. Naturally, that was the end there. We had developed a tremendous plan, segments of which Honeywell subsequently used. It was the "master plan," as we called it, for the entire new product line at GE. We were building up a tremendous staff in terms of confidence, bringing in a lot of new blood from the outside, including IBM. It was cut short and GE exited from the computer field in the sense of being a builder of equipment. They retained their timesharing services operation in Bethesda. I next moved into the private sector and got involved in venture capital activities, acquisition divestiture activities, and certain high-level corporate hand holding operations with various companies through the 1970's. In 1979, I took over as chief executive officer of a company in the field of artificial intelligence.

• • •

AN INTERVIEW WITH

Gene M. Amdahl

Conducted by
Arthur Norberg
April 16, 1986; January 19, 1989; April 5, 1989
Cupertino, California

purl.umn.edu/104341

Photo courtesy of Charles Babbage
Institute (CBI subject file)

Norberg: Dr. Amdahl, can you tell me something about your parents? I know you're from South Dakota originally. Were they a farming family in South Dakota?

Amdahl: Yes, my grandfather homesteaded in South Dakota prior to it becoming a state. So the homesteading would have occurred sometime in the early 1870's. On my mother's side, they homesteaded also and about the same time, also in South Dakota.

• • •

Norberg: After your wartime military service was completed, what were you thinking about doing?

Amdahl: I wanted to be in electronics. I decided I really was fond of electronics, but also wanted physics. I decided I wanted to go back to school, but I couldn't get into the University of Minnesota, which was the one I wanted. They were filled up with so many returning servicemen that they had no openings at all. They were only taking Minnesota residents and I was really a South Dakota resident. So I actually moved into Minnesota to try to see if that would help, but it didn't help. So I missed the first quarter of the fall of 1946. And I applied then to South Dakota State College. I got married just after getting out of the service and occupied myself during that quarter constructing a small house, a portable one, because there was no place to stay at South Dakota State College.

. . .

Norberg: How did you come to choose the University of Wisconsin?

Amdahl: Well, I tried three schools and University of Wisconsin accepted me. I tried Yale and Princeton and they didn't. You know, I'm sure I couldn't compete with the students who had gone to first class colleges and first class high schools. I'm not sure that my college background at that point was a great deal better than some of the really good high schools.

Norberg: I see. All right. So you arrived at the University of Wisconsin in 1948.

Amdahl: Yes.

Norberg: The second thing is the statements that you made about going off to the engineering department and learning about analog machines and seeing what they had in the math department and so on suggest to me that you might also have either gone to the library to see whether anything was available.

Amdahl: I went to the library afterwards. We didn't have any books. The only text on computers that we had, the only book on computers, was a book of pictures that were of the dedication of the Harvard Mark I. It didn't explain anything about the Mark I, just pictures. So that's all we had in the library. At that time, I thought any information on computers was classified, because they were all being done under government contracts. So I didn't know anything about them. I'd read about them in a book [by Edmund Berkeley] called *Giant Brains*. I don't know if you ever read the book.

. . .

Norberg: Then why return to IBM? And what did you find when you did return?

Amdahl: Well, the reason I returned was that I did not find the situation materially better where I went in California. The first company I went to, Ramo-Wooldridge, had the same kind of organization that they had just put into Poughkeepsie, and there was no room for me. They had a role for me to do, but they explained my position as being utility outfielder. That's not necessarily all that emotionally rewarding, because I had the responsibility to write all of the proposals, but didn't get to be involved in the execution of any of them.

Norberg: The same thing happened at Aeronutronic as well when you went there.

Amdahl: To a large extent, yes, although there I had big hopes that since they were associated with the Ford Motor Company, a commercial company, they would be interested in getting into commercial computing. It turned out that their interest in Aeronutronic was to get into the military business, not into commercial. I really sort of misread, and certainly misjudged, what I could accomplish in terms of getting them to make moves in the commercial direction.

Norberg: Now, what was IBM like then when you returned, in contrast to 1955?

Amdahl: Well, in the research area, things were still, you know, loose; it wasn't so bureaucratic there. In some respects, I had a high enough position in IBM so that I was less affected by bureaucracy, but it was bureaucratic now that I look back. But the particular project I had, when I did undertake System 360, was one in which we were really given a fairly free hand to make a lot of the decisions. Later, one of the decisions I wanted to make they wouldn't permit.

Norberg: We'll come to that in a moment. Then do I conclude from that that the work you did on 360 architecture was done in the research facility? It wasn't a project separate at Poughkeepsie or somewhere like that?

Amdahl: No, I went back to Poughkeepsie in 1962 to do that, so it was all done at Poughkeepsie. We brought stuff from Project X along in terms of the plan at the time. In fact, Dr. Emanuel Piore [head of IBM Research] charged me with carrying the responsibility for Project X, that was fine, but I had no budget.

Norberg: Was this typical behavior in IBM to try to woo somebody away from a project they were working on and into a new project, as [Bob] Evans seems to have done with you?

Amdahl: Yes, I don't know that it was any more serious than wooing people away from another company.

Norberg: I would have thought that that's an interesting way to proceed inside a company.

Amdahl: Yes, it is. You could get your hands slapped, and possibly Evans' hand was slapped by Piore. I never knew.

Norberg: Did you work for Piore during those two years—1960 to 1962 directly, or was there somebody between you?

Amdahl: No, the one who was director of research was between us. He was vice president of research.

Norberg: Well, maybe you could describe for me then what the objective was that you were given in 1962 to work on 360.

Amdahl: There were four categories of activity to take place under Fred Brooks. There was architecture, engineering, software, those were under me for initial planning, and market requirements, which wasn't under me.

Norberg: Market requirements.

Amdahl: We talked about market requirements. Market requirements was to be staffed with some people with marketing backgrounds experienced in the field. The software was to be the operating system, that is, the general structure from the standpoint of what the environment was in which this thing was to operate, and specify the software, but not to do all of the software development. It was just to do the specifications. The engineering was to do the timing of the data flow structures for all of the members of the family, and at that point to pass it on each one to a different engineering manager for carrying out the actual engineering projects. But the structure to be defined was to have the performance and cost goals that were to be set for each of those machines. Architecture was to be a continuing activity.

Norberg: What do you mean by continuing?

Amdahl: Well, architecture had to define how the machines were supposed to function, the interface that the machine would present to the user and to all separable parts of the system like the peripherals. Define the instruction set and the access that you had to that system for debugging purposes, for example. It did not specify an interface between memory, because the memory was considered too different between models.

Norberg: I guess I would have used a different word than continuous in this case.

Amdahl: No. It's a continuing function that still exists today.

Norberg: For 360? Or . . . continuing function in that sense. Yes, I would have seen it as the overriding group where most of the things in the other three are defined by what happens in architecture . . .

Amdahl: Oh, absolutely.

Norberg: Therefore, they become sort of the management group, in a sense of the design.

Amdahl: Well, I think that's what Bob [Evans] had in mind, and Fred Brooks had in mind, but it wasn't what I had in mind.

Norberg: Why not? What is it you had in mind?

Amdahl: I had in mind that we should be looked on as helpful to engineering, helpful to software development, not controlling.

Norberg: Why not? Wouldn't it seem effective to control them?

Amdahl: Because you don't make anything happen in IBM very effectively, if they view you as a threat. You'll start to have power struggles. Power struggles were the last thing I wanted to have to be involved in, because the whole undertaking was basically a power struggle within the corporation. Each of the machine families, that is the managers responsible for them, could see their empires coming to an end when the 360 took off. This forced them to do some of the bitterest internal battles you could imagine, particularly between divisions, which now no longer had independence in the product that they were to develop, because we were in one particular division and three of the projects were in different divisions.

Norberg: For a project as complex as 360, I would have thought you'd need to have some group, or some person, making the final decision about, "We'll go this way and not that way."

Amdahl: Well, that was my responsibility.

Norberg: It was.

Amdahl: Yes.

Norberg: So it's not a consensual business that we're talking about.

Amdahl: No, that's right. But what I did was I brought in representatives. I did the data flow first, with some kernel like a person or two in each area. And I did the data flows with them for those machines. But they were not the managers that would come in to take it over. They came in when the time was right to pass it over, which was probably a year and a half later. Those organizations kind of got built up during that period a little bit. Then the managers took over the individual machine models. But they were all brought in with the recognition that they had to be compatible. If they had a problem, they had to resolve it. At the same time, we had established a relationship so that their problems could come to our immediate attention, and we would work together to resolve them. We would work between the members of these groups. Now, many times I was asked to hire more people and I told them it wouldn't work. I wouldn't be able to play the role that I was playing.

Norberg: Did these four groups that you just mentioned to me: architecture, software, engineering, and so on. Did these groups have responsibility for only one of the machines in the 360 family, or for every machine in the 360 family?

Amdahl: The market requirements really interfaced only with architecture. Architecture interfaced, and I had the responsibility for data flows for all members of the family, and the interface to them from that time on, even in World Trade, as well as the General Products Division.

Norberg: How did this work with, say, IBM Hursley [in the U.K.], which had the low-end machines?

Amdahl: I used to travel over there quite regularly, and had people that worked over there for quite some time with them. Some people came over and worked with us on data flow. We talked a lot with them about their technology, found a lot of that very interesting, and tried to spread the gospel in other places about some of the use-ability of some of that technology. Each project, however, ended up using a different technology for the control store, which was inefficient. They had already tested their technology and so had the most experience with it. We also found their participation very effective. So they were represented in architecture, just like people from the General Products Division during the [IBM 360] Model 30 definition. We had two people that went over to Germany and worked with them doing the model 20. They were over there for over a year. In retrospect, model 20 could have been totally compatible, but it wasn't. They elected to do a subset. And we ended up having to do another machine, the model 25 to fill the gap.

Norberg: Well, it seems to me this is defeating the purpose that the company set out to do.

Amdahl: That's right. At that time it was impossible to convince people over there.

Norberg: Over where? In Germany, or in corporate?

Amdahl: In Germany. I think it was in Germany. It was impossible to convince them to try, because they viewed it as verging on the ridiculous.

Norberg: How did they express that?

Amdahl: They didn't really have a discussion with me; they had it with my two people there. On the other hand, it was corrected in the model 25 from that time on.

Norberg: Was Model 20 eventually dropped? Or did that continue for some time?

Amdahl: I don't know.

Norberg: Well, there is one other question that I should ask. How large, then, did the architecture group get?

Amdahl: Considering members that were also members of engineering, we got up to about 20 on the CPU, and probably another 10 on the channel, I/O.

Norberg: That doesn't seem like a lot to me.

Amdahl: It wasn't.

Norberg: But these people were spread all over the world as well, in five facilities, I guess it was.

Amdahl: Yes, and there were about 15 of us that were headquartered in Poughkeepsie all of the time.

. . .

Amdahl: The [architecture] team that I was on consisted of Elaine Boehm and Jacob Johnson.

Norberg: Two people who had worked for you before.

Amdahl: Yes. They had worked for me way back.

Norberg: In the early 1950's.

Amdahl: And we put together a proposal. Gerrit Blaauw and some of his people put together one. One came in from research and there was one or two more. We programmed three sets of data processing applications that we were to compare. We were also to point out the general capabilities that we were trying to achieve with the architecture. He selected ours as the approach that appeared in the System 360.

Norberg: Now was this a foregone conclusion?

Amdahl: No. As a matter of fact, I assumed that Gerrit Blaauw would win.

Norberg: I see.

Amdahl: But I felt that it was really the only way we were ever going to make sense out of that organization.

Norberg: Now, was this proposal that your group made in this competition different than the approach that was being taken in Project X?

Amdahl: Yes.

Norberg: You had developed a new one. So you had gotten over the problem of it being too uneconomical?

Amdahl: Yes.

Norberg: And how did you get over that problem?

Amdahl: Well, we had used a push-down store in Project X. It didn't complicate high-speed operations. It had the effect of being related to formula evaluation. It had been worked out differently, I believe at Burroughs at that time, and maybe if we'd taken their implementations things might have gone a little more effectively at the low end, but the high end wouldn't go as well.

Norberg: Were you aware of Burroughs' activity at the time?

Amdahl: Not in detail. We knew roughly what they were doing.

Norberg: How did you know that?

Amdahl: They did some papers. They had some machines out in the field.

Norberg: Now you have approval to go ahead with your design. Did this win over Blaauw and others?

Amdahl: Yes, they understood why we had done what we did—the combination of both base registers and indexing, so that the addressing structures registers could be made up of an origin and a sequence count using base registers and index registers, but out of a common register set, which allowed the reduction of the number of registers required.

Norberg: Now, did you feel at the time that this would cover the whole range of machines that were planned?

Amdahl: Yes, because we had been looking at how we would do the high end and how we would do the low end. We estimated performance. We didn't do the intermediate ones; they were assumed OK. So we were set then at that point knowing what we would do with the Model 75 and with the Model 30, the two machines we were looking at. We were not looking at the Model 20 at that time. That one hadn't even started yet and we weren't looking at Project X, because that wasn't in the Data Systems Division plan, even though I still had this verbal charge from Piore to keep Project X alive.

Norberg: Had the Hursley people taken part in this competition as well?

Amdahl: Oh, yes. There was a proposal from them and some of those people participated in the architectural planning.

Norberg: How well expressed was the proposal that was put to these groups for competition? Was it two pages, 20 pages?

Amdahl: I think it was just a verbal announcement.

Norberg: And would this have come out of the Spread Report as the objectives for the program?

Amdahl: It had nothing to do with the Spread Report.

Norberg: I realize that, but didn't the Spread Report propose objectives to be achieved?

Amdahl: Oh, yes, the Spread Report did have those objectives, although I never saw the Spread Report.

Norberg: How were the [Spread Report's] objectives transmitted to someone to know exactly what they were doing?

Amdahl: Fred had them, and he was my boss, presumably that was the way I was shown them. He had implemented them in such a way as to make recommendations to our group regarding byte size and addressing.

Norberg: How much interaction then was there between you and Brooks?

Amdahl: A fair amount. After this shootout, if you like, on the designs, Fred was very much concerned that I was going to put Gerrit in a meaningless role. We had kind of limped along at one point, because of format weaknesses, and I wanted to make a change at that time, which would have been a violation of Spread. And I wanted to go to 24/48 words, which would allow us to go to either six bits or eight bits. That, of course, was verboten. I presented that, Fred said no, and I said, "I don't think we can do an effective job on the floating point." Somehow or other, his response made my hackles rise. Probably still over his concern about Blaauw. His not wanting to be there in the first place. Blaauw having suffered what he had to suffer. Anyway, he gave me a direct order and I said, "I want to talk to higher management. I can't really do that." So the next thing that happened I had a meeting in Bob Evans' office, just the three of us. Bob put on the blackboard the pros and cons, and he rated the 8-bit byte as having a weight of 60% because it was different from other vendors.

Norberg: Why? Why not 40, or 100, or whatever?

Amdahl: It was more than 50%, that's all that was important.

Norberg: So in effect, you lost at that point.

Amdahl: Yes. Anyway, I sat there and listened to what he had to say and what went through my mind was that one thing was quite clear, I can lose and I won't have anything, or I can accept this and go this way. I won't get a machine as good as I would have liked, but at least I'll have had a chance to do it, which is a lot better than becoming a nonentity. So it was about the only choice I could make.

Norberg: Now what sort of problems did you have to overcome to do it that way?

Amdahl: There were problems with how you split the exponent. I wasn't really all that happy with hexadecimal and normalizing. You lost definition on truncation. Your truncation error accumulated a little faster. And your range on the exponent wasn't as wide as I would like.

Norberg: What sort of calculations would that have affected?

Amdahl: I think it would have made the computer a much more effective scientific computer. When I say much more effective, I don't know that IBM really very seriously went after the scientific computing. At that point they wanted to do something that was reasonably good for engineering, and could be presented as a scientific computer, but recognizing that not very much money was spent on the scientific end of it. Probably some hang-over from [IBM 7030] Stretch days when you got neither a scientific nor a commercial computer.

Norberg: But I would think that IBM at that point would be looking at the commercial market as the bigger one, and therefore, in Evans' view, the truncation probably was not very serious.

Amdahl: It turned out that had been determined at the Spread meeting, although it had been told to me that it was to be 8 bits, it wasn't really clear to me that that was a requirement at this point.

Norberg: But that suggests the Spread committee had gone rather deeply into architectural considerations in the system.

Amdahl: Oh yes, that's right. But only as to whether or not you could control with microprogramming. Except for byte size and addressing, they didn't go into how a machine should be structured internally. I recall those kinds of implementation concepts were left open.

Norberg: After this meeting, since this is after the proposal evaluations as well, was it a clear path then to the rest of the solution of the problem of developing the architecture for this scheme?

Amdahl: Well, the next part in that particular story was that we had one more meeting with the group vice president, which I thought consisted of . . .

Norberg: A follow-on to the . . .

Amdahl: Only five dollar words which didn't really say anything.

Norberg: Was this a follow-on to the Evans Brooks meeting?

Amdahl: Yes.

Norberg: Was it needed?

Amdahl: Well, it was needed to show top management that the rift was healed. Then Fred also was still not satisfied. He came to me and wanted to clear up what kind of role Blaauw would have. I thought Blaauw should have the role of defining decimal. This was agreeable to Brooks.

Timesharing in Academia and ARPA

J.C.R. Licklider
Ivan Sutherland

Introduction

J.C.R. Licklider was into interactive computing in a big way. He knew what a terrible waste of time and effort batch processing was and wanted to do something about it. That's what time sharing was all about. He felt researchers should have access to a powerful computer, on demand, in new interactive ways, and be able to immediately see the results and share their results with peers within their universities and also at other research facilities via email. All you would have to do is visit CEIR's large-scale data center in the early 1960's to understand why. Programmers would be at our center day and night, seven days a week, in order to get access to the computer. This might take all day, or all night, if we were busy. If there were errors in the code, or data, which there usually were, the programmer would have to start the process all over again. If this seems very tedious and an enormously inefficient use of personnel time, it was. Also, the bill for the computer time at $500 an hour could grow ominously with just a few errors.

University data centers of the time weren't much different, except students were the lowest on the computer totem pole. There had to be a better way. Licklider's solution, along with others, was timesharing. It featured large-scale computers linked to terminals in each user's office. Not everyone agreed that timesharing was a good idea or would work. Some said that it could take most of a computer's resources in overhead just to keep track of users, thus defeating the whole idea. For example, Lincoln Labs installed IBM's 360/67 timesharing system under industry pioneer Oliver Selfridge and rumor had it that it was struggling to support three users at a time.

Maybe, that's why it eventually disappeared. So, there were major technical problems to solve.

That's where ARPA (Advanced Research Projects Agency) becomes key because it had the money to solve the problems and Licklider knew how to work the system. For example, Licklider was at Bolt Beranek and Newman (BBN), then went down to ARPA, and then back to MIT. In essence, Licklider was showing the way. Licklider must have been a blithe spirit, because he formed a psychology department at MIT and was awarding Ph.D.'s before MIT's administration knew anything about it and put a stop to it.

Incidentally, BBN was a remarkable company for its time. It was like a combination government/academic research center/company incubator, much of it focused on computing. Other brilliant people were located there such as Jordan Baruch, whom I would get to know later. Some spun out timesharing companies such as Lew Clapp, or were involved with the MUMPS (Massachusetts General Hospital Utility Multi-Programming System) which is still going strong under different names. Leo Beranek, a co-founder of BBN, is an unusual individual who is still very active at 100 years old. I often see him and his wife, Gabriella, at the Boston Symphony Orchestra where they have been big supporters for many years. Incidentally, he got his start by helping a retired Harvard professor fix a flat tire in a small Iowa town. This led to a fellowship at Harvard as his excellent book, *Riding the Waves: A Life in Sound, Science, and Industry* (2008) recounts.

Investment in timesharing at MIT's Project MAC was underwritten by ARPA. This is where Ivan Sutherland comes in. He is an industry pioneer in his own right as the "father of computer graphics" as demonstrated by his famous Sketchpad system of the early 1960's. He was recruited to run the key office in ARPA regarding such research despite being just 26 years old. He did have a Ph.D. in Electrical Engineering from MIT and had spent time at BBN so he was well qualified technically. Ivan Sutherland, too, is still going strong. He is a co-founder with his wife, Marly, of the Asynchronous Research Center at Portland State University in Oregon. They are designing and testing asynchronous chips, which they see as the replacement to the synchronous chips that the computer industry currently makes and is committed to. It's the system at work again. Ivan and Marly believe that the computer industry can't meet the performance requirements of new computers with such chips without breaking the laws of physics as discovered by Albert Einstein. They are determined to get around the system and do something about it.

J.C.R. Licklider, with the help of Ivan Sutherland, got around the batch processing mentality of the time to introduce timesharing in an effective way in academia. This would lead to the ARPANET (Advanced Research Projects Agency Network) and the Internet.

AN INTERVIEW WITH

Photo courtesy of MIT Museum

J.C.R. Licklider

Conducted by
William Aspray and Arthur Norberg
October 28, 1988
Cambridge, Massachusetts

purl.umn.edu/107436

Norberg: The date is October 28, 1988. We are here in the office of Professor J.C.R. Licklider to talk about his experiences, both in the MIT community and with the Advanced Research Projects Agency in the Department of the Defense. Professor Licklider, we are curious to know how you became associated with the Lincoln Laboratories back in the 1950's.

Licklider: I came to MIT from Harvard University, where I was a lecturer. I had been at Harvard. I was involved in MIT's summer study Project Hartwell and Project Charles on air defense, which led to the creation of Lincoln Laboratories.

• • •

Norberg: What was the nature of the problem of the presentation of data as people saw it in the early 1950's?

Licklider: Well, it was essentially that, here for the first time we were coupling computers with sensors like radar and sonar. It was possible to do things now that just couldn't have been thought about before. We had plan position indicators, and A scopes and stuff like that. But there were many new dimensions now. For instance, in air defense we wanted methods of saving the air situation for successive seconds, and plotting tracks, not blips, and coloring the tracks so that we could see which was the recent information, so that we could tell which way the thing was going; try to get some way of neutralizing the ground clutter, which was relatively stable from sweep to sweep—all sorts of stuff like that. We wanted to process signals so that we could get noise out of the signal with electronics better than we could visually, although we could not take into account its sophisticated relationships. Display was about 80%; control was about 20%. The light gun came out of a group in Lincoln. Then we turned the light gun into the light pen. We never did have mice in Lincoln.

Aspray: In your visits to the universities recruiting personnel, what did you look for in the students?

Licklider: Orientation to theory and experiment. Psychology, at that time, was pretty well divided between experimental and clinical. We were really not in the market for clinical people. We were looking for experimentalists. My bias was toward very bright people. I did not care very much what they knew or what they were interested in. I even made an agreement with all these kids: I told them that if they wanted to keep on working on their Ph.D. thesis project, they could do that up to 50% of their time. But I told them, "You won't want to do that after six months, because this is really an exciting thing that you're getting into." And it was true. They all started off working on their Ph.D. Then everybody left it; there was much more excitement in the new study.

Norberg: Who were some of the people you were able to encourage to come?

Licklider: Bill McGill, who later wound up being president of Columbia; a fellow named Joe Bennett, who, unfortunately, died early. He had a bad heart, but he was brilliant and fluent. Bill Harris, who is still a staff member of the Lincoln Laboratory—one of the few who's still around. Herb Jenkins, who is at McMaster University in Hamilton, Canada.

Aspray: How did you learn about Bolt Beranek and Newman?

Licklider: It was a spin-off of the [Harvard] acoustics lab. I worked in the acoustics lab with Bolt and Beranek, Jordan Baruch, and Sam Labate, who were other members, and they started spending more and more time with their company. They could see the computer was going to be important for them too—they didn't know just how. Here I was really determined to go learn it.

Norberg: Did you hire Bolt, Beranek and Baruch, or had they been around as students?

Licklider: Oh, no, they were senior to me. Bolt and Beranek were two or three years older, I guess. Baruch was maybe a year or several years younger. He was a graduate student at first. But Bolt and Beranek were instrumental in getting me down here from Harvard. As a matter of fact, my first office at MIT was in the acoustics lab. There still is a big space back there that isn't full yet. They simply built an office for me on top of Leo Beranek's office.

Norberg: I guess what I was trying to get you to say was something about how you became interested in digital machinery and moved away from the analog machinery.

Licklider: There was tremendous intellectual ferment in Cambridge after World War II. Norbert Wiener ran a weekly circle of 40 or 50 people who got together. They would gather together and talk for a couple of hours. I was a faithful adherent to that. When I was at Harvard, I came down here and audited Wiener's work. Then there was a faculty group at MIT that got together and talked about cybernetics and stuff like that. I was always hanging onto that. Some of it was hard for psychologists to understand. But Walter Rosenblith was understanding and he did a lot of explaining to me. As a matter of fact, he audited a course down here two weekends ago. There was a young fellow named M. Fred Webster. Routinely we'd talk about it on the way down in the car, and then listen to this stuff. Then on the way back, Walter would more or less explain it to me. (laugh) Digital stuff was big in all of that. Also, there was Whirlwind. I knew about and then visited Howard Aiken's lab [at Harvard]. Once I had the pleasure of riding on an airplane with Aiken, and got to know him enough to be somewhat inspired by that.

Norberg: In what period did you get to know him?

Licklider: It was just about the time that Jay Forrester was getting Whirlwind up and running.

Norberg: Is this also about that same time, when Whirlwind One was . . . ?

Licklider: Yes, I do not remember the timing. Ken Olson, Norm Anderson, and their group had spun off from Lincoln to form DEC, which was a maker of plug-in modules—digital modules. One day, they saw that, my God, we can build a computer. We've got enough parts here. All we have to do is put them together. So they made this thing. Bolt, Beranek & Newman bought the very first one they ever made. In fact, they let us have the prototype while they made the first production machine. So we wound up with this PDP-1. Somewhere along the line when I was early at BBN, Ed Fredkin came to see about a job. It was obvious from the beginning that he was a young genius. So, we got Fredkin working at BBN. At that time he was having all kinds of psychological problems about getting work done. We had fantastically interesting and flexible arrangements, like figuring out at the end of each month what his salary for that month should be. But he was absolutely marvelous. He designed up this drum with MIT in just a few days. Anyway, that was a serious computer. You can make an argument that, although it had better graphics, in other respects it was almost exactly a Radio Shack TRS 80-100 computer. It had about that computing power, a little less memory, and it ran a little slower. Everybody connected with it just sat at the console and did on-line interacting programming and since I was of the first one, I got most of it.

Norberg: This is about the time you wrote the paper on man and information, is it not?

Licklider: The thing called "Man Computer Symbiosis?"

Norberg: Yes.

Licklider: Yes, that was in there somewhere. I do not know what the date of that was. 1960. It was just a statement about the general notion of analyzing work into a creative part that seems to be heavily involved with heuristics and routine programmable parts that you could see exactly how to get a computer to do. That was really based on some measurements I made on myself. I tried to keep schedules and see how much time I spent doing what, and I was pretty much impressed with the notion that almost all the time I thought I was thinking and working, I was really just getting in the position to do something. Also, I had an experience with Jerry Elkind and his manual tracking experiments, which he had done as a graduate student under my supervision (although he was an electrical engineer). He was pretty clear [that] there were some relationships in his data; he had all these things plotted on graph paper. There was a stack of them, and we could never see them all at once, and could not tell what was going on until we put big heavy blobs wherever there was a datum point, and went down to the Sloan building where I happened to have an office at the end of a little mezzanine where you could stand and look down on the floor below. So we redirected traffic a little bit, and put all these graphs down there, we had a hundred or so sheets of graph paper. Then it was obvious what was going on. I was pretty much impressed.

That happened frequently: you do a lot of work, you get in a position to see some relationship or make some decision, and then it was obvious. In fact, even before you could quite get finished, you knew how it was going to come out. "Man Computer Symbiosis" was largely about ideas for how to get a computer and a person thinking together, sharing, dividing the load—mainly heuristic versus algorithmic.

Through the work at BBN, I got acquainted with people in the computer world. Also, through the work of Lincoln Laboratories. So I guess I knew pretty well that there were people at MIT, and Harvard, and UCLA—I remember George Brown ran the Western Digital Network, or something like that, under IBM funding at UCLA. I had a number of notions of where to go. It was not starting absolutely cold. But most of the time that I was at BBN I did not know that I was going to ARPA at all. It happened rather suddenly.

Norberg: How did it happen?

Licklider: Jack Ruina was director of ARPA and was given responsibility for a command and control project that got set up from inside the Office of the Secretary of Defense. The contract was let by them through ARPA to System Development Corporation to do some command and control research. It was envisioned that that would grow. There would be more to it than that one thing. So Jack wanted somebody to do that. Simultaneously, there was a recommendation from the Defense Advisory Board that the Defense Department look into supporting some behavioral research, particularly through some institutes that would be set up to bring behavioral researchers together with better facilities. Jack wanted somebody to look into that; maybe do something about that. Fred Frick, whom I first knew at Harvard in the Psychology Department at Harvard, was in all of this at Lincoln. By that time, Fred was at Lincoln. Fred and I went jointly to talk with Ruina. We were both interested in what he was talking about, but neither one of us wanted to leave what we were doing. I guess Ruina got Gene Fubini to give us a sales pitch and we decided, yes, this was so important that one of us would do it.

Norberg: Do you recall what sort of arguments Fubini used about ARPA and its objectives that might have helped to convince you?

Licklider: Well, part of it was when we got talking I started to wax eloquent on my view of the thing: that the problems of command and control were essentially problems of man computer interaction. I thought it was just ridiculous to be having command control systems based on batch processing. Who can direct a battle when he's got to write the program in the middle of the battle? Fubini essentially agreed 100% with that and so did Ruina. We started seeing that. Here this whole military thing was not developed right. The kind of computing almost did not exist, but up in Cambridge everybody was excited about making it exist. Why didn't we really develop an interactive computing? If the Defense Department's need for that was to provide an underpinning for command and control, fine. But it was probably necessary in intelligence and other parts of the military too. So, we essentially found that there was a great consonance of interest here, despite the fact that we were using different terms we were talking about the same thing.

Norberg: What sort of man was Ruina?

Licklider: In my view, brilliant; for a scientist amazingly competent in finance and all kinds of fiscal administration. As a manager, it seemed to me that he had spent long enough to decide he understood what I was trying to do, and that I would probably work hard to do that, and then just wanted to have a report periodically—was I on track or not? He had much bigger fish to fry; this was a small part of his life. I've told him since that I've felt that that was a kind of benign neglect. Every time I possibly could, I got them to say interactive computing. I think eventually that was what they thought I was doing.

Norberg: Well, why? Why did you want to push interactive computing so strongly?

Licklider: I was just a true believer. I thought, this is going to revolutionize how people think, how things are done. You know, yesterday or the day before I heard a talk about productivity and about improving it 7/10 of a percent per year, or something. I thought we were going to double it or triple it, or multiply it by four or ten or something; and I still feel that way.

Norberg: Why did you believe this?

Licklider: Well, I was one of the very few people, at that time, who had been sitting at a computer console four or five hours a day—or maybe even more. It was very compelling. I was terribly frustrated at the limitations of the equipment we had, but I also saw how fast it was getting better. So I was just a true believer in my own propaganda, I guess.

Norberg: Who else did you talk to about this question of interactive computing before you went to ARPA?

Licklider: Oh, all the guys around here—Minsky, McCarthy, Fredkin (maybe especially Fredkin: he is a tremendous enthusiast), Tom Marill, Wes Clark, Larry Roberts, and Ivan Sutherland.

Aspray: Did they share your view?

Licklider: Oh, yes.

Aspray: Was there a disagreement at all about this in this community?

Licklider: Well, people like Minsky and McCarthy were primarily interested in artificial intelligence, and tended to view man-computer interaction as a neat and convenient thing to make it possible to write AI programs, whereas I thought there was going to be this interval between man's thinking about himself and machines taking over. I do not know how long the interval was, but it looked like a considerable interval, when working with the computer was of the essence. So, in short, I really believed it, and quite a few people in the area here thought that something really great was going to happen. Belmont Farley was another one of the fellows. He worked with Wes Clark on the Memory Test Computer.

I thought the computer money was going to pay for about ten laboratories. Probably the most important thing I could do was get some stuff started very fast; get things committed so it couldn't go away. The other thought was that I really wanted to set this up on three-year funding, because I was not going to be here too long and I wanted to get something set up.

Norberg: Why ten places?

Licklider: I had this picture that Cambridge is a good reinforcing community. There were enough different places doing related things that if you just had a single group doing something, nobody knew whether to believe it or not. But if Harvard had something, and MIT had something here, and there was something at the Lincoln Lab, and BBN had something, and maybe Otto Burnett had something at MGH [Massachusetts General Hospital]—it reinforced. I would have liked to see that happen in Cambridge; I'd have liked to see that happen in Los Angeles or the San Francisco area; maybe one other place. There was always in the back of my mind the idea that, if we could ever get time, we would see if we could not do something in Texas or the Midwest, and create a cognitive center where there wasn't one. I never did really get around to that, although ARPA has tried a couple of times.

• • •

Aspray: Were these contracting organizations already contracting for ARPA for other programs?

Licklider: Yes. In addition, there was something called Defense Supply Service Washington (DSSW), which was a kind of captive of the Secretary's office. If you needed something to happen in a hurry, it was possible to get it to happen. I believe I had one from concept to contract in two weeks. I think SDC (System Development Corporation) started off $9 million, or $7 million. I have forgotten which it was—probably $7 million.

Aspray: Did you have some control over how much they got of that, and when, and what they used it for?

Licklider: I do not know how to deal with this. To be frank about it, I was not impressed with some of what they were doing and cut them back a bit. But I did not do too much of that, because I think all of us are convinced it is easier and better to get more money than it is to take money away from people who spread it around. So they came out of it pretty well; they were a little mad at me, but not terribly.

Aspray: Can you tell us what they were doing?

Licklider: Yes, they were doing command and control research. They were doing database research. One of the really good things they were doing, I think, was that they had the first research, the first thoughtful approach, to how to deal with large databases. They were interested in complex programming, and had a project which was essentially just an excuse for making an extremely complex program, that allowed them to learn how to make them stay on top of complex programs.

Aspray: What did you not like about the work that was going on there?

Licklider: Well, essentially I did not like it because it was based on batch processing, and while I was interested in a new way of doing things, they were studying how to make improvements in the way things were done already. They had what I thought was a pretty great asset. They had one of the four new SAGE computers that the Air Force decided not to go forward with. So there were these four machines, and they had one of them. I hated to see it sit there being used as an old batch processor.

Norberg: So you have a philosophic difference there as to what is going on. Why not encourage them to change, and provide them money for the change?

Licklider: I did exactly that. I even let a contract with a little firm that Fredkin had set up just to give Fredkin time to go take the Cambridge word and transplant it to SDC. Of course, there were drawbacks about that. They did not like to be told what to do. But it did work, in fact. There is a fellow named Jules Schwartz, who is the father of the language called JOVIAL. Really good programmers are fairly easy to spot, especially for other really good programmers. I will not claim to be one, but I certainly was associated with them, and I spotted Schwartz as a really positive character. We supported him to the hilt. We got him to turn a machine into a timesharing system, which I think he enjoyed doing. So, it went well. I did not really have a bad battle with SDC, but I was aware that this was cheating a little bit. I would insist on my philosophy, my vision of what I wanted to happen here, and these people had every right to have their own vision.

Norberg: That's fine. I am just trying to set up an extreme contrast to get you to remember some of these things more clearly.

Aspray: You were clearly committed to this timesharing, or interactive mode of operation. Did Ruina have the same kind of commitment, or would he have been happy if [you] had developed computing for command and control in the existing way and improved upon it?

Licklider: Well, I think his attitude was something like this; that I perceived that command and control really needed some work. It was recognized as one of the three or four main foci of military effort, but we did not know how to do it.

Norberg: This is 1962 you're talking about now.

Licklider: Yes. Well, we needed to get some work going. If we had just done command and control studies, we'd done them well, nobody ever asked too much about them, and then maybe we got a little military interest in them, we would have been reasonably happy. I think he saw that, "My gosh, maybe there is a big theme here. Maybe it is possible to develop a kind of computing, called interactive computing, that will make a significant change in it. That would be great. That's what I'd like ARPA really to be doing." And so, without being convinced it was feasible or anything else, I think he said, "Let's go along with it." I think he also had a feeling, "I have got $50 million or $100 million in getting these nuclear warheads back in; why can't I have 10 or 15 in command or control without . . . " I think he saw it as no big deal, and possibly it would work out doing it the way I wanted to do it.

Norberg: Were there presentations to Ruina, and perhaps to others, in the early months that you were at ARPA?

Licklider: Yes. I even went over to the CIA and gave them a pitch. I had to tell them, "Look, I do not know what you're doing about this. I hope you are doing the following. But let me tell you about what I am doing, and then maybe we can figure some way to talk about what the relations are." I guess it turned out they were not doing it, but I did not know that they were not. I tried to make my presentation so it wasn't too parochial in case they did know about it. Similarly, at NSA (National Security Agency) they really needed what I wanted, and Fubini thought they had it. One of my early jobs was to get in to see that they did not have it.

Norberg: I see. So, did you suggest that people build in both facets, or were you the person who was doing the building in?

Licklider: My first tour at ARPA was too short to build in anything. I did not feel much pressure to make a military case for anything. I tried to stay at the top level of the block diagram, and tried to convince people of the philosophy that in general the same thing is needed. If I had stayed longer, I would have had to be specific.

Norberg: All right, back to the office then. You arrived; you had this money; you had only one contract that you needed to worry about with SDC. How did you go about finding people to do work in interactive computing?

Licklider: Well, somebody gave me a little talk, "Lick, you cannot just go write proposals for people. You're a government employee now; you've got to respond to suggestions." So I took advantage of the presence of those SAGE computers. I could take the initiative of going around and talking to people, "Do you want one of these things, and what would you do with it if you had it?" People were pretty sensible. Nobody wanted one, but it did lead to a lot of discussions; and discussions lead to proposals and so forth. So, I was able to get proposals out of MIT, Harvard, the University of California at Berkeley, Stanford, UCLA, and, oh, where else? Quite a few places; I have forgotten how many contracts there were, but they came pretty fast.

Norberg: To do what? What were these contracts specifically about?

Licklider: Well, some of them were to build timesharing systems, because we needed to have timesharing systems before we could do man computer interaction research. For instance, Berkeley built a timesharing system. SDC built one; MIT built one. That may have been it. There was not really very much graphics. We didn't have the facilities for doing graphics. There were contracts on displays, controls, databases, organization of the main computer interface. Stanford Research Institute did work on these. Doug Engelbart was already working there before I got there, but he was working on a shoestring, and we funded him pretty well.

Aspray: How did you identify these centers? I mean, MIT is obvious, and maybe one or two others are, but you listed a range of places like UCLA and Berkeley.

Licklider: Well, partly it's people; partly the reputation of the university. I had been going to computer meetings for quite a while. I'd heard many of these people talk. There is a kind of networking. You learn to trust certain people, and they expand your acquaintance. I did a lot of traveling, and in a job like that, when people know you have some money it's awfully easy to meet people; you get to hear what they are doing. (laugh)

Aspray: Right. Well, let me ask it in a different way. You do not map one to one onto all of the established computing centers at the time: there is a fairly large center already at Wayne State; there is one at University of Michigan; there is one at Georgia Tech. But I do not see money coming to those places; I see them going to other places. But, am I interpreting what you say correctly when I say, the individuals were more important than the existence of a well-developed computer center and program at an institution?

Licklider: Well, the thing is that we had computer centers all over the country even then. There was a big computer and arrangements for putting in your deck of cards and getting out your printout. But in most of those places there was not much promise for the research I wanted.

Norberg: In that period, somehow, MIT—that is, the community here in Cambridge and Boston—was thinking of computing in a way essentially quite different from people in other parts of the academic community—certainly different from people in industry. It was trying to strive for some sort of discontinuous circumstance where a new world of computing would develop out of the research. What is not clear to me, first of all, is whether others did not have a similar sort of vision. That we would have to inquire about. But secondly, whether or not enough of the required pieces to make that work—the displays, the interfaces, the expanded memories—were seen as part of an overall plan at that time, each piece of which would need to be attacked in order to achieve interactive computing. The way you just described your visits to the various groups suggest that such a vision might have been in your mind, but it isn't clear to me whether it was a clear vision at the time.

Licklider: Well, it surely was not clear. Take this area here. Here's a mass; here's a keyboard. A fellow named Herb Teager thought that you get rid of that, and you put a sheet of plastic down here, because it was an inductive coupling. Go out to RAND and it was the same thing: "It is a sheet of plastic; it is capacitated coupling." My thought was, "It does not matter which they use, but we better have two projects, because people tend to goof up on these." And then the mouse . . . Engelbart had a mouse. There was some difference of opinion about how many buttons there ought to be. "Oh, that's trivial. Why don't we get somebody to do research on how effective a thing like this is. Is this a function of off-set, and comparing this with light pens?" and so on. "Herb Jenkins does that at the Lincoln Laboratory. Maybe if Engelbart wants to do some of that, that's fine. But let's try to think of all of the schemes—horizontal and vertical scopes, languages. Let's not get into the language business, but let's see if there are essentially new ideas about languages." And so on.

Well, I used to draw big sketches on big sheets of paper. Then I would lose them. But I had pretty well wrapped up in me all of the topics that it would take to put interactive computing together. I deliberately talked about the intergalactic network, but deliberately did not try to do anything about netting them together, because it was becoming very difficult just to get them to run. The concept that would say: this is pertinent, this is relevant, and this we can let alone for now; so I would create a network of contracts in which one place might do some subset of things that did not necessarily fit together to make a total system. But if I was going to be successful, I had to have some kind of a system here. Maybe have one place interact with another, get these guys together frequently, and have special Computer Society meetings. We would get our gang together, and there would be lots of discussion, and we would stay up late at night, and maybe drink a little alcohol and such. So I thought I had a plan at that level. I could talk about it to people in ARPA. It was easy to have plenty of topics in the outline carried down three or four levels if I found a guy who wanted it that way. I even invented a way to keep books on how much money was being spent on what, that did not say, you know: "Here's this contract and we will put this in this category." Instead it said: "This contract is dealing with these issues, and the money is . . . " I could take the whole pile of things and say how much money went to each part, and what the interactions were. That blew the minds of the accounting people; they had never seen that. Still, they didn't heckle me much about being the manager there. It was a different dimension. "Oh, go talk to him and he will talk your arm off for two or three hours about that. Better avoid him." So, to come back to your question, it was not a clear vision, as certainly, not that: "We'll plug them all together, and that will be the system"; but, rather, it was a matter of getting a supply of parts and methods and techniques, and different people will put together different systems out of it.

Norberg: I guess it was not the technical side that I was interested in exploring in that question (although you answered it quite nicely), but it was the management side. Did you discuss with them what their procedures were, and did you then apply those procedures to your own operations?

Licklider: No, I viewed myself, and they viewed me as not a very good manager, but didn't think this was essentially a "manage" job. I could always say, "Well, ONR (Office of Naval Research), and the AFOSR (Air Force Office of Strategic Research), and organizations like that are seeing to it that the progress reports get written."

Norberg: So, their objection was a detail objection, rather than a programmatic objection about management, and whether or not you were a good manager.

Licklider: No, they were always kind of amazed that I wanted to travel light. Some of my colleagues liked to have a big office with quite a few people in it. My attitude was, "Time is of the essence. It has gone by, and I don't want to take time to hire somebody. Not when we've got these good people already." There wasn't much time spent on that. The worst thing that happened to me administratively, or managerially, was that there was an old-line bureaucrat in the Secretary's office, who really wanted me to spend my money on something quite different from what I was spending it on. I guess I would repress that guy's name. He got somebody to write a letter saying, essentially, that he didn't see real value in what I was doing. This kid who was picked to write the letter came to talk to me. We weren't close friends, but I knew him, and he didn't want to do this dirty trick. He came around and told me about it. I told him, "Well, gee, Russ, I really don't want that letter to get over the system." And he said, "Well, I think the best thing to do is that I forget about it and you forget about it. I'll let you know if there is any more pressure about it." And it never raised its head again.

Norberg: What was the letter about?

Licklider: It was just an expression of non-faith, or disbelief, that that's not the kind of research we need. I did have a kind of a battle with WWMCCS (Worldwide Military Command and Control System). I'm not sure whether that was really well-formed when I was there the first time, or whether that came later. I'm afraid I flashed out some times in frustration. I said something like you guys are just running a big batch processing center and haven't got your stuff networked enough. It was being run by a guy from IBM whom I vaguely knew. But that wasn't really much of a battle either. They were too busy. They were chronically six months behind on their programming. They didn't have time to fight.

Aspray: Was there a certain ethos about there being an ARPA way of management at the time?

Licklider: I don't think ARPA had convinced itself. There came a time when ARPA thought it was awfully good. I think the first time I was in ARPA that hadn't really emerged much. Ruina was brilliant. [Robert] Sproull, in a different way, was at least as brilliant. The third floor E-ring was populated by very bright people, McNamara's whiz kids, and so forth. So, there wasn't much bureaucratic fighting that I saw. I told you about these two instances, which were the main ones that I could think of. There were problems, like some character came around with a gun that shot little rockets—50 or 100 little rockets—and demonstrated it in my office. The place was left a shambles. There were administrative problems of that sort. (laugh) We were lucky not to be blinded.

· · ·

Norberg: In the early years of ARPA, from its beginning—essentially 1958—through some time later, there was a considerable amount of sometimes open, sometimes not so open conflict between the military services and the director of ARPA, maybe even some of the program people. At least in the early years, there was a sense of impending doom on the part of some of the ARPA people, that indeed, their mission might be wiped out in the Department of Defense. Did you sense any of this when you came, or had that disappeared?

Licklider: No, I didn't even quite realize that was the case. In my area we were cheating a little bit, because when we talked about the military we talked first about ONR, AFOSR, and the Army Research Office. Well, Marv Dennicoff and ONR were close personal friends. I knew if I shook hands with him about something there was no question. Charles Hutchinson in AFOSR. Then the next step would be into operational military that didn't really care much about research programs. We did a lot of visiting of Fort Knox and the interior of a mountain of Colorado, mainly so that we would be surely current about applications. The military development people weren't really in our circuit. I think when it comes to the Strategic Defense Office, or the Tactical Defense Office, or the Reentry Physics thing, or any of those, they had real competitors in the military. But what might have been our competitors were really our agents and our friends. I felt more threat, really, from secretary's offices in the [Pentagon's] E Ring, and not too much there.

There was, for instance, a guy who was in charge of inventory of some kind, I guess. He had 24 databases, and I had a hard time avoiding the assignment of making his 24 databases interactive. So he had the picture that he was going to sit in his office at something, and talk with these 24 databases. I studied it a while and I said, "Oh, my God! Most of them are batch-oriented. There's millions of dollars to spend transcribing records. I've got to stay out of that." It was unbelievable, but he had this kind of a terminal, not hooked to anything, and said, "Licklider, what I want you to do is to hook this up to my 24 databases." He wasn't wanting my money or anything like that, but I could have taken on a responsibility in a relation to him that was just beyond my power to tinker with. I mean, I could tell him, of course, "Ten years from now, if we're successful, you're going to be in command of all of that. That's where were going. But let's not make . . . Sorry."

Norberg: Well, there was one little piece of jargon in there that I didn't understand—the E Ring?

Licklider: Oh, in the Pentagon the concentric rings are A, B, C, D, and E—E is outside. The second or third floor is the most prestigious, depending on if you've got a uniform or not. The Secretary of Defense is on the third floor in the E Ring.

Norberg: I see.

Licklider: And your proximity to the secretary's office is important. Well, first you've got to stay on the E Ring if you're anybody, because they've got outside windows. Then the closer you are to the Secretary's office, the more important you are. I was in the D Ring, so nobody was trying to get in my office. But I was still close enough; I could interact with those bright guys. And they were bright. Oh, what a fantastic bunch of people!

Aspray: At the time that ARPA starts funding computing, the money from the federal government is coming from ONR, from the Air Force, starting to come from AEC. How did your presence disrupt or change the way that the funding patterns came at the time?

Licklider: Well, there was a bad feature, because the amount of money we had, although it was a pittance in modern terms, was pretty much then and its presence could be used, for example, as a reason why ONR didn't need any more money in the computing field. You know: let ARPA do it if ARPA has got all that money. On the other hand, we did have meetings. A gang of people who had some computer money to spend got together. For a time, I think we had a meeting every month. And we were fairly factual with each other about what we had. So to try to answer the question, I think that the fact ARPA had a fair amount of money was inhibitory on the others, but they did help ARPA spend some of its money, and so in some sense they had more than they'd have had without ARPA.

Norberg: Okay. Can you give an assessment, then, of what you think your accomplishments were in the two years in the first tour in that office?

Licklider: Yes, I think that I found a lot of bright people and got them working in this area, well enough almost to define this area. I got it moving. I think maybe the best thing I did was to pick a successor, Ivan Sutherland, who was surely more brilliant than I and very effective, and who carried it on. I think that the main thing ARPA has had is a series of good people running an office, and a fantastic community. I guess that's the word. It was more than just a collection of bright people working in the field. It was a thing that organized itself a little bit into a community, so that there was some competition and some cooperation, and it resulted in the emergence of a field.

Norberg: How do you think that emergence of the community occurred? Was there a particular mechanism that you think stimulated it in that period?

Licklider: Well, let me just make claims about what I did. I think I was a good picker of people. Of course, I realized I could not go give a professor at Irving an intelligence test, but I was just deliberately trying to get the best people I could find, those who were interested in this area, into it.

Norberg: All right, I'm going to ask the question yet another way. Did you set conditions on the awards that you made to these people?

Licklider: Set conditions?

Norberg: Yes, what were the conditions of making a contract with, say, MIT?

Licklider: Well, in that one, my main condition was that they should produce a proposal that would be a statesmanly work, because it was going to be my first one, and I wanted a real good proposal. I wanted interactive computing; I wanted timesharing. I wanted: "Computers are as much for communication as they are for calculation." A lot of these themes in it. Then I wanted assurance there were going to be good people working on it. I wanted a summer study that would bring people from all over the industry that was going to try to shape up this field and make it clear what we were doing. I also said that I wanted a lot of help, although I didn't want that written in the proposal, I wanted a lot of help.

Norberg: What do you mean by a lot of help?

Licklider: I wanted to be able to get an MIT person to visit SDC, or I wanted people to take time off from their research to have meetings to think about how all this was going to go.

Norberg: Did you think about giving a contract to anyone, whether it's MIT or anyone else, which would be a large amount of money that they could then decide how to distribute among the various groups that were doing research? Or was this prescribed before you received the proposal?

Licklider: No, the Project MAC, for example, did not prescribe what the groups should be. The reason for calling it Project MAC, instead of a laboratory, was that it was going to use existing labs to a considerable extent. Existing research groups were going to come into it. MIT had a lot of flexibility in just which projects to do. But it was clear that there's got to be artificial intelligence. There's got to be timesharing. There's got to be interactive stuff like the Teaager Tablet and graphics like the thing called the Kludge that Sal Loventhal did. I would have been very unhappy not to have Sal Loventhal modeling protein molecules, because, to me, that's going to be a dramatic step. I really had to have that, and lots of other things, like the civil engineering Stress and Strudel and those things. I didn't really hear much whether they were in or out. They did exercises on the system and were perfectly good things to develop, but what I needed was an inventory of examples to make things concrete.

Norberg: How closely did you work with the proposers?

Licklider: It ranged. In the case of MIT, Bob Fano worked the proposal. I talked with him at some length on two or three occasions. But I knew Bob very well, and he was a good writer. I felt badly, because this was just absolutely crucial to me, because it was my first one. A lot of people were going to see this, and he had to make a good one. In other cases, I practically wrote the proposal myself, because I could not beat into the head of the research guy that you've got to have milestones. Don't ask why you have to have milestones.

Norberg: Well, the reason that I ask that question is in reading over the MAC memorandum in the spring of 1963, you were organizing a meeting to be held in Palo Alto, which was to take place in early May. A memorandum went around saying that it was going to be impossible for you to be at that meeting, and so could people shift to a week later, because you had to spend a week at MIT—no reason given. "For externally driven reasons," was the phrase used in the memorandum.

Aspray: Let me ask the question a slightly different way. Did you find people who approached you about doing research projects that you thought were technically feasible, and perhaps even important research, that you didn't fund because they were in areas that were outside a few that you were concentrating on?

Licklider: Well, for example, a fellow came to give me a pitch about mathematical technique in engineering. I've forgotten exactly what it was, but it had to do with digital system functions. I knew enough about it to see that this was a real good idea, but I didn't know enough about it to know whether it was original with him, or whether if I talked with other mathematicians that they would tell me, "Oh, yes, we know about that." I didn't fund that, but I did try to help him get connected with people who had mathematics money.

Another example was when a guy had a twist on the general theory of relativity—a somewhat different approach to it that came out looking very similar. I went to the trouble of getting some physicists to study it and advise me. Finally, I decided not to deal with that. But I think Larry Roberts, who succeeded me down the line, did fund it. I think by that time Larry had the excuse that he had some equipment that would facilitate doing it, and he could always say he was using this as a driver. But I don't know whether this is getting at your question. I felt constrained to the general area of interactive computing. I was not afraid to go make little scallops outside it, if they seemed particularly exciting. In a behavioral science I had less limitation than that. I was funding work on pain, and neuronal work, as well experimental psychology. Anyhow, I funded a guy in Toronto that I thought was going to win the Nobel Prize. He didn't, but his work was very favorably received.

Norberg: Let me ask two more questions and we can bring this to a close. First of all, did you, in your capacity as program manager, have any interaction with people in the White House? I'm thinking particularly of staff members for the President's Science Advisory Committee.

Licklider: Yes. At that time there was a thing called the Multinational Force or concept. It looked as though there might even be people from several different countries on the same ship, or in the same group. So how could we declare war if we have got 15 heads of state. Well, I have since written about teleconferencing, and looked at the history. The earliest pieces I found were from our program at that time that we set up in direct response to the White House's request to get hopping on teleconferencing at the Institute for Defense Analyses. I mentioned psychologist Vamos at MIT—he had gone to Stanford by then, I guess—and got him as an external consultant to us. We ran teleconferences. It was very primitive in those days; a teletype machine was about what you had to work with. We'd run conferences face to face, and through teletype, and also, we had some video that was just simulated.

Wiesner was Science Advisor through at least part of that time. I had been very close to him here at MIT. So he gave me some chores to do. I discovered that he was really very sensitive. My bosses in the Pentagon didn't like me working for him; I was supposed to work for them. There was another thing going on at that time. From the library work, I was interested in the flow of scientific and technical information. There was a fellow named Weinberg, the head of the Atomic Energy plant in Tennessee, who had written a document about the national effort in scientific and technical communication, proposing a lot of stuff. So I wrote a kind of a follow-up to the Weinberg Report. That was directed to the White House connection. There wasn't, at that time, anything we had that I could deliver to them.

As a matter of fact, it wasn't till one of my last two or three days in the Pentagon that I had a console in my office. It was connected to computers here and in California. When Ivan Sutherland succeeded me, he had a steady stream of military people, including generals and admirals coming to play with that console. He found that he had to put it in a little room that was big enough for just one person, because if an admiral were sitting at the console, and there were junior officers looking, the admiral was afraid to move his fingers for fear he'd reveal he didn't know what to do.

Norberg: And my last question is, how did you come to choose Ivan Sutherland?

Licklider: Well, I had known Ivan for a while. I thought he was a brilliant person, and he was a true believer in the things I was a believer in (and, in my view, better at it). I had lots of talks with Sproull, and Charlie Herzfeld, and several of the others, about if it is going to be possible for such a young guy to make it in the Pentagon. They worked hard on how to set it up. For instance, a colonel couldn't report to this guy who was a second lieutenant, or something like that. They got enough arrangements made so that there wouldn't be protocol problems—or not too many of them. There is one other aspect of it. Several of us in the field, who realized that Ivan was being wasted in some job in Michigan that he'd been assigned to, got him moved to the National Security Agency.

Norberg: Was he a military person at the time?

Licklider: He was in uniform—second lieutenant. He was such a success at the National Security Agency, and developed such a following there that the ARPA people thought, this is really going to be pretty good to have. That's always been a kind of rough and rocky connection for us. Also, you might say, it wasn't easy to get a successor for me. Most of my colleagues would much rather spend the government money doing research back in the lab than coast another year or two or three in Washington.

AN INTERVIEW WITH

Photo courtesy of U.S. Army (CBI subject file)

Ivan Sutherland

Conducted by
William Aspray
May 1, 1989
Pittsburgh, Pennsylvania

purl.umn.edu/107642

Aspray: This is an interview on the first of May, 1989, with Dr. Ivan Sutherland in the Pittsburgh airport. Let's begin with just a few questions about the time before you came to DARPA. Did you have any experiences with computing, either in your bachelor's degree work at CMU (Carnegie Mellon University), or your master's work at Caltech before you went to MIT?

Sutherland: Well, I had my first experience with computing in high school. So I have been familiar with computers for a long time. I had built various relay machines as a young student, and had built various devices using logic through college, and through graduate school. I had a summer job for IBM after my bachelor's degree. The reason I left Caltech and went to MIT was it was clear that computing at MIT was better than at Caltech at that time, and it was a clear-cut case of the right thing to do.

• • •

Aspray: Had you known J.C.R Licklider at the time?

Sutherland: Yes, I had known Licklider. Not well, but I had known him a little. I knew Licklider from various conversations I had had with him, but I did not know him socially or well. I did not consider him a friend. Later on, I grew to know him much better. The man who was the director of ARPA at that time was Bob Sproull. Bob Sproull had been, I think, head of [a big physics laboratory] at Cornell. I do not know just what he was when he went to run ARPA. His son later became my business partner. He and I are now in business together. But I did not know the son at that time. It was not until some years later that I ever even met the son.

Aspray: Yes. It is a small community though.

Sutherland: Well, the Sproulls are very smart people.

Aspray: What was the mandate for the [IPTO] office?

Sutherland: Well, when I got there the Information Processing Techniques Office was quite new. Licklider had established it two years before—and I think had established the mandate which was basically to support advanced programming methods, which he interpreted to mean, I think, online aids of computing. My understanding of where that mandate came from was a recognition in the Defense Department that billions of dollars were getting spent on software, that software productivity was a problem, and that something needed to be done to improve the productivity of the software world. That problem obviously has not yet been solved.

Aspray: Were systems like SAGE an example of the software problem?

Sutherland: Well, as I recall, the software in SAGE cost more than the machine. It cost more than the hardware. That was kind of a shocker, because people had thought earlier that it would be just simply a matter of programming (SAMOP), which it never is.

Aspray: What did the program look like when you inherited it?

Sutherland: Well, it principally looked like there were a few major contracts. There was the Project MAC contract at MIT. There was a contract at SDC, which was a major effort. There was a contract in place at Berkeley to do timesharing work, which turned into the SDS 940. That was run by a man named David Evans that I got to know through that connection. There was a contract at Carnegie Mellon, which Perlis and Newell basically were the principal characters in charge of. I would say that those were the four base contracts. Licklider had, I think, chosen those contractors on the basis of their general capability. I took the position that the key figures in those contracts were key sources of counsel for me. I felt that those were the kind of senior people in the field, and they had a pretty clear idea as to what good things to do were. I used to call them informally to ask them for advice on various other matters. In fact my task was made quite easy by the fact that Licklider had established a baseline and a direction that the office was going. So there were essentially no great battles to fight. There was no real problem in terms of anybody questioning the quality of the research that was going on. That set of contracts was, I think, quite well done. Now there were critics. Who was the guy who wrote all the FORTRAN books?

Aspray: McCracken?

Sutherland: Was it McCracken? I am not sure if it was McCracken, but there was one critic who was very critical of the whole timesharing idea and the notion that online computing was worth anything. He was quite outspokenly critical of the ARPA program, principally because of its focus on online use of computing. I had had some experience with that personally and recognized the value of it. So I was not concerned as to whether we were going in the wrong direction, and I think events subsequently have demonstrated that it was, in fact, a direction that the industry has largely gone.

I think that I would not have been able to establish a broad scale program of the sort that Licklider had established. I think that he thought it through very clearly in terms of who the good people were. He told me quite directly that his notion of what was needed to form a good program was to get the best people in the country putting their minds to what they thought was the best program. So he did not presume to invent the program out of the whole cloth. What he presumed to do was to select the folk.

Aspray: Yes.

Sutherland: That turned out to be a remarkably wise thing. The principal thing I learned about that kind of research activity is that the caliber of people that you want to do research at that level are people who have ideas that you can either back or not, but they are quite difficult to influence—that in the research business the researchers themselves, I think, know what is important. What they will work on is what they think is interesting and important. You can maybe convince them something's of interest and something's important, but you cannot tell them what to do and get good research. Good research comes from the researchers themselves rather than from outside.

Aspray: Yes. So that also includes their peers. What kind of influence did one contractor have on another?

Sutherland: When I first went to the office there was me and a secretary. There had been Licklider and he had had a colonel as a deputy, but it was felt to be improper for the colonel to be my deputy, so the colonel disappeared into the ARPA staff as opposed to the IPTO staff.

Sutherland: Al Blue was the administrative guy who kept me straight in terms of what I could and could not do, what made sense contractually, how the paperwork had to flow and so on. He was very important.

Aspray: Was he also important in helping you with the inside culture at DARPA? You already had some experience of this yourself firsthand.

Sutherland: The inside culture at DARPA?

Aspray: Or within the DoD (Department of Defense)—the relationships between DARPA and the military agencies.

Sutherland: You know, I have a theory that agencies develop arthritis as they grow older, and that arthritis comes about because various people think that they need pieces of paperwork that at the outset have not been invented yet. ARPA itself was only five years old or something at this time. ARPA had been created as an organization suddenly in response to SPUTNIK. It was created with directors from outside DoD. The directors traditionally had been found outside DoD. They were not bureaucrats, but were typically university folk who were coming to try and do some reasonable technical job for the government with a minimum of fuss. There really was not very much fuss in ARPA. In fact, to get something done, what I had to do was convince myself and convince my boss. He apparently had spending authority. Now, how he in general convinced his boss, who was Harold Brown at that time, is something that I was not party to. But my understanding of the mechanism was that if I could convince the ARPA director that something was sensible to do, it got done.

Now I think that along the way there were a fair number of folk who were kibitzing. I mean, from an administrative point of view, Al Blue had to think it made sense. I do not think that I did anything that was so outrageous that it would be brought into question. But there was really very little required. There were justifications required. There were sole source procurement justifications required. The reason and the background for the operation had to be written. I always felt the principal hurdle to get through was to convince the ARPA director that it was a sensible task. I guess Al Blue and the administrative machinery ran smoothly enough that the ARPA orders got written. Then the actual administration of the contracts was done by somebody else.

Aspray: Right.

Sutherland: So the ARPA order was, in effect, a check, which was written to ONR, or to the Army, or whoever. One of the things that I did was try to get sensible liaisons between which of the services was going to do the administration, and what the contract was. So, for example, we liked using ONR a lot with the universities, because ONR had its own university program and understood university people well. It had a smooth-running mechanism for that. Some of the things involved activities where the Army needed to get involved so we got the Army folk to do some things. Then Rome Air Development Center got involved, and there were a few people there who showed interest in some programs. So, for example, I think when Dave Evans went to

Utah I got a small contract set up with him at Utah, and we did that through Rome Air Development Center. The intention there was to get Rome more in tune with the advanced things that were going on, to try to get technology transfer going more into the Air Force.

Aspray: Why do you think you were chosen for the job?

Sutherland: I believe that nobody else would take it. I believe that over the history of that job it was difficult to find good people to fill it. I think a few good people have been found to fill it and, by and large, it has done pretty well. But I think that the task of filling those positions in ARPA is getting increasingly difficult.

Aspray: What are the reasons for that?

Sutherland: Well, I think they are twofold. One of them is financial, clearly, that the folk that I would like to have filling that job in particular are people who would take a cut in pay of a factor of two to take it. That would not be so bad, except that all of the folk of that sort have various investments in this and that, which they would be expected to divest themselves of. So that makes a very difficult situation. Then the other issue is to what extent the flexibility that ARPA had in the early days remains. I think one of the reasons I was asked to go do that was that I was fresh. I did not have any set of commitments. I was in the service, and from my point of view it was a great assignment. If you have got to be a lieutenant, be a lieutenant in DARPA; it was a fine place to be. It did not change my pay scale any. I think the next two directors that followed me, Roberts and then Bob Taylor, were also kind of in that position. Roberts was fresh. He had just finished his Ph.D. at MIT, and he was just starting out. He was my contemporary. He was able to do something very important at ARPA—namely the ARPANET. That was a very key and important thing to do, but he came in at a time when he did not have a great set of other commitments to give up. One of the ways to fill those jobs is by picking promising young people who are not yet encumbered with all of the difficulties that taking a position like that forces you to give up. But they have to have the ability to trust young people. I mean, Sproull stuck his neck way the hell out, in some sense, in hiring a 26 year old lieutenant to do that job. His neck was stuck way the hell out on a limb. But I think that is something that ARPA might well do. If I were asked to recommend people for that IPTO (Information Processing Techniques Office) job now, the people I would recommend are at the assistant or associate professor level, rather than senior people. That gets more difficult as the bureaucracy gets more complicated.

Aspray: Let's turn to your program for a while. You inherited what you say was a stable and, what sounds to me, a program that you largely had some satisfaction with.

Sutherland: Oh, it was a good program. They were very good people.

Aspray: Okay. So tell me how you went about making the program evolve over time: what kinds of factors you looked for, what kinds of new areas you were thinking about, how you chose people to do these.

Sutherland: Well, I tried to do some things that would seem sensible. There were three things, I think, that I can mention, where I started new activities. First of all, let me tell you about my major failure. Licklider had dreamed about having a network of computers, and in typical Licklider-ese he had called this the Intergalactic Computer Network. "Lick" was a wonderful guy; he had these wonderful words and ideas. He was just marvelous. So I thought I would have a go at that. I got the University of California at Los Angeles, which had three major computers, to put together a program to make a network out of the three. That was never very successful. I think it was never very successful because it was not something that they wanted.

What it took to make networking happen in ARPA was two things. First of all, there was Larry Roberts, who understood in some considerable detail what the technical detail was. He was supported by the Bolt, Beranek & Newman contractors. I think Bob Kahn actually was at Bolt, Beranek & Newman at the time and did much of the actual technical work of making the network happen. So there were some first class research type fellows involved, one in the administrative position, and one in the research position, probably more in the research position, counting those who had a research interest in making it happen. That was an ingredient which I had not been able to find. Now, to what extent the fact that ARPA was interested in networking and had been interested in networking for two, or three, or four years before the ARPANET sort of came into being, to what extent that influenced their thinking, I do not know. You will have to ask them. It may be a little like a sculptor chipping away at a rock. You know, he hits around with a chisel half a dozen times, and then one time the chip breaks off. Now, which of those hammer strokes was important? Only the last one? I do not know whether it was a thing of that sort.

· · ·

Aspray: I interrupted you, or got you off on a tangent from talking about your program. You have talked about a failure and two successes.

Sutherland: Yes, I have talked about the one failure, which was the Network, and I have talked about macromodule work. What was the other one?

Aspray: Graphics.

Sutherland: And the graphics thing. Then the biggest thing I started was the ILLIAC IV (Illinois Integrator and Automatic Computer). I do not know how I got involved in that. Daniel Slotnik came into the office I guess, and he seemed to have very interesting ideas about what to do. I tracked that for a while. He settled down in Illinois, found a job in Illinois and made a proposal. It was a pretty good proposal. I recall calling together a meeting of half a dozen key people. Sid Fernbach from Livermore was there. Herzfeld, who was the director of ARPA at the time, attended. Al Newell might have been there. I am certain that somebody from Carnegie was there. They concurred that it was a good idea, and Herzfeld thought it was a good idea, so we went ahead and did it. I started that program fairly late in my tenure, so it did not come to fruition until several years later. It went on for a decade, or more. It was a major program in the office over a long period of time.

· · ·

Sutherland: Well, the two places that were good in artificial intelligence at that time were Carnegie and MIT. They always have had quite different approaches to AI. I think the reason for that comes out of Newell's background as a psychologist—that the Carnegie folk were always interested in taking protocols of human behavior, trying to model human behavior, and understand what thought was. The MIT folk, I think, were more interested in getting interesting results, no matter how. So it was quite appropriate, you know, that LISP (LISt Processing) was invented at MIT and has become an important ingredient of that. I think lots of interesting results applicable over a wide variety of things have come out of MIT. I think the Carnegie people have been much more scientific in the sense of trying to understand what the relation between computing and thought really is—a much harder topic.

Aspray: Thinking back to that time, were the differences in the two approaches already clear and were their research agendas pretty established about this time?

Sutherland: Oh, yes, it was absolutely clear. You had only to talk to the principal people involved. The difference is clear today. I mean, go talk to Newell, and go talk to Minsky.

Aspray: Yes.

Sutherland: It is perfectly plain. It was then; it is now.

Aspray: I see. It was not clear to me that these were not programs that had solidified in their minds over a period of time.

Sutherland: Oh, I think not. I think if you look at the early papers you would even see that is reflected in the early papers. The kinds of things that they did were quite different. I mean, the MIT people got interested in theorem proving and integration. Slagle did this thing on how to do integration fairly early on. Clearly you do integration by having a bag of heuristics that you apply. You can integrate by parts. You know the heuristics.

Aspray: Yes.

Sutherland: Then you have strategies that you try. Then you get a tree of all the things you could do, and you try and prune the tree back to the promising ones.

Aspray: Yes.

Sutherland: But it is not clear whether the machine does it in the same way that people do it. I do not think Slagle ever collected a protocol on how a human being does integration. He simply plowed in and wrote some code, tried different things, and pruned the tree in various ways and did it with rather little concern about how people think about it. In that same period, Newell and his people were collecting rather thoughtful protocols about how people solve problems, and they were trying to understand whether there were any keys, whether the area could be unlocked by understanding the one existence proof that we had, namely people.

Aspray: Artificial intelligence seems to me a good case for asking this question about its reception within ARPA. It is an area where the research may not have immediate, obvious defense relevance. Can you talk to that point?

Sutherland: Well, it is kind of interesting. I remember when I did my thesis talking to Larry Roberts about stacks and lists. It was pretty hard to understand what they were all about. One of the things we worked on was trying to get the structure of those things better. The idea of a hash table and the notion that you could sort of characterize first programming as something that you just did was unheard of. The artificial intelligence people, I think, pioneered many of the advanced computing techniques: non-numeric programming; dealing with compiler languages; describing languages and so on. I think that that whole effort has now reached a point where it is what is taught to undergraduates as computer science. That has got to have enormous impact. And the idea that one ought to use a list for some purpose, as just the natural thing to do, is something that grew out of that early activity. So I think the defense relevance of the work that was going on then is pretty easy to defend now. But, you know, relevance has a time scale associated with it. If I were the official responsible for a large budget, what fraction of the budget would I be willing to bet on a ten year time scale, or a twenty year time scale, versus what fraction do I want to bet on a two to five year time scale. I think that that is a hard judgment call to make. There was a fair amount of criticism on and off about the artificial intelligence stuff. It has had its ups and downs.

Aspray: From within or without the agency?

Sutherland: Well, I do not recall being hit with too much of that while I was there. But as I watched afterwards, I noticed that there were periods when more AI work was being sponsored, and it was okay to do AI work. Then there were periods where it was not okay, and big questions were raised. I think there was a JASON summer study that was brought to bear on the question of whether it should be done at all. There is always the hope that computers will do something that is really hard. Even when I was in ARPA, the Army had this set of tank and non-tank images, and one of the problems was could you recognize tanks in aerial photographs? There was this wonderful set of tank and non-tank images—I think there were a hundred images. Some of the tanks were half under a tree, and some of them were recognizable mostly because of the tracks, the trail that they leave behind. For 20 or 25 years there has been the hope that some artificial intelligence program or vision program would be able to recognize tanks reliably. The last one of that sort that I became aware of was a [DSB] study done about four or five years ago that looked at one such proposal. The result was not very satisfactory, as I recall. There was a period fairly recently, I think, where the artificial intelligence stuff came under fairly strong attack from within ARPA. Bob Kahn probably was the guy in charge of IPTO at that time, and he probably can tell you about what the events were. I did not get involved in it.

. . .

Sutherland: The proposals that came in were mostly unsolicited proposals. The ones that came in formally, that came in as fat written proposals and so on, were probably too late in the sense that they were already formulated too clearly and too fixed in form to fit into the programs that I had going. The way the office in fact worked was that proposals would be developed over time through conversations between myself and the principal investigator and other people. By the time a piece of paper was written down, it was already pretty much decided what was going to happen. Sole source procurements were possible in those days, usually on the basis of some key ideas that investigators had. We did mostly sole source procurements, and I think that in this particular area that is quite appropriate. The concept that you can go out with an RFP for research activity when what you are buying is the cleverness of a few individuals anyway seems to me to be a conflict in terms, but I guess that is because I grew up in an earlier era.

Aspray: Well, that suggests to me that you were in regular contact with the research community, at least with your PI [principal investigator] community. Were you making many trips to see them? Were there conferences called on a regular basis? Were you on the telephone with them regularly?

Sutherland: Well, I was out of the office more than half the time. Somebody kept score and remarked to me at one time, "Do you realize you are on the road more than half the working days?" I was—and quite purposefully. The way I found out what was going on was by going to talk with the people, and meet with them. When new ideas came into the office I would go and try to visit people at their own site, and talk to the PI and the people that were working for them, and try to recognize whether it was an interesting bunch of people.

Aspray: So new projects came about out of conversations you might happen to have with them on one of these trips.

Sutherland: Yes, or they came about when they came to my office, or in a variety of ways. The three projects that I mentioned worked this way. In the case of the macromodule thing, I had known the people for a long time; as for the Utah thing, Dave Evans had been a contractor of the office, and I got to know him as he was running the project at Berkeley. The project at Berkeley did two important things. First of all, it developed a whole computer system, which SDS (Scientific Data Systems) subsequently sold as the 940, with the design of the SDS 930 basically modified onto the 940. Then it provided a training ground for a whole collection of people—the most notable of whom was Butler Lampson. Who else went through that program? Mel Pirtle, who subsequently ran the ILLIAC project, had gone through that Berkeley program as a student of Evans. So, I had known Evans. I got to know him, and when he moved to Utah he came in and said, "I am going to Utah, I have got these ideas about graphics, and I would like to get something started." I gave him some very modest funding which I think Taylor subsequently increased. As for the ILLIAC IV project, I don't know how it got started. I think he came into the office one day and said . . .

Aspray: Yes, we have heard that the proposal came in over the transom. That was the expression that was used.

Sutherland: Yes, but it did not come in as a document, or it may have come in as a document originally, but that was not what it turned out to be, because Slotnik did not have a place to work. I got to know Slotnik when he worked at Westinghouse. He came into the office and said, "Basically, I want to do these things and I cannot do it at Westinghouse, because they will not let me do it. Where should I go?" I introduced him to some of the university folk. So that one was fairly a long time in the doing.

Aspray: Yes. Were there principal investigator meetings run during your time there?

Sutherland: I recall calling a few such meetings. There was a machine at IBM that had been built that had a very large memory. It had a million words or something of memory. It was the biggest memory around. Some of the artificial intelligence guys wanted to get a hold of that machine, wanted to use it for various purposes. So I called together a meeting of the relevant people and the IBM folk, looked at how we would get a contract in place that would let them use that machine. So, yes, I would say that there were some specialized meetings of principal investigators. I did not make a regular habit of principal investigator meetings. That did not happen until later. I think maybe Bob Taylor started that one out.

Aspray: That sounds right from what Taylor said to me.

Sutherland: Yes, Taylor would have done that sort of thing. He was my deputy, you know; he was at NASA and came over and worked with me.

Aspray: I want to ask you about that in a few moments, or you may even talk about it now if you like.

Sutherland: Well, I did not start any formal set of meetings, but when there was a special reason for one I did not hesitate to get people to them. I remember one meeting that we had in which the subject was character sets. This was before ASCII (American Standard Code for Information Interchange), and there was some problem about how would people communicate, and what character set should we use. Al Perlis put the whole thing in context. He came into the meeting and said, "I am absolutely in favor of character set standards." He said, "My character set is available as the standard." (laugh) Do you know Perlis?

Aspray: I have not met him, no.

Sutherland: He is one of the world's most articulate people. He has got a wonderful sense of humor. This is absolutely typical of Al Perlis. In one sentence he expressed the whole difficulty of getting standards together.

Aspray: Tell me about Roberts coming on board.

Sutherland: Well, Roberts is one of a handful of smartest people I know. He is just very, very clever. I think he had a pretty clear picture of what the computing field was. I knew him really well because we had been graduate students together. I think when I was leaving there was some question about how to get a successor and who the appropriate successor would be, and so on. I remember there were two or three people that we tried to bring in, who for one reason or another either did not want the job, or could not do it, or something. I do not know what the timing was.

Aspray: It would certainly not be very difficult to put the genealogies together of students and teachers, or people who worked on programs, those sorts of things.

Sutherland: Yes. I think the impact of the university research was fairly clear, that the university has a property of disgorging people. I think Licklider recognized that early on, and set the program up as principally a university research program. Now, if I look at what has happened in ARPA since, there is some core base of university research out there, but there is a much larger piece now that is industrially based, and that is still specific, probably, to various companies. I wonder about the efficacy of that, in terms of its long-range impact, and I am not sure that the dollars get the same multiplier over a five-to-ten year period that they could get by doing good university research.

Aspray: Another question that comes to my mind after you said SDC is, what was the relation at IPTO with IDA during your period?

Sutherland: There were some studies that IDA (Institute for Defense Analyses) brought on that were never very big. There were a couple of guys that I used to interact with there. Do you remember any names?

Aspray: No.

Sutherland: One of the things SDC did while I was there was they did this study of online versus offline programming. Are you familiar with this? It was an amazing result. They did a double blind, properly four squares—whatever the psychologists do—the right kind of experiment and ascertained the value of online programming. They asked, are programmers in fact more productive when you give them the terminal to sit at? And the answer is that the programmers all like being at the terminal better, but the differences between good and bad programmers are way larger than the differences between online and offline programming. The bottom line is, if you give a good programmer any damn programming tool, he is a lot better programmer than a bad programmer with the very best programming tools.

Aspray: Okay. Why did you leave the office?

Sutherland: It was time.

Aspray: What do you mean by that?

Sutherland: Well, I went. I said I would stay about two years. I had a career to get on with. It was time to go do something else. If I recall, I left at the beginning of a summer and started teaching at Harvard the next fall. Harvard had offered me a tenured position, and it was too good a deal to turn down.

Aspray: I see. Do you think that the time at IPTO had helped your career?

Sutherland: Oh, absolutely. No question.

Aspray: In what ways?

Sutherland: I got to know everybody. What is maybe more important is everybody got to know me. It was absolutely super from the point of view of getting an insight into what was going on—very important.

I was at Harvard two years. Then I went to Utah to join Dave Evans, and we started the Evans and Sutherland Company with private venture money. I worked at the University of Utah and did some of the research which was at that time supported by ARPA. So my graduate students at the university were ARPA-supported.

Aspray: Fair enough. Now I want to give you an opportunity on tape to make any general comments you want about ARPA and its importance or problems over time.

Sutherland: All right. I would contrast the ARPA approach to sponsoring research with what I will call the NIH (National Institutes of Health) and the NSF (National Science Foundation) approaches, which are basically peer review approaches. It's perfectly true that an office director in a peer review situation can cause to happen any damn thing he wants by who he chooses for the review. Nevertheless, the perception that the peer review mechanism applies permits Congress to say, "Okay, this money will not be wasted because good folk will be watching." You know, a lot of people are watching.

The ARPA approach has never had peer review mechanisms. It has been done basically on the individual initiatives of people in the office with whatever advisors they have chosen to seek. But the director of ARPA and the director of IPTO have had, in fact, a good deal of spending authority. I think that there is room for both of those mechanisms in the government. They are both important. But they are able to do quite different things. When what you want to do is to provide a large base of research to carry a field forward in the steady progress that you want to have in a field, as NIH does, then it seems to me that the peer review mechanism is excellent. For example, it's important that the government put a lot of money into the medical field, and it's important that it be well spent and spent broadly across the country. What the peer review mechanism is weaker at is activities, like in the computing area, where there is a big outburst of things happening, where an insight like that which Licklider had, that online computing is important, or like that which Roberts had, that networking is important, where an insight like that by an individual can make a big effect. It seems to me that that happens mainly in fields where turnover is very rapid, where progress moves quickly, like in computing, where you have had this factor of two a year kind of thing.

Aspray: Right.

Sutherland: Peer review is rather more cumbersome, because it tends not to take those courageous moves. I always felt, when I was in ARPA, that one of the strengths of the U.S. government was that there were multiple funding agencies. If I was a researcher with some computer-related research idea, I had three or four places I could go. If I did not get along with ARPA, I could get along NIH or NSF, or with the Army, or the Navy, or whatever. It seemed to me that a strength of the operation was that there were alternatives. What I hope is that ARPA will not become hide-bound and tied up in a peer-review mechanism which would make it like most of the other agencies, so that it would be unable to make the courageous moves. I do not know to what extent organizational arthritis is setting in. But I sense that there is quite a lot of it. For example, the number of sole source procurement is way down. The need to initiate programs and then go out with RFPs in a very rather formal way, and evaluate the RFPs in a rather formal way, is stifling to individual initiative.

If that is true, then maybe the thing to do is to take ARPA and turn it into a stable peer-review kind of organization and start something else that is not peer reviewed, so that you have a place where individual leadership can be exercised. I do not know who in the government worries about that question. I rather suspect that no one does; that's what happens for a variety of nonstrategic reasons, and arthritis sets in to organizations because the bureau of the budget says, "Oh, we need a new report this year and annually hereafter," and there's enough fuss from various contractors who didn't get selected that sole source procurements go out because there are abuses to that—thousand-dollar hammers—and Congress says, "Oh, we cannot have that." On the other hand, when you cannot have that happening there's a lot of other things that you cannot have happening too. I am concerned about that.

Aspray: Can you give me specific historical examples of areas where the peer review programs did not support an area of research that ARPA did?

Sutherland: Well, I do not think that ILLIAC could ever have started with a peer review. I do not think that the ARPANET (Advanced Research Projects Agency Network) would have started. To get the ARPANET going, one had to move against the grain of the folk. It was a very interesting phenomenon. My observation of it is that the folk who now swear by computer nets—would not be without them for the world—are the very same people who resisted Roberts' influence. Roberts both had the technology in hand and got a good contract, with BBN, to build the network devices with good technical support from Kahn and others. But he also had the clout to say, "Okay, you are an ARPA contractor. I am providing your money. You will install one of these on the machine I am paying for." Like it or not, the ARPANET grew up, and once it was there they loved it. I think it had a big effect on the cooperation of that community. I sensed a decrease in the "not invented here" attitude of groups in the computer science departments at the universities of this country as a result of the ARPANET. I think that that is because people could go to another institution and demonstrate their software, and they could easily communicate with their colleagues at other places. So collaboration grew up where none had happened before; you could borrow software and trade it back and forth. There was a sense of community: "We are the ARPANET users. We have some important thing in common that other people don't have, so we became a group."

Packet Switching and ARPANET

Lawrence G. Roberts
Robert Kahn

Introduction

In 1961, I was hired by a Bell System company, New England Telephone & Telegraph (NET&T) to be a member of its management training program. I was told that 2,000 candidates were interviewed and only 20 were selected. What does all this have to do with Larry Roberts and Robert Kahn? Well, from my perspective, everything. You could only get black phones in those days because that's all Western Electric, the Bell System's manufacturing unit of the time, made. It was a big deal when American Telephone & Telegraph (AT&T) finally introduced phones with color, as well as phones of a different shape, such as the Princess. NET&T made its profit by hiring as many people as it could and then negotiating a percentage of the total costs with the Commonwealth's Department of Public Utilities. This set the rates. The more people NET&T hired, the more money it made, and the more political clout it had.

The same model worked with other Baby Bells across the country. This meant that the communications industry of the time was voice focused and incredibly set in its ways that had worked very well for it. The Bell System was definitely not about change. It was a monopoly. No one at the time seemed to have much of a problem with this except those who couldn't get service for various reasons, including for data communications, or those who tried to compete with AT&T such as Carterphone or MCI. No company had the "muscle" to get around AT&T without some very disruptive technology to handle networking and data communications. Sam Wyly tried to do this with his DATRAN system but he couldn't, despite some very imaginative initiatives including trying to buy Western Union. Transmitting data is a different animal than transmitting voice. This is where Larry Roberts and Robert Kahn come in. Networking of computers was going to be the foundation of ARPANET, but it wasn't going to be easy. Something new had to be invented to make ARPANET possible. It was packet switching. It would also have a profound influence on the architecture of my own company's database/data communications software. That's just one of the reasons I find their oral histories so interesting. I know what an awesome challenge it was for them to get around AT&T and the voice focused communications industry of the time.

AN INTERVIEW WITH

Lawrence G. Roberts

Conducted by
Arthur L. Norberg
April 4, 1989
San Mateo, California

purl.umn.edu/107608

Photo courtesy of Louis Fabian Bachrach

Norberg: Today is April 4, 1989. I am in the offices of Dr. Lawrence G. Roberts, CEO of NetExpress, Incorporated, for an interview about his years at DARPA. I wanted to ask you what occasioned your entry into computing activities at MIT. I know you got your bachelor's degree there as well. How did you decide to enter the computing field?

Roberts: Well, I was already involved in it by the time I got my bachelor's. I did various special projects all the time while I was in school, because the courses were easy, so I just did all sorts of other things. I took a summer job, helping the Computation Center build some equipment to convert an automatic tape unit attached to an analog tape into the 704. That was a project that I just did for them as a summer job. So I got a little involved with the computer. I wrote binary programs on hexadecimal codes, which was painful. (laugh)

• • •

Norberg: What sorts of problems did you work on with the TX 2?

Roberts: The primary project I did, besides lots of support work for this machine and other things around the place, was writing a program that did handwritten character recognition. I published that at that time. It was based on neural nets, which are now becoming very exciting; at that point in time they were also for a short period, and then they died. They have come back. I looked at that technique and developed some for hand-written characters to see if it would be effective. It worked by some odd percent, which was not quite what you would need to do anything useful. That is what everything did at that point in time before it worked. But it was my first published paper in speech in the computer conventions, and so on. I got an awful lot of experience on that computer. The interesting experience there was that I started out looking at this thing, and I couldn't figure out what this typewriter relationship with the computer was. I had no idea of why this thing did. So the guy who had built the computer showed me the prints of all the transistors. I could finally figure out, "Well, that's the machine, and that it's a finite state process, sort of. Then this typewriter connects to it over here and talks sort of at a second level." I sort of learned about operating systems from scratch, because I had to go backwards from the electronics, which I had learned in school, back up to the operating system, because nobody had taught about computers at that time. When I learned that this was an operating system and not the machine itself, then I could deal with it. It was a very simple operating system.

$$\bullet \quad \bullet \quad \bullet$$

Norberg: Do you remember the date of that first funding from ARPA? Was J.C.R. Licklider already there? Were you dealing with him?

Roberts: I was actually dealing with Ivan after "Lick." Well, yes, "Lick" was there most of the earlier time. Then Ivan came in, and he had worked with me at Lincoln on lots of projects. We had worked side by side. So when he got to ARPA, he came back and talked to me, "Well, do you need funding for whatever?" So we worked together to work that out. It was really with Ivan that I did that. That was right at the start of his thing. I myself went to ARPA at the end of 1966. So this was probably 1963 or so.

Norberg: Okay, before we go on to that period, you are alleged to have been thinking about communications and computing issues during your dissertation research. Can you tell me a little bit about that? What I am referring to is a reference that I picked up, I think, in *Datamation*.

Roberts: I've traced back the origin of the ARPANET thinking and work to a conference at Homestead in Virginia that the Air Force put on. The point of the conference was to look at the future of computing. Licklider, Corbató, and I, and a bunch of people from MIT, went to this conference. We sat around talking all night—Al Perlis, and a whole slew of these early people who were doing timesharing. We had all done timesharing; we knew what that was. This conference was in 1962. At that point, I had done all of this graphics work and all of this timesharing work (operating systems and so on), and Corby [Fernando Corbató] had done that, and we had all been through most of what we imagined people might be doing with computers for the next decade. We probably had been through the next two decades in terms of where they are now with graphics and that sort of thing. But we were looking at what came next. I was, anyway. So I talked to a lot of these people about that, not in a formal way, but informally sitting around until I came to the conclusion that the next thing, really, was making all of this incompatible work compatible with some sort of networking.

In other words, we had all of these people doing different things everywhere, and they were all not sharing their research very well. So you could not use anything anybody else did. Everything I did was useless to the rest of the world, because it was on the TX-2 and it was a unique machine. So unless the software was transportable, the only thing it was useful for was written technical papers, which was a very slow process. So, what I concluded was that we had to do something about communications, and, that really, the idea of the galactic network that "Lick" talked about, probably more than anybody, was something that we had to start seriously thinking about. So in a way networking grew out of "Lick's" talking about that, although "Lick" himself could not make anything happen because it was too early when he talked about it. But he did convince me it was important.

• • •

Norberg: All right, so the call comes from ARPA sometime in the late second half of 1966. What was your initial reaction to Taylor's request that someone wanted you to come to ARPA?

Roberts: Well, I hated to talk to him. Several times I said, "Look, Ivan, forget it. I am busy. I am having fun. I am having a great time here and I am all involved in this wonderful research. Why do I want to go waste my time and manage the thing?" That was my reaction until Herzfeld called whoever the [Lincoln Lab] head was at that time. He called me in and said, "I think it's in our best interest that you think about this and it will be beneficial to your career." So he counseled me, after Herzfeld talked to him, that it would be beneficial to get involved with all. I was also coming to the point of view, separately from this research that we were doing was not getting to the rest of the world; that no matter what we did we could not get it known. It was part of that concept of building the network: how do we build a network to get it distributed so that people could use whatever was done? I was feeling that we were now probably twenty years ahead of what anybody was going to use, and still there was no path for them to pick up. It would be much better in the commercial world where they could sell it at least, or something, rather than in this isolated research lab. In fact, we were doing things which only recently started being used in the marketplace in terms of three dimensional projections and techniques. There are other things that have developed much further. But what we were working on in some parts were very much ahead of where people were eventually going to find it economic and attractive to use, and have it really work. But we could not get it out. So I was feeling a pull towards getting more into the real world, rather than remain in that sort of an ivory tower. Anyway, this was a chance to exercise that. And in the course of all those discussions, people made me aware that I would then be exposed to a lot more, because everybody comes to ARPA. They tell them everything that they want to do. So they eventually convinced me that it was a good idea—particularly after Lincoln said that was the best place for me. Otherwise, they were in trouble (laugh).

Norberg: While you were at Lincoln in those years from 1963 to 1966, had you had any contact with commercial outfits that you might have tried to promote these new communications techniques, graphics techniques?

Roberts: No. We had published papers, and I had been involved in the conferences and all of the academic efforts, but I had not had any contact with commercial firms in terms of making it used. In fact, they were so far removed from where we were—IBM was still making non-timesharing machines, and we were well beyond timesharing and into interactive graphics—that there just wasn't a vehicle out there. We would have had to do a lot more than build a platform.

Norberg: What is it you were told by either Taylor, or Sutherland at ARPA, that they wanted you to do? What was the initial task?

Roberts: Well, to run the IPTO (Information Processing Techniques Office), but with particular attention to getting the ARPANET activity going . . . not the ARPANET, but the network activity I had in mind. However it looked. Communications technology.

Norberg: Wasn't Sutherland at this time head of the IPTO office?

Roberts: He was head of it. That was the period that was just before me. When I came, Bob [Taylor] became head—well, he had become head just slightly ahead of that because Ivan did leave, and stayed on, overlapped me a year, I think, while I was Chief Scientist, because I had to go through all this stuff. When I went there, I went there on Lincoln's payroll, because that was the deal that Herzfeld made because their paperwork was going to take time. Nobody did anything, so when I got there I wrote my own application, my own request for employment from the government, and created my own job description. I was Chief Scientist for a while so that I could learn the office and Bob could continue doing the management. So I finished up understanding what was happening, and got involved with all the programs, and saw what everybody was doing.

Norberg: This was a fairly influential year, was it not, for network development?

Roberts: Part of what I did was develop my own view of what the network ought to be and build the plans for the ARPANET. I wrote that first paper which outlined the structure of it and started working with the universities as to how they would be involved.

Norberg: How did that come about? Do you recall any of the details? How did you bring the message to the universities?

Roberts: Well, the universities were being funded by us, and we said, "We are going to build a network and you are going to participate in it. And you are going to connect it to your machines. By virtue of that we are going to reduce our computing demands on the office. So that you understand, we are not going to buy you new computers until you have used up all of the resources of the network." So over time we started forcing them to be involved, because the universities in general did not want to share their computers with anybody. They wanted to buy their own machines and hide in the corner. So, even though "Lick" was very vocal about this subject, I do not think anybody else wanted to be involved. Although they knew in the back of their mind that it was a good idea and were supportive on a philosophical front, from a practical point of view, they, Minsky and McCarthy, and everybody with their own machine—wanted their own machine. It was only a couple years after they had gotten on it that they started raving about how they could now share research, and jointly publish papers, and do other things that they could never do before. All of which was a great boon to them and the artificial intelligence community for sharing information.

• • •

Norberg: Was it expected that you would be able to get these high speed [networking] lines readily?

Roberts: At that point in time, you bought what they called a 50 kilobit line with a very expensive modem that tied a whole bunch of lines together. So you used five lines or something to get it. That's what we did. But there was a price on it from AT&T. It was available under the Telpak tariffs for the government. I could get them reasonably economically because Telpak would let me buy those lines very cheaply. After I checked into the pricing and everything else, I found that I could buy them on the basis that it was reasonable. I did the numbers over and over myself to see what sort of response time and other things they could get, and that looked like it was effective. But they convinced me to look more seriously at it, because I had not done so at that point. They also generated the main packet, which came from England.

Norberg: How were these new ideas sold inside ARPA?

Roberts: ARPA was quite responsive. Herzfeld, Rechtin and Lukasik were very responsive to the whole concept of it. As long as we could find a way to sell it to Congress they were happy.

• • •

Roberts: So everybody was coming with their projects from all over the industry. That was the benefit of being in ARPA. We listened to everybody's projects. Anybody who had an idea. You knew you were on top of the field because you heard everybody's presentation.

Norberg: Was this idea of certain objectives of the nation explicitly discussed by people in the budget meetings, or evaluation meetings?

Roberts: No, we avoided the concept. We had to make it work for the military. That was the selling objective that we had to work under and clearly a particular responsibility. But it was clear to me and the directors that this was something that was serving the nation in every field and clearly serving the military as well. There was hardly any question about that. If we did something which was clearly off the mark as far as serving the military as well, then we knew we would not get good support, and it wouldn't work. Our selling case might be bad. So we did not do things that were too far off.

Once ARPA did try and float one program of building tunnels that Steve [Lukasik] tried to sell and it did not work. Congress turned it down because they figured that although the military needed them for certain purposes, it was much more highways and other things. There was a whole bunch of new technology that could have gotten us hard rock drilling to a point way beyond anything we have done today. We could have gotten it to where we could make tunnels at 10 times the speed of the day. But they said it had to be outside the military and nobody ever was organized like ARPA to do it. So it did not happen. We did make it happen in computing. We managed to keep the focus on the military. They were so dependent on it that anything we did was effective for them and we could sell it with that. Everything we did was effective and beneficial to the military, but they were only one consumer, and we knew that. In every program throughout, I think, even in Congress, everybody understood the game: this was to help the country as long as it was helping the military.

Norberg: That suggests a rather informal way of arriving at programs and assembling dollars to fund them.

Roberts: Well, it was very formal internally with me, because I was looking for the best things to make substantial progress in the field. So I was throwing things out, like I went back to MIT and said, "I do not want to work on compilers any more. Compared to other projects that are being proposed, it's not serving anybody enough. I do not have that much money to throw away. So get off working on things that are not going to produce more than a 10% improvement. I do not need a new language." We even quit working on operating systems after the TENEX (TEN-EXtended) system because it was just not worth building another one.

Norberg: How did this sit with the receiving audience of this message?

Roberts: Oh, the university researchers were upset with that message, because they did not want to quit doing that. The management of the university understood that they did not want interference with research going on either. They wanted the professors to be able to do whatever they wanted. So it conflicted with that. What I told them was, "You can fund that as university research if you think that is appropriate. But we do have a clear direction here: we want to make the most out of our money." Now, there were some [Defense Department research management] 6.2 issues coming in to all this talk, that with the direction of Congress we had to have more and more research that did something; more 6.2 rather than 6.1. But I was even directing 6.2 research to be productive, saying that if it was something we had done over and over and it was now getting only marginal improvements, it was not worthwhile. We wanted something that would really have a big impact if it was worked on, like the networks, or like the speech, understanding, or whatever, rather than something that was going to have much more minor impact. So we directed the research like that, with the concept all along that it had to be a step in front of what the industry was at. That is, if industry was doing it, or they could be doing it, then forget it. Yet it had to be not so far ahead that they would never do it. It had to be two years, three years beyond what they would consider funding themselves. It was very clear what that pattern was after a while and what you could do.

At the moment ARPA is looking at gigabit networks. Industry is now just getting to 45 megabits and ARPA has skipped 100, 200 and gone to a gigabit. We skipped an order of magnitude and tried to jump very far. Is it doable? It may be the right strategy today, but it is a much bigger step than we took. We took more than one step. But of course, nobody was doing anything to do with networks either. So when I started that, the Defense Communications Agency people around me basically said I was crazy, they felt I was absolutely out of my mind.

Norberg: How did they express this to you?

Roberts: They stood up in meetings when I made speeches and booed and hissed and made nasty comments, because they just could not get their mind into a new focus, that this was popular work. The buffers were going to run out. There was just no way it would work. So I remember meetings where people just were caustic. But the computer people were not, so I did not have that from every front.

. . .

Norberg: Can you cite any examples of areas where [ARPA] peer review did not work to the advantage of the program, as you perceive it, of course?

Roberts: Well, in the network program the vote on the ARPANET would have been not to do it. I mean, if you asked all of the PIs they would have said, "No, we do not want to participate at this point. It is probably a good thing to do some day, but we do not think that it is time. We do not think we want to get involved. We do not want to use up our computer." Especially when they knew that their computer was going to be attached to it. But on the other hand, we asked them for support and understanding of the technology and how it would be done and so on, and they helped a lot with that. Once we said it was going to be done, then they were very supportive of the technology. At some point they probably would have preferred that we terminate the ILLIAC IV, because they saw it as a sucking of funds that they could have.

. . .

Norberg: How much flexibility was there in your funds? Ten percent, twenty percent?

Roberts: No, actually there was more on my funds, because the director of ARPA liked the program and—even though Congress might keep ARPA at $250 million or some other number, more or less consistently in those days—he was willing to go in on a request for more for us and less for somebody else, because we had better programs. They were better structured; they were better put together and so on. So the internal competition was to have sound, solid programs that were working well, that were producing exciting results and that he found were effective and that you could also sell to Congress. So by having good results and presenting them well, and having good things to talk about, exciting stories to tell about what we were accomplishing, we were able to get a bigger piece of ARPA's budget as it went from $15 million to $50 million. ARPA didn't change.

Norberg: How did this affect your relationship with the other office directors in ARPA?

Roberts: There was competition. They were all willing to compete and they changed from time to time. They were not being difficult about it. Some of them might have been somewhat less than friendly, but . . .

Norberg: Do you remember your reaction to the Mansfield Amendment in this period and the insistence on greater emphasis on the military mission in DoD programs?

Roberts: It had its impact, and we worked with that. A lot of what I have told you already is in relationship to the Mansfield Amendment and how it affected us. We kept on looking and presenting with the military needs presented. That was one issue. The second issue was to move the presentations and some of the funding away from basic research. In large part it was to maintain the basic research at the levels we had and expand it somewhat, add a lot of element programs, because we saw we could add those more effectively. So for me, the Mansfield Amendment said that there were more 6.2 funds available and we continued to use and continue with the 6.1 [funds] we had. And some of it turned into presentation, like in the speech understanding and artificial intelligence. I turned it into presentations which sounded more supportive of the military roles.

• • •

Roberts: Well, one final part of that process was that then, at that point when we decided it was a goal and we had a proposal that was viable, Al Blue, who was our manager of the contracts, would take it and would work with them to get the contract done. Then there was the whole process in which we worked with one of the Army agencies, or Air Force agencies, or whatever, to do the contract thin. We told them what we wanted, and actually just forced the process through fairly rapidly. It was not a very long process. We had good red tape-cutting capabilities here at ARPA.

• • •

Norberg: Shifting to the one other major contract, were you involved in the discussions with General Electric when they got the subcontract from MIT for developing the 635 timesharing machines?

Roberts: That was before me.

Norberg: Did you have any contact with them afterwards?

Roberts: I had contact with GE, because I was mad because they would not proceed with it. We—not me, but MIT and ARPA—had done this work and gotten the machine to a point where it was valuable. We wanted other military groups or other groups in the community to be able to use this machine, and they would not sell it with Multics. They would not sell that. So I had a lot of fights with GE at the corporate level. We would attack them at that level with our buying power. And we got them to keep them on moving a little bit in that direction, although not very seriously.

Norberg: Did that occasion the shift to Honeywell and the introduction of Multics in other areas?

Roberts: Well, MIT finally made that decision. Their decisions were with their vendors, and we did not have to do much with them in that respect. I observed a lot of that at MIT before I even came to ARPA, but what I got involved in with ARPA was the remaining stuff with getting Multics and seeing if we could make any use out of it, because it was a valuable commodity, but we never could. So we eventually concentrated on TENEX, which we could get production of and military supplied. So TENEX was a major operating system activity. I did not realize how much we had gotten involved in it early on. It was actually probably a lot of my support, but I had not conceived of it as supporting ARPA systems that we had around the office. I was doing programs at those places, and that was what they happened to do with some of their work to do their work. We wound up with an operating system and then had to put money into getting it to where it was. Then I started negotiating with DEC and other people to support it, to create it. They took it on and made it into one of the versions of PDP-6, because we could not afford to continue with that endeavor. We had to get it into commercial. So in many cases I got involved in the commercialization of things, if possible. That is where we got involved more with them. I don't know which case you're thinking of with IBM. You had mentioned IBM.

Norberg: Well, IBM got the contract with Lincoln for the timesharing machine after they lost the original on the . . .

Roberts: Yes, that was while I was at Lincoln, not at [ARPA] . . .

. . .

Norberg: I would like you to wax philosophical for a moment about the influence of IPTO specifically and ARPA, generally, on the field of computer science. What do you think the influence of IPTO was during your tenure as head of the IPTO office, and in general over the last 25 years?

Roberts: Well, I think that the one influence is the one I mentioned in relation to the net, that is, the production of people in the computer field that are trained, knowledgeable, capable, and that form the basis for the progress the United States has made in the computer field. That production of people started with "Lick," when he started the IPTO program and started the big university programs. It was really due to "Lick," in large part, because I think it was that early set of activities that I continued with that produced the most people with the big university contracts. That produced a base for them to expand their whole department, and produced excitement in the university so students went to those departments and more students went to computing than ever before. The numbers were astounding. It was partly due to the success of industry, and partly because it looked like the field to go into, because there were jobs. But the reason that there were jobs was also partly due to the fact that these jobs were there in industry which we had funded in the research area. So it was clear that that was a big impact on the universities and therefore, in the industry. You can almost track all those people and see what effect that has had. The people from those projects are in large part the leaders throughout the industry.

But the change in the government over time made it such that we could not change and influence in massive form when I was there. In other words, I continued funding the universities with the more basic research throughout my period as much as "Lick" had, and somewhat more. But I could not get it to $50 million for that. It had to be other things. Nor would it have been necessarily appropriate, or necessary to get it to that level. So it stayed more or less at the level that "Lick" had established at $15 million, or something like that. Lately it has actually pressed much higher, to where that may be in trouble because of ARPA's current view. Over the last several years, the universities have been having tremendous trouble in getting the same level of funding and that may hurt. So that is one area.

Secondly, it has created unique technologies which have led in each sector, like artificial intelligence. That is why we have expert systems. Without it, we would not have expert systems or anything like it. It is still going to take another decade or two to figure out how valuable that would be to computing. But they are starting to be used in virtually all complicated systems, management programs now. I suspect that people are finding them very effective.

Thirdly, we clearly would not have had the networks in the same time frame. Eventually somebody would have developed network technology. They tried in England with Donald Davies. They had the ideas, but they did not have the money. As a result they never got anywhere, because they could not get it funded. So it was critical to have the money to fund it, and make something happen that was visible so you could see the result of the experiment. Industry was so set against packetization as opposed to channelization—and still is, almost—that there was just virtually no way for AT&T, or the existing industry to do anything about channelization. When I was at GTE, I tried to get a new switch built, a packet switch, and I got it through as long as I was there. There was always a fighting faction from the channelization groups at the labs. As soon as I left though, they won with the president, and the project got killed, because there was not the political presence to do that. That same thing has happened at AT&T. It has happened at every major place where they have tried to do a packet project for voice.

It clearly will work for voice. It is the right approach for voice. There is virtually no one in the industry anymore that believes that it is not the right approach but nobody's built a switch, because the engineering groups are just threatened. They have one technology that they know. They do not want to lose their position to some other group within an organization and they fight it. They kill it. I have been approached by small companies who are in the multiplexor business who say, "I need somebody, as an outside corporation, to do a project because we cannot do it internally. Our people are channelized thinkers. They think in channelized stuff. It is just impossible to build it in."

This unwillingness to change is still a problem within industry. So what happened by doing the ARPANET with computing people and with going in and just getting new contractors who started from scratch to do it, was probably something that made a major shift in time. It was too big a shift for people. That is the biggest benefit of such a program: being able to go out and do something which is a major shift in thinking— that would not happen at IBM, or AT&T, or somewhere—because it is the next thing to do once you are ready. And maybe they will do it, two years later than when you did it. That is not so valuable. The ILLIAC IV probably was not as valuable, in that respect, because the machine used ECL [Emitter-Coupled Logic integrated circuits] for memory and everything else. But it was valuable in the sense that it introduced parallel processing, which nobody was willing to undertake.

In as much as it would just be a computer that is faster than anything else, we would be wasting our time, because they will get there. Faster is better, and everybody knows it. And there is a question in my mind what the program that undertook faster semiconductors could accomplish. Although I was not involved in that, so I do not know exactly what the impact was. But anytime you are just leading industry by a few years in what they will get to, you are not changing the world that significantly. What we did where we could were things that would take a different thinking. So you had to start a project that had support all the way through to the funding. You could not get cut on this new concept, like parallel processing, like artificial intelligence, like networking. You could go all the way through the completion and show what the result was without getting killed in the process. I think GTE must have spent $50 million on the switch that eventually was killed, which is more than we probably spent on some of the programs internally. But they could not get it through to completion where anybody ever saw it. It is just absolutely critical to have unfailing support throughout the process; that is, basically the financial support to be able to finish a project, even if it was within IBM, or AT&T, or something. If we could have funded it within AT&T, it would have worked because they would have had the outside funding.

Norberg: If you identified one characteristic about IPTO that contributed to these successes in programs, where the people added to the stream and the innovative projects developed into something worthwhile for the economy and the nation, what would that characteristic be?

Roberts: Well, the first characteristic is that the office had bright minds, people who were short-term oriented, and were young people who saw important possibilities in the field. The second was that the office had little red tape. There was the possibility of fast development of programs, and fast approval of projects.

AN INTERVIEW WITH

Robert E. Kahn

Conducted by
Judy O'Neill
April 24, 1990
Reston, Virginia

purl.umn.edu/107387

Photo courtesy of Louis Fabian Bachrach

O'Neill: I want to focus on your network experiences. You described sending a letter to Larry Roberts, when he was already at DARPA, talking about your interest in networking. What happened after that? How did you get involved in working with the ARPANET?

Kahn: Well, I had been doing my own work in that area while at BBN, unaware of the fact that DARPA was interested in networking at the time. So I had a set of memoranda that I had been generating on various aspects of networking. It was for my own research project. Larry responded to that letter by inviting me down to chat and find out who this stranger was that sent him this random letter out of the blue. I learned from him at the time that he was seriously thinking about creating a network across the country. You have to remember, I was a fairly young person just on a leave of absence from MIT at the time, so I guess I hadn't fully digested the idea that one would actually be able to make one of these things really happen.

O'Neill: Do you remember what time this was? Roberts came to ARPA in very late 1966, December of 1966.

Kahn: Sometime in 1967. That was my recollection.

O'Neill: So Roberts told you at your first meeting that he was interested in actually getting a network project started?

Kahn: He had gone to DARPA (then called ARPA) to actually make such a network happen, and he was in the planning stage for it. I thought that some of the ideas I had could be of use in that project. We chatted a bit about what I had been up to. There had really been no very direct interface with him up until the time that DARPA actually issued an RFP. I guess that was what he had been working on at DARPA. DARPA issued an RFP back some time in the summer of 1968—June or July, if I recall. And I remember getting a copy of that just as soon as it came out, and we at BBN put together a proposal that eventually won.

O'Neill: So between the time that you talked to Roberts and the time that the RFP or RFQ came out in mid-1968, you didn't have any interaction with the community who were working on developing the RFQ? There were a series of meetings and different people being involved coming up with the requirements for the RFQ in the detail that came out eventually.

Kahn: Roberts certainly had asked me for any of the papers that I had. After we had our first meeting, he said, "You know, if you can share any of your stuff with me, I'd be happy to see it." Well, I think I sent him some of the stuff that I had been working on. But I had no direct interaction with Larry during that period, at least that I can recall. I think he met with people like, there's a fellow named Frank Westervelt from Michigan, there's a guy named Elmer Shapiro from SRI (Stanford Research Institute). Larry had even given a contract, I think, to SRI to help him draft the RFP.

O'Neill: So Roberts had your papers and they may have been circulated within that group.

Kahn: He certainly had my papers. In fact, as I was writing stuff I generally would send it to him. I can even recall sending him one paper that basically said whatever he did with the network, he ought to have a long line involved in it up front so he could find out whether the network would work with long-distance lines or not. Because everybody was thinking about small scale experimentation. I was afraid if they only did a small scale experiment that it might work in the small but fail in the large. So I felt they ought to set the initial structuring of it to be consistent with what the eventual network would look like. Worry about the network on the scale that you really want to operate it. You know, if you are going to deal with real errors make sure you are going to encounter approximately the same number you would expect in a reasonable number of configurations. It seemed to me at the time that the longest lines you would ever want in a network would be roughly a few thousand miles long. So put in one or more of them initially, just to see how it would work. Larry was talking to lots of people at that time. I mean I don't know all the people he would talk to, but having been in the ARPA office later, the number of people that you come in contact with could be enormous. He could have been talking to thousands for all I know.

O'Neill: When you started working on the ARPANET at BBN from 1969 to 1971, how did you see your role in the group that was developing the IMPs [Interface Message Processor] and implementing the network?

Kahn: Well, originally I wasn't even planning to get involved in the implementation. You have to remember I started out as a professor in the EE department at MIT. In fact, the main reason I had gone to BBN was to spend some time working on more practical kinds of things than just mathematics. The thing I had chosen to work on was networking. Having now written the networking proposal, I was fully prepared to get back into research and leave it up to other people to go build this thing. But it became very clear to me, shortly after we had gotten the award, the set of issues that were involved was very complicated relative to what you normally find in a typical engineering project. In fact, my being involved in it was actually far more important than I originally thought because I really played a key role in bringing it all together architecturally. It was a design role that was very essential to what was going on.

O'Neill: You are talking about during the time of writing the proposal?

Kahn: Yes, and afterwards too. I took the lead in putting together the technical part of the proposal. The whole thing was sent out of the systems division that Frank Heart ran. There were a lot of people worrying about things that I didn't know much about, like subcontracts with the computer vendors and the details of building the hardware because that was not really my specialty. In terms of the conceptual parts of it, that is really where I was main contributor, I think. My notion originally was "Help them get the award; let them go build it and I will go back to doing what I was doing." But I pretty quickly came to realize that that just wasn't a practical notion. There were too many things that had to be thought about. System design was going to be a continuing factor; it wasn't just something you did once up front and then forgot about. There were really a very small set of us that were directly involved in the actual development of the network, and I was one of the key people. Some of the others were Severo Ornstein, principally responsible for the hardware, and Bill Crowther, principally responsible for the software. He was helped by a fellow named Dave Walden who subsequently became president of BBN Labs.

What finally triggered my going over there was an activity that involved simulation. Along with another colleague at BBN, we developed a simulation program that could be used for evaluating network performance. Most of the really interesting issues to me about networks were how they were going to work, because this was a really new area. Nobody had any experience in knowing how networks would actually function in practice: how did routing algorithms work, how did congestion control algorithms work, how did flow control work, how did buffering work. All of those kinds of things were critical issues back then. The simulation system was developed to give us a visual clue. I mean, this was a rather innovative development—remember this was at a time when interactive graphics were not par for the course. I mean, there were no such things as workstations. Timesharing was pretty new at the time as well. To be able to get an interactive environment with graphics displays of networks was a major coup in its own right. We had a very powerful facility; my thought was to use it to explore some of the issues.

BBN at the time was structured into two parts. Leo Beranek ran one part of the company having to do with acoustics and the old line of physical sciences work that BBN had originally started in. They did acoustical design of concert halls and things like that. The other half of the company was run by Jerry Elkind who subsequently left BBN, briefly went to MIT, then went out to Xerox for many years. Jerry had several divisions underneath him, one of which was Frank Heart's division. So he was Frank's boss.

O'Neill: This was all after the proposal had been accepted?

Kahn: After the proposal was won, right. So in some sense I found myself sort of like somebody on a slide being asked "Why did you go down the slide?" Well, once you are on the slide, gravity just sort of takes you. This was a situation where I would have been perfectly happy to do the work in the research division. So I, in fact, picked up my office and moved over to the systems division. Formally, I was still in Jerry's division, only physically in another location. I never knew quite how the payroll was handled at that time, so I can't tell you all the machinations.

· · ·

O'Neill: While you were working on the network project, what was your interaction like with ARPA and with Larry Roberts?

Kahn: It became very tight. Larry and I developed a very good personal relationship. In fact, he later hired me to go to DARPA. It was a very interesting relationship because Frank Heart, who ran the group in which I was physically residing, also had an interface with Larry. So Larry was, in effect, talking directly to two different people in that group. I was not usually privy to his discussions with Frank, so I don't know what the two of them talked about. But it was a separate, and in some cases, independent channel, because Larry would often call me as easily as he would Frank. I had quite a number of interactions with him, but they were usually on technical matters, planning for the future, "What do you think we ought to do about this," "I got this thing, I need to respond, can you handle it?" That sort of stuff. And oftentimes he would send things up for me to think about, you know, go talk to a group of people on such and such, or whatever. We had a pretty good relationship. Of course, I later became director of the same office, so I had the same position that he did. But that was some number of years later. Larry actually left DARPA in 1973.

Steve Levy was a vice-president of BBN at the time. Steve was involved in new financial opportunities for BBN at the corporate level. I had been pushing BBN to get into the commercial networking business for many years, going back to 1969. Originally it was a recommendation to a small panel that Jerry Elkind or Steve Levy had been chairing. I made subsequent recommendations along the same line to the senior management at BBN, but they had never done anything with them. And, in fact, one of my reasons for accepting the DARPA job was because it just didn't look like BBN was interested in capitalizing on any of the technology we had developed.

O'Neill: Do you know why BBN wasn't more receptive to the idea earlier? You said you mentioned it originally in 1969. Were you given reasons at that time?

Kahn: Not really. You have to understand what kind of an organization BBN was. It changed fairly radically somewhere along the line. BBN was a kind of hybrid version of Harvard and MIT in the sense that most of the people there were either faculty or former faculty at either Harvard or MIT. If you've ever spent any time at either of those places, you would know what a unique kind of organization BBN was. A lot of the students at those places spent time at BBN. It was kind of like a super hyped-up version of the union of the two, except that you didn't have to worry about classes and teaching. You could just focus on research. It was sort of the cognac of the research business, very distilled. The culture at BBN at the time was to do interesting things and move on to the next interesting thing. There was more incentive to come up with interesting ideas and explore them than to try to capitalize on them once they had been developed. I think that the administration at BBN would have acted on my proposal earlier if they could have figured out what to do, but the payoff wasn't sufficiently near, and the understanding of what to do with packet networks didn't really exist in industry. So they just sort of let it go. I think "it was ahead of its time" is the right way to put it.

O'Neill: So until they were prodded in 1972 by another company starting to capitalize on it . . .

Kahn: Well, composed of their own people . . . a non-sanctioned spin off. I think BBN was protecting its interests more than anything else. But they suddenly decided that this was something they really ought to do. I think it was reactive largely. They set up

Telenet, which lost money for a long time. I remember Steve and I talked about Larry as being a potential guy to run it. I just wasn't interested in getting into a business setting at that time. I really wanted to stay with R&D. Somewhere in the mid-1971 time frame, I picked my office up and moved back to the research division again, because we had largely gotten to the point where the networking development effort was stable. We had done the critical phase and from then on it looked like whatever else . . . it's like getting to the moon. Once you get there the first time, you at least know that it is doable. But there was still a lot of development work that needed to be done to improve the network performance. I wanted to move into other areas, like understanding what to do with the networks—maybe some of the more basic research aspects of it. So I went back into the research group, but that only lasted for about a year. Then, ultimately, I finally went down to DARPA. I showed up there in early November of 1972.

O'Neill: When you were working out the plan for Telenet with Steve Levy, did you recommend Larry Roberts? Did you talk to Larry Roberts about what was going on?

Kahn: I never talked to Larry about it, but I did recommend him. Steve had asked me on several occasions who might be a good choice to run it. It seemed like a very natural thing since Larry was the guy who was the prime mover of the network in the first place. While I was involved in most of the technical parts, Larry was the political mastermind during the project. He got a lot of support from Bob Taylor, who ran the DARPA office when Larry first arrived.

Kahn: So he was actually at DARPA for four or five months after he announced that he was intending to leave. When he left at the end of September, his successor had just been named. It turned out to be J.C.R. Licklider from MIT who came in for a second tour. He started the IPTO office in the first place back in the early 1960's and actually showed up to stay in January of 1974. So there was a period of three or four months where the office really didn't have a permanent director.

O'Neill: During this time were you running the network project?

Kahn: *The* network project. You have to understand that the way DARPA was organized, it had a lot of different programs—and the ARPANET was one program. One of the things that I chose not to do was to run any of *the* network project. Having just come from BBN, I wanted to get into new things. In fact, the agreement that I had when I went to DARPA was I would set up a program in flexible manufacturing. I was intending to make a clean break from networking. Apparently quite a bit of money had been set aside, or planned, or budgeted, for the new program, but when I got there it had been canceled by the Congress. So the program somehow disappeared in real-time right in front of my eyes. I remember Larry coming to me and saying "Look, I know you didn't want to work on networking anymore, but you know more about it than anybody else around and that's where our main efforts are going to be for the next several years, so why don't you just go do that." So I did, but I got into all the new efforts. The actual running of the existing ARPANET program was left to other people. Of course, people used to talk to me about the network, so it wasn't exactly as if I was isolated from it. However, I was never the official program manager for any of the old existing programs.

O'Neill: I would like to back up and ask a few more questions about your time at BBN. We talked about your interaction with Roberts and your direct connection with him. What about with the other contractors working on the ARPANET? I am thinking of the people at the Network Measurement Center.

Kahn: I had most of the external interactions with people in the community. You have to remember that here were a bunch of people in the research community who were expecting a network to show up and didn't know what it was. That is why I wrote that document [Report 1822]. I also used to talk to them quite a bit by telephone. Dave Walden and I went out and spent quite a bit of time on the West coast trying to do some of the early debugging of the network. The very first installation was out at UCLA, where Vint Cerf and I had our first opportunity to work together on measurement and testing.

Although I had quite a number of interactions with the different groups who were involved, they organized themselves pretty well, partly through the workings of the ARPA office itself. One of the critical issues that came up then was, "Suppose these machines were all connected to the net somehow—how would that all work?" I mean, how is a machine going to be able to move a file from here to there? How would that work at the host level? And a mechanism got set up to address this issue. I think Barry Wessler, who worked for Larry Roberts, was one of the key guys that put it in place, along with a fellow named Steve Crocker, who was then at UCLA. Steve organized something called the Network Working Group, whose job was to get host-level people together, to discuss what they were going to do, what things they had in common, and what standards were needed. In particular, they were to come up with a protocol (or set of protocols) that would allow machines to talk with one another. Steve ended up chairing and coordinating that whole process. But it was, in fact, a very broad group activity. And it started a series of working notes called RFCs which still continue to this day.

O'Neill: Were you a part of the Network Working Group?

Kahn: I sat in on some of the meetings, but I did not consider myself a prime mover in that activity at all. Often times I was there to represent the network, to tell them what we were doing, or explain things that were written in some documents. Occasionally I would contribute a note to the series. But this was mainly a group of people who were more involved at the host level, and I was more involved in building the net that would move the bits between the hosts. Vint Cerf was definitely involved at that level. In fact the original paper that was written about host protocols was co-authored by three people: Steve Crocker, Vint Cerf, and another fellow named Steve Carr who was at Utah. Carr later just disappeared from the scene and I never heard of him again.

• • •

O'Neill: How would you describe Donald Davies' work in England on networking?

Kahn: You could think of it like a terminal IMP. In fact, that's very much what it was except that the terminal IMPs had all these network protocols in them that he probably didn't have in his implementation because it was fairly simple early implementation. Donald Davies was a very creative guy; he thought a lot about interesting ideas of how networks should be built. He clearly had the concept in his head of what packet networks ought to look like, and he had done it independently in England. I believe Larry Roberts will probably tell you that Donald had a big influence on him. In fact, I think the term "packet switching" came from Donald's work. We had been calling it message switching before, on the notion that what computers did was send messages into these network nodes, which broke them up into packets, sent the packets through the net, and put them back into messages at the destination. So we were thinking of the network as a message switching system—but the term packet switching eventually stuck.

O'Neill: Do you recall when it started to be called that, when the terminology changed?

Kahn: Well, we wrote the very first paper on the ARPANET IMPs in 1970, and we did not use the term packet switching in that paper. We also called it the ARPA Computer Network, so the term ARPANET was not yet in use, and packet switching was not quite in the vocabulary yet. I mean we referred to packets, which would be switched from here to there, but the term "packet switching" was a term we didn't actually use. I think that it was probably a year or two later that it actually stuck, maybe 1971, or early 1972.

O'Neill: I've been trying to identify when it actually appeared. I haven't been able to find anything.

Kahn: Leonard Kleinrock, Howard Frank, and I wrote a paper on "Lessons Learned," that was 1972. That was the first attempt to bridge the gap among theory, simulation, and engineering. We came at it from three different points of view. Len specialized in theoretical analysis. Howard ran the group that was doing all the topological analysis; that was all done by simulation. Where should one put the lines and how much bandwidth was needed—things like that. I was the focal point for the engineering aspects of the network design. When we all got together to try and figure out how to write what we had learned, we all would agree, "We don't know how to build nets today that are bigger than about 30 or 40 nodes." And everybody would say, "Right." "Can we craft a sentence that says why?" And I would say, "The reason we can't is because the lines fill up because you are passing too much routing information back and forth." Howard would say, "The reason is because today's simulation systems can't handle more than 30 or 40 nodes. You can't get answers back." Len would say, "The reason is that the denominator of this formula goes to zero when rho equals such and such." Everybody had a different view of what was important, because they were focusing on different things. That was actually a very interesting paper that we wrote. It was the first attempt to get the lessons learned out in writing. It would be interesting to look in that paper and see if the term packet switching shows up.

O'Neill: How did you become familiar with Paul Baran's work at RAND? Why did it show up in 1968?

Kahn: Probably Larry had mentioned that there was a report series that RAND had generated. The RAND work was not published widely because it was mostly for defense purposes. Paul Baran's reports were first published internally at RAND. So it could very well have been hard for people to get hold of. I don't think the report series was published externally. If they were, I don't know where. However, aspects of this work were published in the *IEEE Transactions*, if I recall.

· · ·

Kahn: How do you do routing, what do you do when congestion occurs was one of the main points of contention early in the days of the network. It was my contention that we had to worry about congestion and deadlocks. What do you do when the network just fills up? Things might come to a grinding halt. I was busy at work designing mechanisms that would prevent that from happening or, if it did happen, that would get you out of it. The prevailing feeling of my colleagues was it's like molecules in a room; don't worry about the fact that you won't be able to breathe because the molecules will end up in a corner. Somehow there will be enough statistical randomness that packets will just keep flowing. It won't be able to somehow block itself up. It was a significant point of contention.

When Dave Walden and I went out to the West coast at the end of 1969 or early 1970 to test the net, the very first thing that we did was run deadlock tests. And the network locked up in twelve packets. I had devised these tests to prove that the network could deadlock. There was no way to convince anybody else, particularly the person writing the software, that the network was going to deadlock—except by doing it. And even that wasn't sufficient as it turned out.

O'Neill: Okay. Let's move on to 1972 and the ICCC demonstration of the ARPANET. How did that idea come about? I know you had a large role in organizing it. Was it suggested to you as a project? How did it get started?

Kahn: Well, I can give you my view of it. I had been thinking for a while that it would be useful to have some kind of a demonstration of the net. My recollection is that in early 1971 I had suggested to Larry Roberts that we try to put on a demonstration at the Spring Joint Computer Conference in 1972. That never developed, but Steve Crocker called me back soon thereafter and said there was an opportunity to actually put on a demonstration at a new conference called ICCC (International Conference on Computer Communication) in the fall of 1972. Larry had made a deal with the conference organizers that if they were willing to put up the space, he would somehow arrange a network demonstration. I mean, I think I proposed to Larry that they do a demonstration. I think the fact that we did it at ICCC was his idea. It is entirely possible he thought it up independently. It doesn't really matter. The fact is, it was clear to a lot of people that having a network demonstration was a good idea. Because in the middle of 1971, despite the fact that the ARPANET had been able to deliver packets for a year and a half at that point, there were almost no useful interactions that were taking place on the network.

O'Neill: Why was that?

Kahn: Well, it would be like having a highway system that was perfectly capable of handling automobile traffic, except there were no cars around, or no on-ramps and off-ramps. The reality was that the machines that were connected to the net couldn't use it. I mean, you could move packets from one end to the other. You could run all the test programs you want. The network nodes could even send test traffic. I could sit at the teletype at one place, connect it to an IMP and talk to somebody at the other end, but none of the host machines that were plugged in were yet configured to actually use the net. That was one of the main reasons why I was thinking that a demonstration would be useful. It would put some pressure on the community to make the connections useful.

We had a meeting at MIT during the summer of 1971 at which I recall putting a matrix up on the board. The rows were the names of host machines. Like number one was UCLA, number two was SRI, number three was UCSB, number four was Utah, and so forth. So we listed all the machines, and at that time there were probably something on the order of twenty-ish machines available. The columns indicated the minimal things you could do over the net. Like you could connect, or you could actually get a herald back—herald meant you could get the protocol to open a connection to a process. Or that you could actually run a program, by "a program" I mean at least one. You could do something once the herald came up. Or perhaps you could run an arbitrary program. We had about ten columns that denoted various stages of ability to do something. It would be the equivalent of, "You could drive your car up to the front door. You could actually walk from your car and grab hold of the door handle of the front door. Or, you could actually open the front door and walk in the lobby. Or, you could walk from the lobby into the office, or you could actually sit down in an office." It was sort of that level of penetration into the machine. And we filled out this whole matrix and there were perhaps six entries in the first column, and maybe three entries in the next column, and maybe one entry in the third column, and nothing else. So the fact of the matter is that—maybe it was ten, five, and two, I don't remember. But the fact of the matter is that this was an incredibly sparse matrix. The hosts basically couldn't use the net. My thought was "Look, we've got to fill in this table, and make the network more usable; otherwise the demonstration is going to be a bust." That was my logic. But at the same time a main reason for having the demonstration in the first place was to make it all work. So that was the process that actually got the utility of the net up from ground zero to some reasonable level.

O'Neill: What, in your opinion, was responsible for the sparseness of the matrix?

Kahn: Well, you have to remember every site needed to do something to get connected. One, they had to figure out how to build a hardware interface between their computer and the network. Almost all that hardware was special purpose. Sometimes that took six months or a year; in some cases they built it in-house. Then behind that you needed to build all the software. Somebody needed to implement the network protocols in those machines. That was fairly complicated stuff. I mean it wasn't like you bought a package from Lotus back in that time. Some creative scientist on the staff wrote the code, which had to be interfaced to the operating system. This was absolutely uncharted territory. And people needed some motivation to get it done. The demonstration was actually motivation to do it.

O'Neill: Okay, so the demonstration really worked in two ways. Before the demonstration, it worked to give more sites incentive to put cars on the highway.

Kahn: It gave them an incentive because it set a target to shoot at with a public deadline, a target that really couldn't be put off.

O'Neill: Then the actual demonstration was to a wider community who could look at the ARPANET and see that it was functioning.

Kahn: That's right. That was the event that made the world take notice of packet switching, because up until that point you couldn't see it anywhere. All you could do was read an arbitrary abstract paper somewhere that said, "Here is this new way to do computer communications." A lot of people were skeptical in the early days. I mean, breaking messages into packets, reassembling them at the end, relying on a mysterious set of routing algorithms to deliver packets. I'm sure there were people who distrusted airplanes in the early days. "How are you going to ensure that they are going to stay up?" Perhaps this was the same kind of thing. I think ICCC was the watershed event that made people suddenly realize that packet switching was a real technology. We had thousands of people who went through that—I don't know what the exact number is—at least a thousand who went through that particular exhibit.

O'Neill: After the 1972 demo you went on to work at the DARPA office as program manager, and you explained how you had not gone to work on networking but ended up working on networking projects. How did the idea of the Internet come about? What was the problem that you were trying to solve?

Kahn: One of the very first efforts that I undertook when I got there was to develop a technology that was like the ARPANET technology except it was based on radio communication. So the idea was to build a net that could link a number of entities, computers let's say, where each of these entities could be, in principle, on a moving platform although they could also be stationary. But the communication was by radio. So instead of machines linked to each other by wires, they would be linked by broadcast radio. A given node would broadcast its radio packet and a nearby node would pick it up and relay it. There had been an effort supported at the University of Hawaii in the late 1960's, early 1970's called the Aloha System. I think it originally got its money from AFOSR (Air Force Office of Scientific Research), then DARPA became a big supporter of it.

So my first question was "How am I going to link this packet radio system to any computational resources of interest?" Well, my answer was, "Let's link it to the ARPANET." Except that these were two radically different networks in many ways. I mean, all the details were different. I don't mean conceptually they were different. They were sort of the same genre. Just like, say, Chinese and Americans are of the same genre except one speaks Chinese and one speaks English, one lives on one side of the world, one lives on the other side, they go to sleep during your daytime, etc.

The details of the two networks were rather different. The ARPANET ran at 50 kilobits per second and the packet radio system ran at 100 or 400 kilobits per second. One had thousand bit uncoded packets; the other had two thousand bit packets which could be coded. The ARPANET assumed that once you sent something it was delivered with 100% reliability. If it didn't get through, the system was broken. The other assumed that much of the time you would never get anything through, even though the system was working. The protocols that were designed for the ARPANET wouldn't work over the packet radio net because when a packet entered the packet radio net, the only thing the ARPANET would have told it was where it came from but not where it was going.

So the packet radio net had no further information to know where to route it. If a packet got lost along the way, the ARPANET hosts would come to a halt. Well, in a radio net you can get interference and so some loss is natural. So we really had to rethink literally the whole issue of host transport protocols. Vint Cerf and I jointly came up with the TCP/IP (Transmission Control Protocol/Internet Protocol) concept as a new transport mechanism as part of an architecture for internetworking. DARPA then gave a contract to Vint at Stanford to actually implement the TCP/IP concept—along with small efforts at BBN and at University College London. Vint had the lead for developing the specification.

O'Neill: What were the other two contracts for?

Kahn: The one at University College London was part of an effort over there to explore remote use of the ARPANET and to implement a TCP/IP protocol on their machine. I think it was a PDP-9 at the time. BBN was under contract to build a piece of the packet radio system (called a station) that needed portions of this protocol. That was the first embodiment of the notion of a gateway. We needed to implement a protocol that would work across the gateway. Eventually we all took the Internet technology pieces and created a separate program in DARPA for it. But originally, all that work was done as part of the packet radio program. I subsequently hired Vint Cerf to come to DARPA and actually run the Internetting Program. That was in 1976, and by that time we were already three years into it. So he took it from a fledgling effort and turned it into a major national activity.

O'Neill: Did you go to Vint Cerf with these problems and discuss them with him because he had previously done the host-to-host protocols? Why Vint Cerf?

Kahn: Two reasons. One, Vint and I had worked very effectively on the original IMP when he was at UCLA. So he knew about the ARPANET; he was one of the three people who were involved in actually writing the original paper on the NCP (Network Control Program), so he knew that pretty well. I had a good view of what the linkage between the packet radio system and the ARPANET should look like. And I knew what the protocol roughly wanted to be, but there were all kinds of details that needed to be worked out; what are all the issues that you have to worry about in linking this to the operating systems, which those folks had already solved. So I needed somebody like Vint to be able to represent that part. Of course, Vint was very facile at thinking through the rest of it as well. So it just took one session before the two of us were on the same wavelength as to what we needed to do. And he and I just jointly worked it out from there.

• • •

O'Neill: We were talking about the interaction with the military and how they started using timesharing, not directly but by having it available from industry.

Kahn: That was the typical method that was used before by the particular office that I was involved with. This approach was somewhat different from some of the other offices, however. If you are working on, let's say, technology for an improved airplane, the Air Force would probably understand instantaneously not only why they would need it, where it would fit in, but they might be part of the process of helping to develop it. It is harder to see how some of these advanced computer technologies could have been handled the same way—at least in that timeframe. Maybe now it is different because more people in the military have backgrounds and expertise in computer technology. There were very few in the early 1970's. One of the things that happened as a result of the ARPANET experience was we managed to get DCA (Defense Communication Agency) to take over the day-to-day operations of the net. So here was a case where we actually took a finished piece of technology and literally got an operational part of the Defense Department to run it. So that was a way to actually transfer technology and to make them aware of it. But it really came after the fact. I mean DCA was not part of the actual creation of the technology, although it became probably the largest user in Defense of that technology after the fact.

• • •

O'Neill: Once they started understanding the technology and what it could do for them, did they request changes to it? Was there any feedback? Did their requirements affect how you then proceeded?

Kahn: Yes, in many ways. Dave Russell, who became IPTO director after Licklider left, was instrumental in making those test bed programs happen. He handled a lot of the interfacing with the folks at Fort Bragg. We set up the second program with the Air Force Strategic Air Command out at Offutt Air Force Base on a similar kind of problem, except in an Air Force context. We had a number of other examples of test beds. Dave Russell was an Army colonel who understood the implications of all this technology for the military. He was the office director for the period from August 1975 through August 1979. He was a marvelous point of liaison with the military in that he articulated both the technology point of view as well as the military needs. In fact, during that whole period, I think we opened up a greater dialogue with the military in terms of these test bed programs than we ever had just through technology alone. The agency director at the time, George Heilmeier, was very supportive of these test bed programs. So that was a very important development in the history of the office.

O'Neill: Okay. Let's move on to the conversion effort to TCP/IP, which as I understand it, happened in January of 1983. First of all, were you active in working to get TCP/IP established as a DoD standard in 1980?

Kahn: The answer is yes, except that I did it in the role of Office Director. Vint Cerf was probably more involved than I was, because it was part of his program. But, in fact, a lot of the drive to get the protocols standardized came from the fact that the ARPANET itself was growing. I mean the ARPANET, after it transferred to DCA, suddenly became a vehicle where a lot of other military sites could now get on easily—just go to DCA. It was their normal way—they didn't have to deal with a research agency.

By the 1980 timeframe there were already a large number of military sites on the ARPANET. And by 1983 the number had grown so large that the need to split it was becoming urgent for many reasons. Many of the military sites were beginning to depend on the net for operational purposes. Their day-to-day business really depended on it, and they felt, I think rightly so, that there were good reasons to keep the military application of it separate from the research and educational aspects. If you have nodes in the network on university campuses and if there were some major outbreak, it would be hard to guarantee that something couldn't happen to the network. By 1980, there was real interest in somehow making sure that this net was a stable, dependable facility for the military. And the protocol that was most widely used at that point that could lead to an eventual partition of the network was TCP/IP. There was still quite a dominant use of the old NCP (Network Control Protocol) technology. But if there was ever a hope that we could split the net into multiple pieces, we needed to switch over to the internet protocol because connections between multiple nets needed an internet protocol. So the protocol became a DoD standard in 1980 and Vint played a role in that. The sweep of events at the time was such that DoD really had to decide what guidance to give people who were connecting their computers to the net as newer sites came in. "What do we tell them?" So they finally decided to standardize the protocols, because it was really the only game in town at that point in time.

O'Neill: Do you recall if there was much resistance to adopting a standard?

Kahn: Well, there had been a move afoot in Europe to develop a competing—I say competing although I don't know that officially that was the way it was viewed—set of protocols within the oversight of the International Standards Organization (ISO). There were two standardization bodies over there: CCITT (Consultative Committee for International Telegraphy and Telephony) tended to deal with the lower levels, the physical connections, and then the ISO dealt with the higher levels. I just think there was a sentiment on their part to do their own thing. They just didn't want to adopt an American development. So they proceeded to develop their own. They came up with a reference architecture in the mid-1970's, which was actually a very important contribution because it gave people a way to think about protocol layers. It had certainly been in our consciousness, but we had never articulated it quite that way—and they did. That was a real contribution.

But their seven-layer reference model didn't say how any of the layers should be implemented. Interestingly enough, in their original seven-layer model, they did not have an internetworking layer because they assumed end-to-end circuits. It was the old telegraphy model of the world, or telephony model. But later on they decided to add internetworking so their model became more compatible with what was going on in the U.S. They developed their own standards. X.25 was one of the early protocols for interfacing computers to networks. That protocol came out of some of the early needs of the commercial world to define interfacing standards. Four PTTs (national postal, telegraph, and telephone services) were involved in originally agreeing on the X.25 standard. There was some pressure by the late 1970's or early 1980's to have us use the ISO protocols, except that they weren't really well defined, and there were few compatible implementations. We were dealing with protocols in the U.S. that had been around for six, seven years, and had been through three or four major versions. A protocol conversion, even if it were well defined, would have cost many millions, if not tens of millions of dollars given all the sites involved. So there was no motivation or incentive to do it. That was really the only competing pressure at the time.

O'Neill: In terms of organizing the conversion—as I understand it you were quite involved in that.

Kahn: Well, Vint Cerf had been running the Internet program and he left in October of 1982, just before the conversion. But I picked the program up after he left and actually managed the transition. I handed the project over to Barry Leiner in September of 1983, so actually I managed the Internet program right through the transition for just about a year.

O'Neill: What were the big problems with the conversion?

Kahn: Well, I think the biggest problem was just getting people to believe that it was real. It is like any major change; it is not real until it happens. We sent messages to everybody, alerting them to the timing and yet one week before we were still getting messages, "Is this really going to happen next week?" or "Let us know if you decide to really go ahead with this." The day after we did the transition, people were saying "Hey, how come I didn't know about this?" or "It was impossible for me to convert; I need another six months." We would say, "You had two years lead notice; why is it that suddenly you need six more months?"

So we actually had to deal with the fact that not everybody was able to convert on day one. In fact the way we actually handled it was to allow an overlap of both the old protocols and the new ones for a short period of time, and then by special exception we allowed a few sites to continue using the old protocols, particularly where there was no interest on their part in ever converting. Like military sites, where the only party they wanted to communicate with was one other party or for some reason they were passing classified traffic, and there was only one type of device in the world that would do it and it required the old protocol. Something like that. That was by far the biggest problem—just getting people to take it seriously. But managing it was traumatic for a while. I mean, the phone was ringing off the hook every few minutes. Every day someone new would complain, "I used to be able to do this, and now I can't." Shaking it all down was also a problem. Even the places that thought they were going to convert properly suddenly found that while theirs worked with the three or four places that they thought it would, or had tried it out with, it didn't work with some others. So there was quite a bit of time required to smooth out the rough edges.

O'Neill: It sounds as if you actually used to network to communicate with people. Is that how you sent messages and tried to coordinate? Did you ever try to bring people together?

Kahn: More often than not, critical problems were handled by telephone. But when you are dealing with a lot of people, it is just a matter of keeping them appraised as to what was happening, sending out notices, schedules, debugging problems, coming up with alternatives. We would advise, "Look, not to worry because in two weeks the following will happen, and you'll be able to do this"—helping everyone separately think through their unique situation.

O'Neill: Who else was working with you on this?

Kahn: At that time? The whole community.

O'Neill: I'm sorry, I meant at the DARPA office.

Kahn: Just me pretty much during the transition. You have to remember that that office was really small. We had about ten technical people and a few secretaries.

O'Neill: I thought with something as large as the conversion, you might have drafted a few other people to help out.

Kahn: Not within the office. Before Vint left, he had put in place a number of mechanisms to help with the management of the whole Internet process. He had created something called the Internet Coordination Control Board (ICCB), or some such thing.

O'Neill: Is that the Internet Advisory Board?

Kahn: That eventually became the IAB. Vint is now the chairman of the IAB. But when we started the Internet program in the mid-1970's, originally it was just me in the office running the program. After Vint was hired, it was just Vint running the program with me to kibitz. He was so good at what he did that he basically had everything in his head. What I worried about was what would happen if he got hit by a truck? Number two, what would happen if he would ever have to leave? And number three, how was anybody else in the community ever going to be part of the thinking process?

So he set up, after some discussions, a kind of kitchen cabinet, if you will, of knowledgeable people that he would convene periodically. These were mostly the workers in the field, the key people who were implementing protocols. He would sit down with them and discuss what his plans were and get inputs from them. But it was basically Vint driving that whole process. There were a lot of strong personalities involved, but Vint was so knowledgeable about what was going on, he could have made all the decisions himself, although they gave him a lot of good input. When he left, that group stayed intact. I didn't particularly require it for myself, since Vint and I had created the Internet protocols and he and I had it all in our heads before it all started. But in terms of the plan and in the evolution of the research program, it was pretty clear that whether it was Vint or myself or whoever was going to be there in time, you really need inputs from the research community because, in the final analysis, the problems that needed to be addressed would have to reflect problems that individual groups were having. "Here's a thing they wanted to do; the Internet should help with this. Here's another thing they wanted to do . . . " So that process became increasingly important as time went on. And, of course, in formulating what the program would be during the year that I had taken it back over again to run, I relied heavily on the group for inputs.

When I handed it over to Barry Leiner, he had had no direct experience in that area. He had taken over the packet radio program from Vint when Vint left. When he eventually took over the Internetting program too, he was primed for it. The issues are very unique in that particular discipline. This group was very helpful to him. Barry was the one that reorganized and renamed it the Internet Activities Board, because it had grown so large by that time. When Vint was involved, the discussions had become so interesting to everybody that the people just wanted to come to hear them. Oftentimes those meetings were held in conjunction with other planned events, like the satellite program that I was running where we would have meetings of people internationally. So he would have one of his ICCB meetings in conjunction with that. Often there would be fifty to a hundred people that would want to sit in as observers just to hear the discussion. Because of that, it almost became unmanageable. When Barry took the program over he said, "I don't want to run a planning group of several hundred people." So he created a smaller body called the IAB, thinking that it would remain small. The problem was that pretty soon people who suddenly weren't getting invitations to ICCB meetings because it no longer existed suddenly said "Hey, what happened?" And of course they found out there was an IAB, and then they wanted to come to its meetings. The IAB ended up supporting an Internet Engineering Task Force and an Internet Research Task Force, both reporting to the IAB. The IETF, which Phil Gross chairs, is now a very large open organization. A typical meeting will have hundreds of people. The IRTF is much smaller. So that is sort of how all that evolved. In any event, Barry Leiner took over in 1983, and he ran the program until he left in 1985.

Photographs

Figure P.1   John Cullinane behind a "dumb" terminal, a big improvement in interactive software development at Cullinane Corporation at the time. (Photo courtesy of Cullinane Corporation/Cullinet Software, Inc.)

Figure P.2   **Wilkinson Lecture at the Digital Computer Museum. John Wilkinson, John Cullinane, Charles Bachman, Maurice Wilkes and Gordon Bell (left to right) at the Wilkinson Lecture reception. This was the fifth Pioneer Lecture at the museum and was titled *The Pilot Ace*.** (Photo courtesy of the Computer History Museum)

Figure P.3   **New York Stock Exchange listing. The woman with the big smile is my wife, Diddy, along with Board members and company executives. This picture was taken on the floor of the New York Stock Exchange with Cullinane Corporation shares the first trade of the day. It was a big deal as we were the first software products company to be listed on the NYSE.** (Photo courtesy of New York Stock Exchange Archives)

Figure P.4   **Belles of the ball. Two pioneers in their own right at a Cullinane User Week: my mother-in-law, Mrs. Agnes Haverty, and my mother, Mrs. Margaret Cullinane, with good friend Larry Broderick.** (Photo courtesy of Cullinane Corporation/Cullinet Software, Inc.)

Figure P.5   A Board meeting of Cullinane Corporation (Cullinet Software, Inc.). Seated left to right are company executives Frank Chisholm, Bob Goldman, Phyllis Swersky, Board members George White and Pat Grant. Standing left to right are Board members David Rubin, Bobby Orr, *Dick Bloch*, John Cullinane, Joe McNay, Sol Manber, and Bill Eidson. (Photo courtesy of Cullinane Corporation/Cullinet Software, Inc.)

Figure P.6 Good friends (left to right): Jon Nackerud, his wife Joan, and Betty Grant. Jon was an early and key Cullinane Corporation Vice President, handling the West Coast. Eventually, he would become Founding President of Relational Technology, Inc., which would become Ingres. Betty Grant was a very successful Cullinane Corporation Regional Manager in the Upper Midwest. (Photo courtesy of Bill Casey, Vice President, Cullinane Corporation)

Figure P.7   **Left to right, Bill Casey and Tom Meurer, two early and key vice presidents of Cullinane Corporation.** (Photo courtesy of John Cullinane)

Figure P.8   **Nelson Mandela visits the John F. Kennedy Library after 27 years in prison. He is greeted by Senator Kennedy and Stevie Wonder with John Cullinane, MC of the event, in the background.** (Photo courtesy of John F. Kennedy Presidential Library and Museum, Boston, Massachusetts)

Figure P.9 Founders of the "third university in Cambridge," Bolt, Beranek, and Newman, Dr. Richard H. Bolt, Director of the Acoustics Laboratory, Dr. Jordan J. Baruch of the Laboratory's research staff, and Dr. Leo L. Beranek, Technical Director of the Laboratory, in the anechoic chamber at MIT. They are discussing a travelling microphone which automatically records the distribution of sound entering the chamber through a test wall. (Photo courtesy of MIT Museum)

Figure P.10   **Grace Hopper in front of UNIVAC magnetic tape drives. She holds a COBOL programming manual in her hand.** (Photo courtesy of the Computer History Museum)

Figure P.11   **Mark I's wartime team (early 1945). U.S. Navy officers (second row, from left):** *Ensign Richard Bloch*, **Lieutenant Commander Hubert Andrew Arnold, Commander Howard Aiken, Lieutenant Grace Hopper, Ensign Robert Campbell.** (U.S. Navy photo)

Figure P.12   **Harvard Mark I computer. From left: Robert Hawkins, Howard Aiken and *Richard Bloch*.**
(Photo courtesy of Charles Babbage Institute)

Figure P.13   *Ivan Sutherland* (seated at right), developer of Sketchpad, an enormously important system as an early demonstration of interactive computing. (Photo courtesy of MIT Museum)

Figure P.14   **MIT symposium on Engineering Analysis of Speech Analysis. From left: Walter Lawrence, Martin Essigmann, and *J.C.R. Licklider*.** (Photo courtesy of MIT Museum)

Figure P.15   **BBN IMP Development Group, including (left to right): Truitt Thatch, Bill Bartell (Honeywell technician), Jim Geisman squatting, Dave Walden squatting, Frank Heart standing behind Dave, Ben Barker standing behind Frank, Marty Thorpe standing beside Frank, Will Crowther squatting, Severo Ornstein in Bob's shadow, and finally *Bob Kahn*. (Bernie Cosell was absent from photo.)** (Photo and names courtesy of Dave Walden (CBI photo 1565))

Artificial Intelligence and Changes at MIT and DARPA

Marvin L. Minsky
Michael Dertouzos

Introduction

Many people have had a problem with the term "artificial intelligence." I think it may be poor branding. Regardless, it has come to mean many different things to many people. Even Marvin Minsky has three descriptions for it. Over time it took on a "what's happening now" quality as it worked its way out of academia. It was even promoted in some unusual ways. For example, a big billboard in Kendall Square, near MIT, once called it "Artificial Intelligence Alley." Eventually, AI seemed to fade, but it keeps coming back in different forms, such as expert systems. Any imaginative use of computers can be called artificial intelligence.

Marvin Minsky's oral history covers artificial intelligence in great detail with observations about ARPA funding and how the whole process worked that provide valuable insights, as well as the importance of timesharing. He comments on the importance of BBN as well as the movement of some key people to the Xerox Palo Alto Research Center (PARC), which he refers to as BBN West. This is very interesting because PARC would have a big impact on computer hardware and software development on the West Coast, particularly with graphic user interfaces. Xerox, ironically, wouldn't benefit much from all this great research work that PARC was doing, but others such as Apple would.

One imaginative experiment that Marvin Minksy undertook was to recruit three composers to see what would come of it. Why composers one might ask? Professor Anthony De Ritis, brilliant head of the Northeastern University music department, composer, and a high tech entrepreneur, has been consulting with the Chinese to help them find ways to make them more entrepreneurial in the future. They believe the process of creating music lends itself to corporate innovation. Ironically, of the three composers that Marvin Minsky recruited, two faded away and one created a bestselling book for children.

Michael Dertouzos appears late in the game but has an objective view of timesharing and artificial intelligence. A Greek immigrant, he has a very good sense of where the industry is heading and what MIT should be doing in computer sciences. Timesharing, in his opinion, had run its course after 30 years. Also, he recognizes that Project MAC was created as a project by Professor Robert Fano to be able to recruit faculty more easily—time to focus on new areas of research with a Laboratory for Computer Sciences. He questions the division between AI and computer science since, in his opinion, they are really the same thing. However, he also comments on the major changes at DARPA when it comes to funding new research. This is a very important development.

AN INTERVIEW WITH

Marvin L. Minsky

Conducted by
Arthur L. Norberg
November 1, 1989
Cambridge, Massachusetts

purl.umn.edu/107503

Photo courtesy of MIT Museum

Norberg: It's very difficult to decide where to enter the question of what is AI, and what sub-areas of AI we should focus on in looking at the history of its development.

Minsky: Well, I think the problem is . . . nobody knew what AI was. I have three definitions.

Norberg: That's exactly where I'd like to start. I'd like to ask you if you can review for me the determination of AI objectives in the late 1950's.

Minsky: OK. The simplest one is: how could we build a machine that thinks and does all the sorts of things that you would say is thinking if a person did them? So that's one question. Another question is: is there a theory for this? Could we understand principles of intelligence or something like that? Those are not quite the same thing, because somebody might think maybe there are some general principles of problem solving that apply to any machine that can solve hard problems, whether it's a person or not. But the third one, and the one that's really the most effective definition, is very weak, namely that AI labs are the places where young people go if they want to make machines do things that they don't do yet and that are hard to do with the currently existing methods. So in that sense, AI is just the more forward looking part of computer science. That's the definition that makes sense in terms of the history.

At one time they were doing advanced graphics of one sort or another and then that becomes a little industry of its own, or they were working on speech recognition and that becomes a separate thing. From the very start AI labs were obsessed with making machines that could see. So there was the early vision work. A lot of the early vision work was somehow associated with AI. Although my friend Russell Kirsch at the National Bureau of Standards had been doing it as early as 1954 or 1955.

Norberg: Vision?

Minsky: A little bit of computer vision with the SEAC (Standards Eastern Automatic Computer) machine. Nobody used the word AI yet. He was the kind of person who could say, well, everybody's having their machines crunching numbers, can we have one that can recognize patterns? Of course, the electrical engineers would dispute that and say, we've been making sensory systems all the way back to World War II. I think if you could get a portrait of an AI lab at any particular time you'd see that only a few of the people are trying to make a thinking machine and other people are just trying far out, new kinds of software.

Norberg: Was it clear in those days of the late 1950's that this is what people were doing?

Minsky: Certainly when we started the MIT AI Lab, the goal was let's see if we can make a machine that will have common sense and solve the kinds of problems that people do. Now, Newell and Simon in their Carnegie Mellon and RAND places had similar ideas. The main goal of their work was to imitate thought; for some reason they decided to call it complex information processing. They didn't like the term AI really, but I think that was sort of justification for the labs and the way they got funded and the way they explained it to people. But this other part of just being in the forefront of new computer techniques and hackery and getting the machines to do all kinds of new things was just the informal thing that actually happened.

Norberg: How did support come for these groups? Let's just stick with your group for the moment.

Minsky: Okay. It was very simple from my point of view. McCarthy and I met—he might have a slightly different version of it, we were walking down the hall and we met Jerry Wiesner or Zimmerman or someone, and he said how's it going and we said well, we're working on these artificial intelligence ideas, but we need a little more room and support for some graduate students. So then a room appeared a few days later, I believe under the auspices of the Research Laboratory of Electronics (RLE), which had a block grant, so did Wiesner and/or Zimmerman. I don't remember quite who, but they could simply decide let's give them a room and some assistance.

Norberg: You people didn't have to be concerned at all with money.

Minsky: Zero. Right. We had people like Wiesner and Morse who just did it. In 1962–1963 when it was starting to get large, and we were starting to need a lot of money for our own machines, the Project MAC miracle happened and Project MAC got $3 million a year and we got $1 million a year. I don't recall ever writing a proposal for that.

Norberg: But in the meantime, quite a number of memos came out from the AI project which was in RLE and the Computation Center.

Minsky: Yes. We started this idea that whenever anybody got a good idea, they should write it out. There wasn't any idea of wide publication but the memos got numbered and there got to be several hundred of them before long. Memos three through eight are missing; nobody has a copy.

Norberg: Well, how did this interaction with Robert Fano then go on?

Minsky: It was just incredible. We just managed everything sort of informally. I think the unique thing about our lab was that it was co-directed by McCarthy and me. Whoever was in would make whatever decision had to be made. Then McCarthy went to Stanford and Papert came to MIT and we continued that.

Norberg: How did this interaction between you and McCarthy go on? This seems rather haphazard, if you'll pardon the word.

Minsky: Oh, yes. Well, we had known each other quite well in graduate school in 1952, 1953, and 1954.

Norberg: What sort of relationship was that? Did you work on problems together, did you take classes together, dissertations closely allied?

Minsky: No, dissertations were pretty different; it was a social thing. First of all the [Princeton] mathematics department was rather small; everyone knew each other and everyone had many common interests. I was a bit interested in topology. Differential topology was his main concern. There was another mathematician named [John] Nash that I worked more closely with. I never really worked with McCarthy on anything mathematically. There was Lloyd Shapley. Shapley and Nash were the key people in the RAND Corporation game theory business and Martin Schubeck was an economist, also a mathematician. The whole cluster of these people all worked on different things and talked about them to each other.

Norberg: But, now, how does this then develop into a relationship of the kind that you're describing to me?

Minsky: We used to talk about how you could make thinking machines. I had been working on it longer than anyone else because I was enamored of Warren McCullough and people like that. And then I went to Harvard at the end of graduate school. I went to Tufts for six months—an ill-fated, ambitious project—and then I got the junior fellowship at Harvard. McCarthy went off to Dartmouth, which was sort of a nice miracle there. You know what happened? You could say, how come Dartmouth was prominent in computer science? What happened was that, as I understand it, the four professors all retired about the same year.

Norberg: Four people in mathematics?

Minsky: At Dartmouth. So, Dartmouth called up and said what do we do? Where's the best mathematics department? They called up Princeton and asked someone, perhaps Lefschetz who was the Dean, I don't know, said we need mathematicians, and they got four of them. Kemeny came as, I don't know if he was chairman yet, but he had finished his degree a year or two earlier than the others, I'm sure Snell and McCarthy. But they got four young mathematicians all at once, and McCarthy was already interested in the possibilities of computers. Then we didn't see each other very much for several years, but we got together again in 1956—well, just two years—and McCarthy organized that AI conference. We kept in closer touch then. My fellowship got ditched in 1957 and I went to Lincoln in 1958, MIT in 1959. McCarthy came down there the year before, and we decided to start a group because we were both working on common sense reasoning.

Norberg: At this time, how aware were you of the work that was going on elsewhere? Such as at Carnegie Institute of Technology, at SRI (Stanford Research Institute)?

Minsky: I was very, very current on the Carnegie Mellon stuff—it was the best stuff being done. I don't remember when I established connections with SRI.

· · ·

Norberg: I want to go back to the idea of objectives again and how one decides what AI is in this period. It seems to me that the three definitions you gave, if we choose any one of them, are fairly broad definitions, and at any time in a new field the broad definition provides some indication of what sort of problems one might work on; how does one decide which ones to address first?

Minsky: Well, first, we didn't do the same thing. John decided that a way to understand common sense would be to try to make a mathematical formulation of it, and so he went in the direction to use mathematical logic notations. I think calculus was the most well-established tool, and most of his students went along in that direction. I didn't think that that had much future, still don't. So my students worked more on trying to make machines solve new kinds of problems. I had one student (Henry Ernst) working on how to make a mechanical robot find objects on a table; another student, Jim Slagle worked on a machine that could solve integral calculus problems. Manuel

Bloom is another student who worked on the theory of ultimate computability, which didn't have much to do with AI, but I had also been interested in this.

Both McCarthy and I shared another interest, which was the foundations of computation and the basic mathematical principles of computers. Again, we worked in somewhat different directions. I worked on the theory of Turing machines and Manuel worked on his thesis, which was the first one to start developing this idea of computational complexity: when could you make one program twice as fast as another and at what cost. But then, the big difference was that I started working with a student named Tom Evans to make a machine reason by analogy, and that was very different from what the logic people were doing. Dan Bobrow worked on making a machine understand algebra problems in English. So I was going more in the heuristic direction of taking problems that people could do and just picking out interesting ones and trying to get machines to do them.

Norberg: Where were the various heuristic methods coming from?

Minsky: These were coming from us and from Carnegie Mellon.

Norberg: Were those methods used elsewhere?

Minsky: No. You see the basic difference between AI programs and other ones, and it's not really very profound, was that in typical computer programs you would have to say in advance what should be done. In the AI programs you'd say, well, if you're stuck, try different things, generate a list of things to try. So, that was the basic idea of search, which I think is sort of the characteristic difference between AI and other things. But then the searches got too large, so you'd invent heuristics. One kind of heuristic would invent new things to search; another one would discard them. Generally, discarding was more important. Nobody had ever made machines do that.

Norberg: Was it just the memories were too small or were there other problems of accessibility and reliability as well?

Minsky: Well, the time-sharing project came out of the AI things because of the accessibility problems. So, I suppose you could say we felt very badly limited by accessibility.

Norberg: Came out of the AI?

Minsky: Yes.

Norberg: Could you be more explicit about that for me?

Minsky: McCarthy developed these things, first at Bolt, Beranek & Newman and then at MIT, so that we could debug our programs better.

Norberg: So, just because McCarthy did this makes it AI or because it was associated somehow with an AI problem?

Minsky: I never used the word AI. That's somebody else trying to structure this rather integrated project of trying to get machines to do more. See, if you can take the first definition of AI, then timesharing is AI because nobody had done it very well. Developing timesharing had the same role in our minds as developing LISP, mainly how were we going to get our programs to be developed and run.

Norberg: I guess what that makes me think is that you would classify any new area in computing as on the frontier and, therefore, somehow associated with what we, people like me, now associate with AI.

Minsky: Well, that was my first definition. The AI labs were filled with the kind of people who wanted to do new things, and now there were such people in other labs. But they were handicapped because there was only a couple of them in each lab, but if you looked in the MIT lab we had a dozen people, each of whom was trying to start a new domain of computation. People whose names aren't very well known yet—Greenblatt, Holloway, Tom Knight, and William Gospers, each of them were pushing in some direction on this frontier. So it was an atmosphere. I got it from McCullough's lab, because there they were interested in the nervous system, but they were inventing new algorithms before computers. Those were the leaders of cybernetics before AI.

Norberg: What were other people doing in that period that we would call computing?

Minsky: Mostly ordinary science, as Thomas Kuhn puts it.

Norberg: Let me try to pull it out in a slightly different way. Do you remember in the early 1960's various meetings that you went to?

Minsky: Yes. I remember one which was in some great place in Virginia where we went skeet shooting. (laugh)

Norberg: You remember the skeet shooting, but do you remember what went on at the meeting?

Minsky: Not in the least. Hardly anything . . .

Norberg: Not at all? Because there was such a meeting held in . . . I want to say Hastings, Virginia, but it's not Hastings, it's around the Wye Plantation, in which the Air Force apparently sponsored the meeting. There was some discussion about the directions in which the Air Force program, and various computing programs of the military services and the Defense Department, ought to go.

Minsky: I presume that we decided those people were going nowhere, what should we really do? For the first time we were in some place to spend actual hours together instead of meeting in the hall.

• • •

Norberg: Can you tell me something about the interaction with J.C.R. Licklider ("Lick")? When did you first come into contact with Licklider?

Minsky: I don't know. Oh! Of course I know—as an undergraduate, it must have been in 1948. I took a course called Physiological Psychology. I think that's in the Bernstein article.

Norberg: It is.

Norberg: What sort of projects did you consult on out at BBN?

Minsky: I don't know how they pulled this off, but you see what they had at BBN was making money on acoustics and there was a miracle in there. That place was like a university psych department. I'd come over and it would remind me of what it was like in the basement of Memorial Hall. They had different people working on different theories of perception. There was a sort of close bridge to the acoustics because somebody would be working on how a subject perceived how loud a sound is, and, let me see, it was pioneering in cognitive things. Dan Bobrow and other students would work on other things. I think it was getting funded by AFOSR (Air Force Office of Scientific Research) or something, so BBN didn't care, since the project was paying for itself anyhow.

Norberg: What sort of opportunities did this provide for your students?

Minsky: It meant that students could go there and earn some money while they were pursuing their studies and still do the same thing.

Norberg: Which was fairly traditional at MIT, it seems to me. I remember in the 1920's and 1930's that that was going on with professors having some consulting relationship with the various companies—Raytheon comes to mind.

Minsky: That's right. Now, I think at this time Licklider was full-time there. He had been at MIT for a while, I think, then he was at BBN. He didn't come back to MIT until later in Project MAC.

Norberg: After he left IBM, after one or two years.

Minsky: I didn't know he went to IBM.

Norberg: He went to IBM from DARPA and spent almost two years there before coming back. So you had this relationship. We got onto that because we were talking about the train ride and you becoming involved in Project MAC.

Minsky: You see, you're putting things together for me again because part of the chemistry that made that work was probably that Licklider and I had a great deal of confidence and respect from my college days. He was just an assistant professor then himself, so there wasn't that much difference. I don't know, was he 10 years older?

Norberg: You mean back in 1948?

Minsky: Yes. So that we knew each other a lot.

Norberg: With all this new amount of money, this million dollars now that's available ostensibly for AI in 1963, how did that change your outlook or vision for the research laboratory?

Minsky: Oh good. That hits what we were talking about in the proposal thing. What was the limitation of AI research? In 1958 or 1959, the limitation was that the 704, the IBM machine, was more or less fast enough for what we wanted to do, but it didn't have enough memory. By 1962, the programs were starting to occupy two core loads, which means you would have to run something and then re-load and run something else—32,000 words of memory were beginning to be a pain. Our staff was getting sort of slowly larger; it didn't expand dramatically. Mostly the people we had in the project in the late 1960's were undergraduates who had grown up in it and stayed with it. That's another maybe unusual feature. So the million dollars came in very smoothly because we spent most of it the first year on buying, I forget what, but we got our own PDP-1, which was a few hundred K dollars with all the stuff, and then before long we got a PDP-6, which was DEC's next big machine. My impression is that you might look at that money, which lasted quite a few years, a million dollars a year, and the first few years it was spent mostly on equipment as we needed it, and then more on people. So although it sounds like a huge influx of money, it was not used for ultra-rapid expansion, but it was very luxurious. If there was somebody we were interested in, we could invite them to come for a year, absolutely. There was hardly ever a chance of deciding should we do this or that; we could do both. This was all without any planning, but the hardware got less expensive as the people got more expensive.

Norberg: How did the new hardware change the nature of the problems that were being worked on?

Minsky: It just meant that you could write bigger programs. I think Joel Moses and Bill Martin started writing MACSYMA (Project MAC's SYmbolic MAnipulator) in 1965 or 1966, and those required the biggest machine available because MACSYMA was a huge LISP program that would hardly fit. What we did then was we went and spent another million dollars to buy more memory for the PDP-6. So we negotiated a contract with a company called Fabri-Tek and got the largest memory in existence, except secret ones.

Norberg: How many people using it at the same time?

Minsky: Usually about 20.

Norberg: How was the field evolving at that point? Were the objectives changing in any way, considering the new interest on the part of the Defense Department in this research?

Minsky: No, I don't think so. There weren't any sudden transitions until about 1972 or 1973. What evolved in this period was that the emphasis moved. At the end of the 1950's the problem was we knew how to solve some problems like proving theorems by making a big search and we needed heuristics to make the search smaller. And then, at least in my side of the thing, we began to sense that heuristics would not really go very far when you had a big tree. So, the emphasis shifted to saying, in order to solve a problem the machine has to know, has to have built-in knowledge of what's relative to that field. We gradually turned to finding new ways to represent knowledge and building up these knowledge bases. That led to these kind of expert systems.

Norberg: And you said that transition is in the early 1970's?

Minsky: Well the transition of saying, we've got to get the machine to have the knowledge for doing these things, that's in the middle sixties.

Norberg: That sounds early to me.

Minsky: Yes. Well, the thing like MACSYMA had virtually no heuristics at all. We started to get knowledge about algebra and rules about when to apply them, so it did very little searching.

Norberg: What was the meaning in your comment when you said, until the transition in the early 1970's? What transition were you referring to?

Minsky: Oh, that was when the Mansfield Amendment and things started, and we had to start writing complicated proposals to ARPA justifying what we were doing and had to find some relevance, things like that. It got to be rather painful. Eventually Papert and I quit, because we couldn't stand that, having to be able to manage it.

Norberg: What sort of justifications were given before that?

Minsky: Didn't have to. Before that, people like Larry Roberts, Ivan Sutherland, and Bob Taylor were the interface. They would explain to their superiors why this was relevant, and they never bothered us at all. You see, in the late 1960's when . . . when did Taylor leave?

Norberg: 1969.

Minsky: So then he went to BBN—I shouldn't say BBN right? (laugh) Because Xerox was BBN to us. Dan Bobrow went there. Licklider had left so Xerox [PARC] was the new BBN and Bob Taylor went to BBN West as far as I was concerned. But at about that time, the pressure was starting to come from ARPA that IPTO couldn't insulate us from. We would actually meet with [Eugene] Fubini and people about how to reformulate a proposal so it would be acceptable. That's when we both quit.

Norberg: Do you remember any examples of this? As to how you reformulated it to make it acceptable to the Defense Department?

Minsky: As I recall, the compromises were almost invisible, so I can't remember any specific things. Sometimes we'd say well, this vision system would be usable to spot cats in the bushes, but I don't think I ever wrote any of those. Then we would have to make milestones. Actually, it wasn't so much that it was military, as that it was bureaucratic. We'd have to say, we hope to get this vision system doing this by October. But I sort of attribute it to the idea that they were having more Congressional oversight and having to cover their tracks. In the early 1960's that just never reached us.

Norberg: Who had to be satisfied about the research?

Minsky: Beats me. (laugh) You know, I've met the directors of ARPA since then and they always said they had perfect confidence in me.

Norberg: Well, I guess I wasn't referring to the ARPA people, but how does one get validation for one's research in this new area of AI in the 1960's?

Minsky: You mean, as opposed to whether the proposal is acceptable?

Norberg: Yes.

Minsky: That's a funny question; it almost never came up. Everything we did was new and you didn't have this question of even why does it really work.

Norberg: That suggests to me, though, that there's no peer review process going on within this avant-garde area of computer science.

Minsky: There's no formal one; there was an internal one.

Norberg: How did the internal mechanism work?

Minsky: Their idea was it's impossible. A computer only does what it's programmed to do. You can't solve problems, unless you cheated by dumping the solutions in, I mean computers don't have souls. It's a religious idea and it's still there a bit. But the point is that it meant that the AI people were a sort of beleaguered minority. I think people like Newell, Simon, people at Stanford and SRI, and us as forming a kind of circle. So, the peer view doesn't exist in the other sense, but there's a sense that what we do has to be very good or these vultures will get us. One great feature was that if you discovered something you'd call them up the same day and say, hey I found this way to . . . why don't you make GPS [General Problem Solver] work on this kind of difference instead of that.

Norberg: This is calling up Newell or Simon or one of those people.

Minsky: That's right. So, we'd always be on the phone, and I think there were no secrets. That meant if you had a bad idea, you'd probably get peer reviewed in a minute instead of in a journal a year later. Now that's changed a bit. Not so much that the skepticism has gone, although most of it's gone, but because of this damn commercial problem. I have a student who's made an optical score reader, reads piano scores rather well, and somebody else somewhere else might have one, so they might say, I don't want the details of this to get out. Ray Kurzweil was a student of mine. I could never find out whether his optical character reader worked.

Norberg: Is that because he intended to manufacture it?

Minsky: Yes, and he was protecting it and copyrighting it and keeping it a secret. It was really annoying. I mentioned the optical score reading. There is a kid named Alan Ruddenberg (?), he's in exactly the opposite situation, because MIT has just established a kind of proprietary rights agreement that students have to sign. Ruddenberg wants to give the software away free, they don't want him to.

Norberg: That's interesting. That is a shift, certainly.

Minsky: He's really furious. They're withholding his RA money until he signs the agreement.

Norberg: Well, now getting back to this reviewing process of being on the phone continuously . . .

Minsky: And email. We were the first ones because of Larry Roberts. We simply used email for ordinary social . . .

Norberg: What I was trying to say, and trying to see if you would agree with me on this analysis, is that it seems to me that the present AI community, however we define what we mean here by community, the people who claim to belong to the artificial intelligence research community, seem to me to have a different attitude toward publication, for example, and how you evaluate publication, where many things appear in proceedings and preprints rather than in published articles and in reference journals. This seems to arise from the kind of interaction you're talking about. That it's more important to interact with your colleagues in the same field than it is to worry about whether there is this trail behind you that you can point to as your productivity. Would you agree with that?

Minsky: Well, there's both, because there's also the usual thing of people publishing incremental versions of their thesis . . .

• • •

Norberg: There is certainly an increase in bureaucratization within the Defense Department in those years; whether we ascribe it to the Mansfield Amendment or some other phenomenon. But, that having happened, what happened to the activities here at MIT that you were involved in? How did the size change over the next twenty years?

Minsky: I don't know exactly, I could look in the progress reports, but I think when Project MAC started, then there was a sort of steady growth and by 1973 there were probably 50 people, 40 or 50, and it continued to grow. So now there's probably about 120, and it's at least two and a half floors. But, also, there's a discontinuous point where LCS (MIT's Laboratory for Computer Science) absorbed first the MAC lab group and Jerry Sussman. The boundary between the AI Lab and LCS is indistinguishable now, and the whole thing is very big.

• • •

Norberg: What areas of AI would you think have the most promise for demonstrating development and influence?

Minsky: There are things that you can still identify as AI and things that just happened to start developing in AI. A good example of the latter is modern complexity theory. When you take a course in computer science now, or if you go to graduate school, there are four areas, and one of them is called algorithm theory. Algorithm theory is actually not how the algorithms work so much, but how you judge how efficient they are. I was very interested in the question of why does it take longer to compute some things than others. I got MIT to hire Albert Meyer, who was very good at this. He sort of headed that section. You might think it would be the business people who would say "What's the fastest possible way to sort." But as far as I can tell, the important thing in business is how can I get a sorter that's slightly faster than the competitors'. I don't want to discover one that's very fast, or else we'll all lose money. (laugh) It's sort of funny. But that's what we're going through. So that's an important direction in theoretical computer science that came from other places too. Shmuel Winograd at IBM was interested in that.

Norberg: What sub-areas of AI would be the best ones to focus on to show development on the one hand and influence on the other.

Minsky: Maybe robotics. As far as I can remember, modern robotics came almost entirely out of AI groups, but maybe that's a wrong judgment. I know people in

Pennsylvania, at Ohio State or somewhere, who were trying to make a walking machine and it crept along. Nothing much came of it, but the idea of a robot with a vision system so it could see something and grab it, I don't think that happened anywhere else. We started doing it. SRI started doing it at Stanford, then somewhat later Carnegie Mellon. I think in the next century that's going to be a very big thing. Right now it's impressive, but in fact, it hasn't dominated in the field. In industry you never lost a part once you've got it. It's always clamped or tied to a belt. So vision systems are used more for inspection than for assemblage. But generally the incentive for making more versatile robots has always come from AI.

Norberg: Okay, so that's two examples.

Minsky: Speech recognition is a good example. That was done partly at Bell Labs for 40 or 50 years and never got anywhere, and a little bit of it was done in AI labs, mostly the Raj Reddy stuff at CMU (Carnegie Mellon University). But Reddy got started because he was a student of McCarthy and he was interested in speech, and I persuaded him to see if he could do it without using Spectra.

Norberg: Is that a relatively late development in comparison to robotics? Say in the 1970's?

Minsky: Speech? As far as I can remember Reddy's was the first one. Then there was a five-year ARPA program to push a speech program, which didn't pay off much. It took a couple of generations of speech machines. Yes, I'd say that's a little pocket and someone decided to put a lot of money into it, and it might have been a little too early. Speech is coming along now, but it seems that a lot of it is due to computers being a hundred times faster and algorithms only a little bit better. That's debatable. For example, OCR—Optical Character Recognition, a lot of AI people worked on that and a lot of inventors worked on it in different places. For example, Pat Winston's doctoral thesis was on it. Warren Titleman's thesis. He was one of the people from BBN. And now you can buy OCR machines that are actually pretty good. I tried one yesterday, put a full page in there and it only made a couple of errors; it was a magazine article with several pictures. It even got the captions to the pictures and put them in a separate file, it didn't confuse them with the text.

Norberg: How about natural language processing?

Minsky: I would certainly say that the AI people have done more on that than the linguists. Linguists tend to study syntax and avoid the question of meaning. So, the commercial natural language systems were mostly versions from people trained in AI labs, and they're not very good yet. But within a restricted domain they're pretty good. My feeling is that another 20 years is necessary because you can't deal with language unless you have the conceptual representation of what the words mean, and that's a big job.

Norberg: What's the basic problem there, can you tell me that? We have meaning.

Minsky: Well, that's the point. To get the meaning, you have to solve a lot of the old problems of philosophy. For example, Douglas Lenat in his psych project in Austin is trying to build a big database that has conceptual representations of all the sorts of things every child knows. It's a terrible job.

Norberg: Is it an accumulative task or does, every once in a while, the researcher come up against some new conceptual understanding that means you go back and you have to redo the whole thing again?

Minsky: Very good. Excellent. It was supposed to be an accumulative task, and they've had to revise it twice so far. Now they've got quite a few people entering knowledge, and I feel that they made a big mistake at a certain point, and they're going to have to do it over again. But Lenat thinks it's good enough, so that when you have to do it over again it will know enough to help. I hope he's right.

Norberg: (laugh) I hope he's right, too.

Minsky: See it knows a lot about things and classes of things. It knows that dogs are kinds of mammals and it also knows that animals have to eat and stuff like that. What it doesn't know is in the functional domain. It doesn't know that chairs are for people to sit in. And it's very important, I claim, that you know that, because to understand why a chair has legs, in fact why isn't a box a chair?

Norberg: Besides vision and speech as two good examples of AI development, I guess I would have chosen something like problem-solving and knowledge based-systems as the third area.

Minsky: Oh! The general development of expert systems is certainly the most productive of all. The problem solving has not developed into an industry exactly because I think it lacks this common-sense knowledge base, and the whole world has to wait for things like Psych to work so that the machine just knows something about what you want done and what it's for. But the expert system, that's a very interesting thing because expert systems, you know in the commercial sense, these are these rule-based knowledge-based systems. The knowledge is put in the form of procedural rules, which say if you want this then do that. They're not quite like GPS, because they don't use differences. But what's important about that is that with one of these expert system shells, a person can write a problem solver by hand and you might be able to do something in a few days that would take a regular programming house a year to do. So, it's wiping out conventional programming. Instead of writing this big, tricky program that has procedures that call other procedures in symbols you can't understand, you have this set of rules which say what it should do and then it just reads the rules. So it's sort of a computer; it's like you didn't need a compiler.

In the early 1980's, Ed Feigenbaum was the one who basically declared that rule-based systems were good enough for practical use. Some members were telling him you're out of your head. They are just going to be always breaking; they're not rugged enough. But he was sort of right, and they actually started some companies because Feigenbaum invented the idea. Also, I think, that there was a special profession called knowledge engineers who would interview experts and formulate their decision rules and use things so they got investors to buy these companies.

I'm sort of amused to see that the reputation on Wall Street is rather bad. They say AI companies are losers; they cite Symbolics. Of course, Symbolics didn't even do that kind of software. Although the AI business you can invest in didn't do well, you look at a company like Arthur Andersen where half of its income comes from programming in this way. Basically the only thing Feigenbaum might have been wrong about is that the knowledge engineers are not such a highly developed skill and someone else can learn that in a fairly short time. So you're right. The expert systems probably have the largest impact on the computer industry, because I really think they're going to eat up most of the programming jobs. It's just so much easier than writing a program. It's not very good if you want to write an actual low-level program that converts a certain file into something that could go out on a certain printer. You could write that as a rule based system, but it would be too slow.

Norberg: Okay, so graphical techniques would not necessarily be included here.

Minsky: Yes. Ivan Sutherland's Sketchpad is the best graphic design program ever used, but it was never replicated. It's a miracle that's still being rediscovered. We have this permanent state of wonder that there'll be another, commercial version of Sketchpad. Some company up in Burlington made one recently but they ran out of budget so it's not available.

Norberg: If I understand Sketchpad correctly, a number of the things that are included in the program, such as the window technique that Sutherland included in order to pull out sections of the bridge design that he was working on. If you think of the programs that now use that as a regular feature, then why wouldn't you say that Sketchpad had a substantial enough influence on development?

Minsky: I think it probably did. People saw it, and they invented their own. The critical thing in Sketchpad was that it had internal constraints; so you could say this angle is twice as big as that one; as far as I know, no drawing program has that yet. It's quite easy to implement. It has this problem: if you have a set of constraints, then you have to have a program that solves them simultaneously and that could be hard. In fact, the way Sutherland did it was to take each of the errors and square them so it would be positive, and do a relaxation. I draw my lecture slides on MacDraw or something like that, and I'm always furious because I really want this thing to be twice that size at all times and I want to be able to move this. It's very funny that nobody's done that.

Norberg: I wonder why.

Minsky: I don't know why. So you could say it inspired a lot of graphics.

Norberg: Well, it's certainly seen as the starting point in what happened in computer graphics.

Minsky: The first spell program, for example. Some kid at Stanford wrote the spelling program, and he attached it to all of our editors and the whole environment of word processing comes from AI. It's a big industry that's never called AI. I'd say it's interesting that people haven't seen that.

Norberg: Going back to the statement you made about AI being out there on the frontier continuously . . .

Minsky: I know that when I came to MIT, Jerry Wiesner in RLE (MIT's Research Laboratory of Electronics) had decided he would have McCullough. McCullough wasn't a professor, he didn't want to be; he had been a professor at Illinois. He kept getting people. He had a guy named Manuel Serillo who was a Mexican conceptual artist. Serillo was making different theories of perception, and no one understood him very well. But Jerry got him; this might be a new deal. So when he was running RLE, he would collect people that he thought might be important for the future. I think it is inherent in the nature of artificial intelligence. Sure, you're trying to make machines that can think so you need ideas about thinking. In Project MAC, I hired three different composers at different times in the hope that they would, I guess, seem more articulate than other musicians. They didn't pan out.

Norberg: Was that to do computer music or to do things generally?

Minsky: I was hoping they could do computer music and bring some new viewpoint. What happened was usually very ironic. Alan Fort was a composer, who's now head of the music department at Yale, and he wrote a book on SNOBOL (StriNg Oriented and symBOlic Language) programming. He got so interested in computers that he didn't, in fact, contribute anything to us.

Norberg: I want to go back to the comment you made about email, when you said that in the reviewing process email became very significant as a replacement for, I presume, the telephone and regular mail, postal service. How did it affect the interaction among people?

Minsky: Good question. And when was it realized? Because, I remember when people were talking about building the network. I think the idea in most people's minds was that if there was a program somewhere else, we could use it. See, the network was going to be a computational network. Mostly we used the network to get software from somewhere else, if you want, as a mail system, not as a computer. But, I would say, as soon as the thing started, we started sending mail to one another, and the glorious thing was the ARPANET because when Danny Bobrow went to Xerox . . . I don't remember whether the mail was working yet, when did Taylor go to Xerox?

Norberg: About 1971.

Minsky: So the network was in place by then?

Norberg: Yes, in 1969.

Minsky: So when I had a question, I'd email to Bobrow and just ask him. It was as though he'd never left.

Norberg: But how does that differ from the telephone? I mean, could you ask the same question over the telephone?

Minsky: Yes, but they wouldn't be there. The difference is that e-mail is always answered. Usually within a day or so. But with a telephone they're not there, they say they'll call you back and they don't. It's very different. Also, it's more concise. You write the things and say, no I meant this. It's very nice. Then there's a sort of illegal aspect, which is that it's used for all sorts of social things—the bootleg lists of the good Chinese restaurants. One day I just noticed that I had gotten messages from all three children; Henry was teaching a course in LISP in Japan, Margaret was somewhere else, and Judy was somewhere else. It was this little family affair we had on the email, and we keep in touch that way. I probably am better connected. Until the last few years. When I started writing *Society of Mind*, I sort of stayed home and just worked, which was good, I didn't pay any attention to the world. But I bet that up to that point I was in closer touch with my students than a typical professor.

Norberg: There must be a number of examples that you could cite that are important contributions to, now, non-AI activities, as a result of the work in AI. What are a few examples of that sort of contribution? Timesharing is one you mentioned before.

Minsky: Yes, timesharing, and word processing is probably the most important of all. I'm sure word processing would have happened once timesharing happened, and certainly it would have happened once personal computers happened. So there's some inventions that are inevitable. Arcade games: a big prototype was the Space Wars that we had and, in fact, at some point we had to ban it, because it was so popular. The ban on Space Wars must have been about 1965 and it wasn't until 1975 or 1980 that personal computers were cheap enough that you could have it again. So there's an invention that would have been made in 1975; if Steve Russell made it in 1960 that's just a sort of historical anomaly. So, you could say that the arcade games, computer games, came out of AI and the adventure games came out of the network for some reason, once people had timesharing. But that's a kind of indirect thing. Very direct tools are things like Mathematica, which people buy for their computers, and applied mathematicians have these nice tools.

Norberg: Are there no specific tools that were developed?

Minsky: Yes. In fact, C has just become the most popular programming language in the world—in UNIX—and UNIX has not got this yet. We consider UNIX to be a world-wide disaster setting things back a few years.

Norberg: You said that the other day and I wasn't quite sure what you meant.

Minsky: It's very primitive. It puts you back in the early 1960's. Everyone tells me that in four or five years they'll get back to the Project MAC way of doing things. The designer of UNIX didn't understand the importance of having a nice transparent program.

Norberg: Is that possibly related to the problems that Bell [Laboratories] had in continuing to be part of the Multics project?

Minsky: Well there is this little fragment of history which is that John Pierce didn't like AI in any disguise. But he's been gone a long time, Arno Penzias is the director now, and he likes the idea of AI. I don't think he's gotten around to following up on it, but I'm not sure.

Norberg: Anything in data structures? Do people develop databases differently now because of AI?

Minsky: Well, almost everybody uses frames for representing ordinary knowledge, when they do ordinary knowledge. That's a popular thing. Some of the expert systems are critical. But for big commercial databases it doesn't pay to use anything fancy. I think that the right person to ask about that would be someone who knows.

Norberg: Do you think the AI field is now too big?

Minsky: Sure. In general, but the field of making these common sense databases is too small. I think they have to synchronize the various areas that are too small.

Norberg: Would you like to separate them out from AI and call what's now become AI something else? I guess what I'm asking you, is that now part of conventional computer science?

Minsky: Yes, I guess so. I think expert systems activity is not returning very much scientific knowledge. But you know, you've got this problem when you decide to separate something. You don't want to get rid of the money cow, because you can hide basic research in large projects. If they're out in the open, they are vulnerable. That, again, was a strange feature of that golden age of the ten years after Project MAC where the whole thing was full of basic research. I'll bet if we hadn't done those things like networks, word processing, and timesharing and so forth . . . It turned out that basic research actually produced a lot more useful stuff per person than applied research, but it's very hard to judge that now.

Norberg: Well, if we look at the contributions of DARPA in terms of the things that they funded, it would seem to me that we would probably argue that most of the things that people cite as being the significant contributions tend to be out of basic research or at least a technique to stimulate basic research.

Minsky: Well, what else did IPTO fund? I know ARPA is a billion dollar enterprise, so most of it I never heard of.

Norberg: How would you characterize the contributions at DARPA? We're talking about just computer science.

Minsky: Well, I told you in the elevator, or whenever it was, my impression was that it was probably equal to all of NSF (National Science Foundation). It's just that all the good people I know are in the DARPA circuit. Every now and then I meet somebody who isn't in our network and I'm sort of surprised—I didn't know you could do good work out there. (laugh)

Norberg: I certainly understood your comment, but I think what most of the people who have listened to the DARPA crowd in Washington want to say is that somehow that program was unique. What I'm trying to find out is what about the program would contribute to uniqueness.

Minsky: Well, I don't know if it's unique, but I'd attribute the great success and influence to the initial heads of that office, namely "Lick" and was it Roberts or Sutherland?

Norberg: Sutherland next, then Taylor, then Roberts.

Minsky: Anyway there was something miraculous about that particular string of people. I didn't know about Taylor much, but I know the other three were in this position of molding the thing, and really had a lot of good taste about what were the important problems to look at. That's very rare.

Norberg: How would they know the right problems to look at, do you think?

Minsky: I guess we'd all work together. (laugh) My problems are the ones that I think are the right problems. (laugh)

Norberg: All right. So, that means that convergence between the research community and the people in those offices handing out the money is an important element.

Minsky: Right. The easiest way is if one of the people will actually volunteer to go there and help. For some reason, they got many of them. You usually can't get any.

Norberg: Up through [Bob] Kahn that certainly worked.

Minsky: That's right. Now if Kahn hadn't—I don't know how Kahn did so well. But he did and he hadn't been in it very much before then.

Norberg: Well, he was another BBN person who went down there.

Minsky: Okay. So getting a great director of an office. Marvin Denicoff's personal influence also sort of roaming around the projects and sometimes deciding what was going well. I don't know what he did about it, but . . .

Norberg: That would be from the ONR (Office of Naval Research) side.

Minsky: That's right. That was a piece of luck, having a contract administrator actually know about the personal lives of these people in a quiet, sympathetic way. I have a feeling he must have told some of them they were wasting their time. Who knows?

Norberg: Did you see a difference between the programs of places like NSF and NIH, in computing now, and a place like DARPA/IPTO?

Minsky: Yes. On my few visits to NSF, I would meet people who were trying to do a good job, but they didn't know what was going on. It was a kind of review process in which you have to have either a peer review process or a benevolent dictatorship.

AN INTERVIEW WITH

Michael L. Dertouzos

Conducted by
Arthur L. Norberg
April 20, 1989
Cambridge, Massachusetts

purl.umn.edu/107245

Photo courtesy of MIT Museum

Norberg: Today is April 20, 1989. I am in the offices of Professor Michael L. Dertouzos of the Laboratory for Computer Science (LCS) at the Massachusetts Institute of Technology (MIT) for an interview on the development of the laboratory and its relationship with the Department of Defense's Advanced Research Projects Agency (ARPA). I think the way to begin is for me to ask you if you would tell me something about your range of activities in, say, 1970. What sort of research were you involved in? Who were your colleagues?

Dertouzos: I was doing research on computer-aided circuit design, which had started with Project MAC, of course. My doctoral thesis was on threshold logic. I was one of the first people to use Project MAC for my book. My book that came out in 1965, which I have here, had all the tables done by Project MAC's timeshared system. In fact, this was CTSS (Compatible Time Sharing System). You might be interested to know that I never learned how to program on the older systems. That was my first system, so I never knew how things got better. Closer to the 1970 period, the other piece of research I did was on analyzing circuits. I had worked on programs that, if you gave the computer a description of the circuit, a linear circuit with transistors, resistors, and capacitors, then the programs would give me the performance of a circuit in time, in various other parameters. Then you could analyze them and vary things and gain an understanding. It was CAD (Computer Aided Design)—one of the early examples of CAD. It used to be called CIRCAL (CIRcuit CALculus). That was what I was doing. I was using, of course, a lot of the MAC resources.

• • •

Norberg: During this period of the early 1970's, do you remember what your interaction was with DARPA people?

Dertouzos: Yes. I very well remember meetings of DARPA people coming here. And I remember (Edward) Fredkin and them disagreeing with each other.

Norberg: Disagreeing about what?

Dertouzos: Fundamentally, they were fighting about who tells whom what to do. I remember Fredkin felt that DARPA was trying to dictate too much to him at the Lab's review. Later, I never found that to be a serious problem. To this day, DARPA is extremely interested and open to creative suggestions from the field. Sometimes they have their own suggestions, which are very good; for example, Morse Code. We took that suggestion right out of DARPA and worked on it.

Norberg: I see. I did not realize that.

Dertouzos: To this date they are open to suggestions from the field.

Norberg: Was Fredkin reticent to approach the DARPA people, where you seem not to be?

Dertouzos: I don't know about that. I do know that I embraced them and they embraced me. We have had our differences over the years, but we have been able to work together as an extremely good team.

Norberg: When you took over in 1974, the organization was still called Project MAC.

Dertouzos: Yes, I renamed it.

Norberg: Do you recall how much of the Laboratory's activities were consistent with the overall program of DARPA at the time? We are speaking of 1974 now.

Dertouzos: There was no such thing as a strong DARPA driven component.

Norberg: Here or there?

Dertouzos: Here or there. I remember one of the first things I did was to visit DARPA. At the time Licklider was in charge, and I said . . .

Norberg: This would be his second time.

Dertouzos: Yes. So, I am going to be director of the Lab. I want to understand what it is that DARPA does. I went and got a tour, a show, an exhibition, and a discussion of what they were after. I remember finding things very, very vague at that time. Later, as time went on, I began to understand how DARPA operated. Smart people within DARPA and smart people from outside keep formulating a changing pattern of ideas, and you find almost no differences. You will find that these outside and inside people have their ideas gel at about the same time. And I think part of it is they influence each other. They coalesce in these new directions. I can go back and pinpoint them for you.

Norberg: Be my guest.

Dertouzos: Sure. Well, let me start back at one of the first discussions I had. I remember being at the roof of the George Washington Hotel right next to DARPA, around 1976. I was with Al Vezza and Joel Moses, who was then Associate Director of the Lab. The next day we were going to visit DARPA. I said, "Look fellows, you know, the world is going to go to distributed systems." That was in 1976. That was a long time ago. Distributed systems were unknown, so you have to define them: lots of computers at different places connected by networks. You see, the ARPANET was known. But it was only known as a medium for logging onto other computers and a way of doing Telex (faxing in today's language). Nobody thought that you would have computers all over the world that would have to interact with each other, understand the same language, and be a community of machines. In many ways that was one of my inspirational thoughts and hopes in 1976. Now, I am not going so much for the credit here, although a bit of credit is deserved too.

Norberg: (laugh) We'll take care of that.

Dertouzos: But I am really trying to explain to you the mindset at DARPA. So I went there the next day and I explained. I gave my impassioned plea and my description of where the world was going, and where we think we should take it. I talked about distributed systems, the power of networks, of machines. I talked about the information marketplace, how machines and people would trade things with each other, how it would help mail in this country, the transaction services, the rendering of legal services—the whole bit. When I finished, I remember the fellow in charge (I think it was Colonel Russell . . . maybe it wasn't) made the statement, "Look, we think all this is nonsense, but you are the director of LCS and you may be right. You have $300,000. That is what you asked for; you are going to get it. Get it started."

Norberg: Yes. Well, can we back up just a little bit? How did this proposal of yours compare with their distributed information systems program that was going on at that time?

Dertouzos: There was no perception of distributed systems as I just described them. They viewed distributed systems as entirely different things. I mean, they were thinking of sensors in the field. They were thinking of fusion of information from various places. They did not think of distributed systems as powerful equal entities that would negotiate in some form of open-ended fashion. The image I presented to them was much like that of people in society, much like offices and stores, and entities like our own selves. We do not give each other all the details we have. We just do enough to communicate so as to achieve our goals. I said, "We need to understand the semantics of the languages and the systems that are going to do all of this." Of course, DARPA did not think that this vision would play. Yet, there was this belief, this sense that if there is a group of smart people at MIT who want to go that route, damn it, we are going to let them go.

So that is one example. A second one is multiprocessing. We talked about multiprocessing. There was a time, believe it or not, when DARPA did not want to hear about multiprocessing, about several machines working on the same thing. I could not get them to fund Jack Dennis. Slowly we came to the point where they not only espoused the whole multiprocessing notion, but to where Strategic Computing (1983 to 1993) was formed with multiprocessing as its core. Now this takes us to a period that is quite a bit later, and starts around 1979. Arvind (Mithal) came from Japan. He brought the fifth generation plan with him. I got on the horn and started screaming. I wrote to our computer corporation presidents. I went to visit the Defense Science Board. I started working with Cooper and with Kahn (Bob). I was not alone. There were other people around the country feeling the same way. Soon we were sitting around the table, and we were putting together the key ideas behind SC—Strategic Computing. If you try to see who started this or where it went, you will find it distributed equally within DARPA and outside. Multiprocessors fared very well in that program.

Norberg: Who was the IPTO director at that time when the Strategic Computing program got started?

Dertouzos: Bob Kahn.

Norberg: What sort of interactions did you have with Kahn?

Dertouzos: I remember Kahn telling me (it may have been very close to that meeting): "You guys have had a pretty good record over there at MIT and you, in particular, Michael, just seem to have a good common sense about where things ought to go." Then he said, "You know, on the other hand, you guys are not always right." But there was basically a respect on Kahn's part for what we had done—in other words, an openness and respect. There was also a respect from our side for what DARPA would say. For example, near that period one of the DARPA people said, "Why don't you solve the Morse Code transcription problem?" And we said, "What do you mean? It is obvious. You know in Morse Code: dit-da=A; da-dit-dit-dit=B." They said, "Oh, no.

Make me a Morse Code machine that will work with intelligence and will understand things in a noisy environment." This was driven initially from DARPA, yet we ended up making a very important contribution. So there was this distributed period; then there was the multiprocessor and Strategic Computing theory. Let's see, what program came more recently, after the strategic computing?

Norberg: In DARPA or in MIT?

Dertouzos: In DARPA. We really do not have one yet. The more recent movement is Squire's movement, which has not panned out yet.

Norberg: I don't remember one in between Strategic Computing and now.

Dertouzos: No, there hasn't been one. There is one now. It is the one that led to the OTA (Office of Technology Assessment) study. It involves the National Research Network and things like that. We tried, at various times, to push DARPA in other directions— for example, theory. They did not want to touch this. The only time it succeeded was with Jack Schwartz last year. For the first time he started thinking of theorizing.

Norberg: Why do you think they did not want to do theory?

Dertouzos: I think they felt the issue of turf. They felt that NSF ought to be supporting that. That is the basic scientific apparatus of the country. Also, it is hard to predict where theory research is going to go, and it is not quick in its results. Whereas at DARPA, a young manager would get an idea, "Hey, let's have a project," and that gave the agency a lot of strength. They had no peer reviews, nothing to worry about, a lot of things that could guarantee bad quality under other circumstances, but as long as the people on both sides were good, it worked. You see, in a way, this is why DARPA people were very good, and the field was very good in those days. I mean, they only dealt with MIT, Carnegie, Stanford, where, by the mechanisms that these institutions had, there were only good people there. If any one of these factors were gone—bad people in DARPA, or bad people in the field, this could have been the scenario for disaster.

Norberg: Tried to do what?

Dertouzos: To make industry change its mind. Neither Fano, nor Licklider, nor the team of people that were in those days the gurus of the various labs—the McCarthys of this world, the Allen Newells—were very industrially oriented. The generation that is now running the DARPA sites, many of them are or have been corporate players, owners of companies. I started my own little company; Ed Feigenbaum has started two or three; Nils Nilsson has started his company; Raj Reddy has started his company. You are looking at a team of people for whom industry is not so far from academic work.

Now, Fano and Licklider and Corbató—our good friends from that period—went out and said, "Here is how you should do it." They tried to convince them, but they did not speak the language of industry, and industry said, "Goodbye, we are building the System 360. Thank you very much." And who says they were wrong? They made more money on the 360 (laugh). You know, timesharing lasted a good 30 years and then started giving way to personal machines.

Norberg: I want to again go back to the 1974 to 1976 period, because I am interested in seeing whether there are some trends here. Why did you rename the Laboratory?

Dertouzos: (laugh) Well, there are three reasons. First of all, MAC sounded like a hamburger.

Norberg: At that time it would have.

Dertouzos: Also, "Project" was a trick that my friend Bob Fano did to get people to come here without coming here. If he had called this a lab or a center, people would have said, "My God, I am not going to leave RLE or one of the established big centers to come to this fledgling place." So Fano, in his wisdom, said, "Project MAC. Anybody can participate in a project." However, it was untenable for me, when I was trying to build a laboratory that would be a forefront center for computer science research. Second, MAC was losing in meaning. It did not mean anything to people. It had some nice value in terms of tradition. But after a while, you have got to change with the times. So I put on a search, I probed. Joel Moses, Associate Director for the lab helped. We put up a lot of names, and we chose the Lab for Computer Science. I am glad we did it.

Norberg: How did you convey this new objective to the people who were then associated with Project MAC?

Dertouzos: When you run an educational institution like this, like (Bartlett) Gamatti said, "You have to run it from a medieval throne—even in a 20th century environment." (laugh) So you must appreciate that if I were to stand up and say, "This is what I am trying to do," I would have had a revolution. Basically, what I did was I spoke about it. I said, "This is what I feel the important interactions are." Then step by step I made the right moves. There was something very important about the laboratory's faculty: they would hear something and they would say, "No." Then they would hear it the second time and they would fight it. Then the third time, if it had good components, it would be their idea. Now be careful. Many times I was all wet, and they would come back and clean me up, and correct the all-wetness. And I listened. So this is a bilateral thing. We have moved with a great deal of teamwork around this lab. After a while I gained credibility here, and then they trusted me.

• • •

Dertouzos: The AI Lab existed then, as you know. That was the sin of our forefathers— Licklider and Minsky. They decided to split the labs up. In the history, there was a period there . . .

Norberg: Pardon me. Was there something wrong with that split-up in your mind?

Dertouzos: Yes and no. First of all, in terms of what it ultimately meant, there was nothing wrong, because we were so big that we could not have run as a single center. There are 380 people at LCS, and there are probably 250 at the AI Lab. So it would have been too big. In terms of keeping cohesiveness and keeping the community together, however, we might have stayed closer together. You see, the distinction between AI and computer science is artificial. There is no such distinction. Well, people behave like there is—even knowledgeable people. That is one of the things I have fought since day one. We have plenty of AI in this lab. This lab and our sister lab have plenty of what you would call computer science. So it was a little bit intellectually dishonest to make that distinction. There was a point where DARPA tried to help us unite. Colonel Russell and others at DARPA were putting on a little pressure. They did not like the way the AI lab behaved. We were a little more corporate, a little more organized. The AI culture was a little more disheveled: do what you wish and this is how you get the best result. Both places were getting great results, but one was doing it IBM-style and the other one was doing it Apple-style, if you wish. DARPA did push a little, but not hard—very gently, but that did not work out for a variety of reasons. So that is part of the history, too.

• • •

Norberg: Now there is good deal more computing around the MIT campus, such as Project Athena.

Dertouzos: Project Athena we did precisely to bring computing to the educational and instructional side of campus. So now, of course, with personal computing and with the networks around, the scene is pretty much as we had predicted in our 1979 report. Then we predicted that we would have by now, 10 years later, around 5,000 machines, 4,000 or 5,000. We are right on target.

• • •

Norberg: I want to go back when I asked you about your interaction with the people at IPTO and at DARPA

Dertouzos: Let me give you the style. I will paint it like an impressionistic painting rather than a precise picture for you. There is a sense in my head that in those days we were able to get things done a lot more easily.

Norberg: Those days, meaning early 1970's?

Dertouzos: Meaning essentially all of the 1970's. You would basically pick up the phone and have a discussion about a new idea. You would get a reading as to whether the new idea made sense. You would go down to Washington, spend a couple of hours, and it was done. Then the bureaucracy maybe took two months. Up until 1983 or 1984, we could submit our proposals in August, and have full funding in place by the end of the year. Okay? I will trace it, but I think it goes all the way to 1985 or 1986. You would go to the PI meetings . . . I remember, in fact, as a young Turk, taking over a meeting and discussing future directions and everybody being happy about it. A lot of things came out of this—a sense of common language. I mean, when I am together with Ed Feigenbaum or Raj Reddy, or Nils Nilsson, we all have a sense that we are the same community. Oh, we may disagree on small things, but you know, we feel French. All of us feel French. DARPA is French.

Now, several things have happened. Some things have changed. First, the bureaucracy that has entered that organization is much greater. Now it takes a year, even for a place like MIT, to get a proposal through. The freedom of going down there with a quick idea and getting going is no longer there, because now there are all these bureaucracies set up, in the interest of fairness, for small people and big people to compete on equal terms—all of which has a lot of validity. But then, of course, who says that you've got to be fair if you have got to be inventive. Then there is this tendency, which started for no good reason, which I call the systematic broadening and the systematic destruction of the strengths of DARPA, which was to take what was great and worked, and start chopping it up based on absolutely no rationale. So now you find 300 universities competing, or 300 contractors competing, in inky-dinky chunks. If you go to the PI meeting today, it is a big mass affair where you go hear big people speak. And there is no longer a sense of give and take, of "Let's get together; let's pull this. What do you think of that idea?" There is just too much variability between the people who attend. I am very consciously trying to not be the old man with the old man syndrome of "It was good then and bad today." I am trying to be as objective as I can, because even today, good things are happening.

Norberg: Given the ability of the Department of Defense to act rapidly if they want to, why should this continue to be the case once it is recognized to be a failing of the system?

Dertouzos: The first factor is the succession of people who got into DARPA. Each one had his own agenda. Some came from the aerospace establishment. They did not understand computers, and they wanted things to go like they did in the aerospace business. So they had that agenda. Other people came in and were reluctant to go up to Congress and say, "Computing is the only thing left in this damn country. We lost steel; we lost textiles; we lost electronics. Are you going to support us?" Nobody until recently has gone to Congress and said this with this conviction. And, to be sure, there is some rationale behind this weakness. After all, why should the DoD be the agency to mind for U.S. competitiveness? Well, it has done so and it's the only game in town. Enter now, the bad boy—the bureaucracy and the requirements—and everybody uses that as an excuse for all that happened.

Norberg: Do you think something like *Made in America* will turn this around?[1]

Dertouzos: I know that if one good person were to go in there, he could clean that place up in six months.

Norberg: Well, considering the number of good people that are around, why won't people go?

Dertouzos: I can answer that for you, because I have been Chairman of the Advisory Council to DARPA for years. I have gone after people myself for the job, and others have come after me. One is a damning statement for all of us. We are not cooperative. So people like me, and people like my colleagues, will not stop doing what they are doing and go do something that is perhaps less exciting for a couple of years in the interest of helping the U.S. First, there is a component of lack of cooperation that *Made in America* brings up. Second, however, there is a very practical component: money. I had people in the palm of my hand who were ready to take this job if I could only get up there and pay them the $150,000 that they required, or the $160,000; yet all I could get for them was $65,000. These are successful people with children. These are people making $160,000. There is no way to get them. So, you have got to be financially comfortable or independent like Bob Kahn was. Bob was one of the superb people that we were lucky to have there. But if his dad did not have a medical forms business, we would not have had Bob Kahn, and where would the computer industry be today? It is almost as fickle as that.

Norberg: Kahn seemed to me to be a man with a mission, at least with respect to networking.

Dertouzos: But what allowed him to have the mission was his financial independence. I mean, Kahn did not need anybody's money, and he was at DARPA 12 years, which was a boon to all these programs; the SC [Strategic Computing] and everything else was a result of that.

---

1. Michael L. Dertouzos, Robert M. Solow, and Richard K. Lester, *Made in America: Regaining the Productive Edge* (Cambridge: MIT Press, 1989).

Norberg: Do you think that that was not a problem in the 1960's when people like Licklider and Sutherland went there?

Dertouzos: That is right.

Norberg: The salaries were less.

Dertouzos: That is right, the differential between outside and inside, a) was smaller and, b) more significantly, the field was so much in its infancy. The excitement was so high that the sense of what you could achieve with the steering wheel called DARPA was much greater. Now, you know, computing is 10% of the GNP, $400 billion, hardware and software combined. And you are just sitting there. Industry and everybody else control this $400 billion, and you have got a little chunk of $120 million, and another $100 million in applications. What do you think you can do now? That's the first. Then you have got a two-to-one ratio on salary; then you have got the bureaucratic procedures; then you look inside and the personnel is not stellar. If you are a top notch person and you are also not very cooperative, you know this is going against several gales.

Norberg: It strikes me that you are painting a very pessimistic picture for the future.

Dertouzos: I do not think it has to be pessimistic.

Norberg: Ah, but that is not what I said. I said that you were painting a pessimistic picture.

Dertouzos: I am an optimist; I want you to know this. But yes, I paint it pessimistic because the field is leveling out. The field is not growing as fast as it used to. It has become more mature. Computing is now accepted; it is not a fringe field. Even the kids that we get here are normal (laugh). They are no longer the wild geeks, the unwashed. We get normal kids (laugh), so something is wrong. So how can I but be pessimistic?

Norberg: Where are all the wild kids going, incidentally?

Dertouzos: They are sitting still now. They are waiting for the next higher technology.

Norberg: I am sorry. I didn't mean to interrupt you.

Dertouzos: No, no. It is a perfectly legitimate question. Look, all they have got in this country at the peak of intellectual activity now is biotech, material science, and computer science. These are the three hot seats. And material science is not that exciting. So biotech and computer science are the queens. That is the leading edge. And biotech is not getting that many geeks either. So both fields are beginning to level out. Maybe there will be a new one—I do not know, maybe fusion; who knows? Look, if we could spin salaries off and make it possible for people to live on them, you could find good people. I think that it is a question of survival; if you have two or three kids and all that, you cannot live on the stupid salaries they give. So if you can satisfy that, as a minimum, then I think you can find dedicated people who will do the jump. So I am not pessimistic, if we tend to it.

Norberg: If you were in my position trying to assess the influence of the IPTO portion of DARPA on developments in computer science, what sorts of things would you focus on?

Dertouzos: I would say, first of all, that if we look at the computer field as a whole, I can peg for you the major contributions in the field. So I would say the microprocessor, the personal computer; I would say artificial intelligence; I would say languages like FORTRAN, compilers, LISP; I would say advanced work stations, distributed systems, the whole networking from local to broad area networks; multiprocessing; and work in theoretical advances. Then I would say, "How much of this do I credit to industry, and how much do I credit to DARPA, and to NSF?" I would credit NSF with a lot of the theoretical advances, period. Regardless of what they say, I would stop there. I would credit industry with the microprocessor, with making the computer a commodity, a staple commodity like bread that you go out there and buy. I would credit DEC with doing this with the PDP-8 in the mini era, and credit IBM with doing this with the PC. I would further credit Xerox PARC with that whole invention of the Apple Macintosh personal computer world, and then I would credit Apple with the continuation of that. I would credit our semiconductor industry for the invention of a whole bunch of other special purpose devices that have really played a major role. Then I would turn around and I would credit DARPA with timesharing, with the whole field of artificial intelligence, with the LISP language, with a lot of the pioneering work in distributed computing, with multiprocessing, unquestionably, and with networks. Then I would sit and weigh these two parts on a scale and say, "Look, we are all human. I may value something more than the other, but those two are not far from equal, my friend. DARPA has been responsible for half the computer field's evolution in the world."

Then if you ask what we at MIT, and Stanford, and Carnegie have been able to do by educating the cream of computer scientists throughout the world, you can attribute a lot of this to DARPA. Without DARPA, would we have had such strength? Would we have had this vigor? I look at this Laboratory—25, 26 years in existence and see steady funding. I have tried to get funding from industry. I would say that the effort and the difficulty of getting $100,000 from industry is maybe five to eight times higher than getting it from DARPA. Where would we have been if we had to get funded from industry? We may not have generated as many computer scientists, as many good people, and so forth. So I think the impact of that organization has been tremendous. They are the closest thing we have to a (Japanese) MITI (Ministry of International Trade and Industry). If I am bitching about something, it is because forces unknown are trying to change that. They are trying to change something that is working perfectly all right, or they are trying to question it by virtue of turf, you know, "Should they be doing this and all that? Isn't their function the military?" When we are working with a tool like the computer, it is like pliers. Do you care if the pliers are going to be used to pull nails, or if they are going to be used on people's teeth? (laugh) The intent is a human purpose; it is a mechanism that we are talking about. I think DARPA has a profound influence . . . Unquestionably, it has had a profound influence on the computer field.

Norberg: Do you think that the DARPA influence in LCS will continue?

Dertouzos: I think it will continue, because LCS by now is so broad and big that it is inconceivable that it will do things that are not in line with what DARPA at any time thinks is in line. I think we still have our problems. For example, I think LCS is the only place, I repeat, the only place that is resisting doing things with as short-time horizons as DARPA is pushed and is pushing to do. Kahn predicted this. He said that LCS is going to be the only place that is going to be able to hold on because of its established record and all that. How long we can do this, I do not know.

Norberg: That is interesting. Does that mean that places that Carnegie and Stanford are giving in already?

Dertouzos: Oh, yes. Carnegie is working on systems that are in use today. I have always felt that if we start working on things that are current we are dead, because we are competing with industry. We have got to stay at least ten years in the future. How long we are going to do this, I do not know. But I will tell you, we are strong enough now to where if DARPA decided to go loose on us we could survive.

Creating Something Great in Unusual Places

Joseph F. Traub (Carnegie Mellon, Columbia University)

Introduction

Joseph Traub's oral history was particularly intriguing to me. I knew that Carnegie Mellon had become a big name in computer sciences, and still is. In fact, Michael Dertouzos said the big three were MIT, Stanford, and Carnegie Mellon. How did this come about at a time when there was great controversy in academia about where computers belonged? There would be some bitter turf battles fought over it. Some thought computers should be in the mathematics department. Others, thought engineering. Then there were those, such as Joseph Traub, who thought computer technology was so important that it should be in a new department called Computer Science. He created a great one in Pittsburgh, Pennsylvania, not something one would have expected at the time. Pittsburgh in the 1960's wasn't Cambridge, Massachusetts, or Northern California. How did this happen?

This is a question I have often pondered as I witnessed my company's database system being installed in some very unusual organizations. Why was this happening in the places I wouldn't have expected? On the surface there was no rationale for it. Over time, I concluded that somehow, some way, one good person was at these sites and set the whole process in motion. It could happen anywhere, all you needed was that one good person at the right time and right place. As a result, his, or her, organization became skilled in and benefited from advanced database technology, while others fell behind. This was particularly true of universities.

I once wrote a book for entrepreneurs with tips for managing in good times and bad. One chapter was called the "Nines and Sixes." Readers seemed to really like this chapter. Nines are those people who work for an organization whom everyone knows are the best, have good judgment, anticipate problems, take corrective action in time, etc. Every organization has eights and sevens, which are ok. With some good supervision they can be very productive as well. Sixes are trouble. Sometimes a six would be hired in my company and he/she would say something in a meeting that was a dead giveaway. I could see the look on everyone's face when it happened, and I groaned because I knew I was stuck with doing something about it. Sixes are the ones that will take your organization right off a cliff. Worse, sixes gravitate to sixes. In the process, they drive away nines. This often happens in a fast growing organization and then others later wonder, "What happened? How did things go so wrong?" I once mentioned this syndrome to Joe Tucci, Chairman of the Board of EMC. His response was, "I know what you mean, the empty suits."

Joseph Traub operated like a classic nine who attracted nines. His oral history demonstrates how he got around obstacles, found good people, and accomplished great things at Carnegie Mellon and Columbia University that I am sure some people thought wouldn't be possible. He has much wisdom to offer the reader and excellent insights as to why some universities have elite computer science programs and why others, who should, don't.

AN INTERVIEW WITH

Joseph F. Traub

Conducted by
William Aspray
March 29, 1985
Columbia University, New York

purl.umn.edu/107684

Photo courtesy of Charles Babbage
Institute (CBI subject file)

Aspray: This is a session on the 29th of March, 1985, with Joseph Traub in his office at Columbia University. It is the third in a series of interviews, and the main topic of this session is institutions in computing. Why don't we start by talking about why certain universities—Pennsylvania, Harvard, and Columbia, which had strong early activities in computing—didn't develop into first-rate research and teaching centers in computer science?

Traub: It seems to me that in each of the institutions that have become the major centers one can usually identify one or two people who were responsible. I'm speaking of people who really cared about building institutionally.

There was a program at Carnegie Mellon in 1962; there was a precursor to the Stanford department also in the early 1960's. Purdue may have already had something like a department, though I'm not sure it was called a department by 1962. Certainly there were departments at Stanford and Carnegie in 1965. The beginning of academic computer science is in the mid-1960's or perhaps early 1960's in the United States, to the point where now practically every major university in the country has a computer science department, or, in a couple of special cases, an electrical engineering and computer science department.

Because that's all happened during the time I've been active, I can see who was responsible. For example, why should Stanford have been a leader? I think it was due to one man, George Forsythe. He had the vision that this was going to be a discipline, and the energy, and obviously support from some key people. George was a man of great character and moral force who made that happen. At Carnegie it was Perlis, Newell, and Simon initially. When Perlis left, I went there at a crucial point that I will come back to, which could have been a turning point for the department. But first, I'll identify the people. Perlis, Newell, Simon, and myself in terms of the builders. With MIT, I simply don't know. You could say it was a great science and engineering school and, therefore, it was inevitable, but it didn't happen early at Cal Tech, for example. It's just now happening at Cal Tech.

At Berkeley, there were two departments; and two departments are perhaps worse than none, because there was a bitter battle between Abe Taub, who headed a department (he's a mathematician who'd been recruited from Illinois to head the computer center and to build a computer science department in the School of Letters and Sciences), and Lotfi Zadeh, who was the head of the electrical engineering and computer science department; or perhaps, it was called Electrical Engineering, but had people working in computer science. In the late 1960's the country watched while this bitter battle was waged at Berkeley between the two departments. Engineering wanted it more than Letters and Science, and Engineering won. There's an Electrical Engineering and Computer Science Department of great distinction, with a Computer Science Division, so it's got to be Zadeh who gets much of the credit. He was the winner, certainly, in that battle of getting Berkeley to form one department, and that's now a department of great distinction.

At Penn, I don't know the history of why they were not successful, despite their enormous head start with the Moore School. It's only recently that Penn really has made a push under Joshi, who is the chairman of computer science. But for a long time there was only limited activity.

At Columbia, where there was the IBM Watson Laboratory early on, which in fact was one of the few places in the United States where one could do research in computing in the 1950's, there has been a long history of not being able to get going in computer science. There were various efforts made. Mathematics tried at one point: mathematics said, "We can do it." There was an Electrical Engineering and Computer Science Department. There was a group within Mathematical Statistics. I'll talk more about the Columbia history later, but I'd like to say now that it simply couldn't get going. What finally happened was that there was a Dean, an extraordinary man named Peter Likins, now President of Lehigh who said, "This is the most important thing that I can do as Dean." There was Associate Provost Norman Mintz, now the executive vice-president, who very much supported this, and Peter recruited me. That was five and a half years ago, and now Columbia has one of the major departments.

There are two possibilities in answer to your question: there was no one willing to devote a fair amount of his life to building the institution, or there was such inertia in the institution that one couldn't do it. It could have been either, or some combination. Certainly at places that were successful it seems to have been one person, often with very little institutional support. For example, the amount that Carnegie Mellon University put into the department annually in 1971 was $200,000. At Stanford, my recollection from when I visited there in 1966 is that the total budget from the university was on the order of $150,000. There was very little support. It was the key people—one, two, or three people—who built the great departments.

Aspray: When you started, you spoke just about people, and then you broadened it to talk about institutional support at least in the sense of the willingness of a few administrators to allow somebody with some ambition or initiative to come in and do things. What about financial support from the computer industry or from the government?

Traub: When one looks at the best departments today and at their history, it turns out that the agency most responsible for major chunks of funding was the Advanced Research Projects Agency (ARPA) of the Department of Defense. That is not to say that the National Science Foundation hasn't helped: it has heavily supported basic research in computer science. In fact, fairly recently, over the last five years perhaps, it has started a program called the Coordinated Experimental Research in Computer Science, giving major funds for equipment. Also more recently, IBM in particular has been extremely generous, for instance, to Columbia.

Let me start with ARPA, because I think they're crucial. The Information Processing Techniques Office of ARPA was led by a group of visionary directors—J.C.R. Licklider, Bob Taylor, and Bob Kahn—who felt this was enormously important for the country and identified the few places in which to put major resources. For example, at Carnegie Mellon, to return to the budget in 1971, when I showed up, the budget was $2 million for the department—$200,000 from the university, $1.8 million from DARPA. There had been major funding at Stanford, for instance the AI lab, and major funding at MIT. In fact, the Big Three—Carnegie, MIT, Stanford are usually called that in computer science, though I don't know who coined the phrase; I don't know whether I did or somebody else, but it's simply part of the lingo and it has been for a while—all had major and long-term infusions of DARPA money. By long-term I mean for the last twenty years. At Columbia, we are now one of the top five in terms of DARPA funding. Berkeley, by the way, is the fourth. But Berkeley has gotten mammoth funding, and that has been simultaneous with their move into the top group. I know how crucial DARPA funding was to Columbia.

Now, let me mention IBM because they have been so important somewhat more recently. For instance, at Columbia—which is what I know best—when we first started this department, even before I came here in the spring of the previous year, Peter Likins and I went up to IBM to talk to Ralph Gomory, Vice President of Research, and to talk to the Director of University Relations. Likins indicated that I might be coming to Columbia and asked if IBM would be prepared to help. It turned out that, two years before, Columbia had approached IBM. IBM had laughed and said, "Get your act together first." Pete now had a real live candidate, and he went up and said, "If Traub comes here will IBM help?" I wrote a proposal in November of 1979, my first full year. In December, we had a gift of $600,000 to attract faculty and students. I can tell you something that hasn't been announced yet, which I've just found out, early next week the President of Columbia will be receiving the initial check of a $4 million gift from IBM for the support of this department. IBM has been enormously generous.

Aspray: The other thing I've wondered about often is the relationship between academic centers of excellence and major regions of computer industry. For example, Route 128 and MIT, and Stanford and Silicon Valley. Carnegie Mellon doesn't seem to fit that very well.

Traub: Oh, you're just a little bit behind the times.

Aspray: Maybe I'm wrong.

Traub: You're just a little bit behind. Let's start with Stanford and MIT, and then take Carnegie. There is no question about it: the high technology belts are directly associated with the great universities, and in fact in the case of Stanford one can make a direct trace from Frederick Terman to some of his students, such as Hewlett and Packard whom he urged to go and do their thing, and to Fairchild Semiconductor and the spin-offs from that. But it was directly from Frederick Terman at Stanford that the vision came which eventually led to Silicon Valley. And Route 128 is certainly due to MIT. There's also the Research Triangle area, and more recently, although it's too early to see what will happen, is MCC's (Microelectronics and Computer Consortium) move to Austin to be near the University of Texas.

Carnegie Mellon is very interesting. There is Pittsburgh, the absolute epitome of the Industrial Revolution, blue-collar workers, and so on. In the early 1970's, Simon, Newell, and I were talking about "The greening of the University through computer science," and then eventually changing Pittsburgh and western Pennsylvania. So we built a great computer science department. We then strengthened nearby departments, such as electrical engineering, mathematics, and psychology. When Dick Cyert became president, he had the vision that he would use computing to change the university. Today I think in some ways Pittsburgh is the most interesting example. I became aware of Carnegie in 1971. At the time, it was a respectable but not great science and engineering school. Carnegie Mellon, Lehigh, RPI, maybe Case Western, were all of a class. It had just been fused from the Carnegie Institute of Technology and the Mellon Institute of Industrial Research. That is, it was forced on the Mellon Institute by the fact that apparently the Mellons were no longer prepared to fund the Mellon Institute.

That was the picture, in the early to mid-1970's of Carnegie Mellon. It was a respectable engineering school, nowhere in the class of Cal Tech and MIT as an engineering school, nowhere in the ball park of the Ivy League, Stanford, Berkeley, and so on as a great university.

Aspray: But it is true, for the case of Carnegie Mellon, that it grew strong much more quickly than an industry built around it, whereas these seem to be happening coevally in the case of MIT and Stanford?

Traub: Forty years ago Stanford was referred as "the farm." It was viewed as a school for rich kids and wasn't taken very seriously. It was only in the post-war period that Stanford became a great university. Silicon Valley came later. At Carnegie, it all happened in the last 10 or 12 years; we're watching it happen.

Aspray: But, for example, in the Boston area, as MIT developed, there were a number of closely related things going on—many spinning out of the war, actually, through the Rad Lab (Radiation Laboratory) and such. But there were people whom they could call on; there were companies they could call on for local support as the program at MIT was starting to get built up. They could place many of their graduates in the immediate area. It doesn't seem to me that Carnegie Mellon could that easily draw on the Pittsburgh community as it was growing in the 1960's the way that either Stanford or MIT could.

Traub: There was a $5 million gift from Richard King Mellon that gave a chair to Herb Simon and did some other good things for the university, though I don't think it was crucial to the future of the Computer Science Department. What I used to say in the early 1970's is that what's extraordinary about Carnegie is we don't deal with any company within three hundred miles of us. That is, our closest contacts were with DEC up in Massachusetts, with Xerox in Palo Alto, and later on, by the late 1970's, with IBM. That was to change, of course, with Westinghouse being involved with the Robotics Institute in 1980.

I used to say to people at Stanford, "Look, you guys have it so easy. You've got great quality of life, you've got a great university, and you've got all that industry. We don't have any of the three." Then later I really realized, in fact, that that is one of the things that gave Carnegie it's absolutely unique flavor in the 1970's: we all put everything into the department, because there was no place else to put your energy. There was no place to consult, there was no industry, there wasn't that much to do in the city, so we put it all into the department. In a sense, it's one of the reasons Carnegie was so good and so cohesive, whereas at a place like Stanford there were so many distractions, both in terms of scenery and other companies. So, you're absolutely right. Carnegie was not fostered by local industry, but it created high tech in Pittsburgh.

Aspray: Why don't you tell me the story of the building up of Carnegie Mellon's computer science program?

Traub: In the academic year 1970-1971, I was on leave from Bell Labs at the University of Washington. In fact, I had a tenured professorship there, although I was still on leave from Bell Labs. I liked Seattle very much in terms of people, but I felt somewhat isolated scientifically. The nearest major city and great university were eight hundred miles to the south. I talked to Alan Perlis in January or February of 1971 and he mentioned they were looking for a head. An executive head, rather than a chairman, is what it's called at Carnegie. We made arrangements that I would visit there on the way back from the Spring Joint Computer Conference in Atlantic City. I visited Carnegie in February for a day, met the faculty, and was so taken with the faculty and the students that I said I'd stay an extra day. I remember having lunch with a number of the faculty and the administrators and being asked questions such as, "Should there be an undergraduate program?" and I'd say, "Well, that's a difficult issue. I should hear the pros and the cons." It was a very comfortable visit and Perlis said, "I will be in touch with you on March 1." On March 1st I was offered the headship to Carnegie.

Aspray: Before you go on to that, tell me something about the diversification of funding.

Traub: For instance, within a couple of years we succeeded in getting $1 million a year from the National Science Foundation. I wanted to get the percentage of ARPA money down, but ARPA put in so much money that it was hard. Even some years later, ARPA was still supplying something like 60% to 65% of the budget, but then it was 90% and more. In fact, when ARPA went through some hard times, or at least when it wasn't putting its money into the academic sector in the mid-1970's, we suffered a cutback from $1.8 million to $1.5 million, with a threat of going down to $1.2 million. It was a time of concern. But we got money from NSF and from ONR (Office of Naval Research). We got some industrial funding.

Then I managed to convince the university to increase our budget. That wasn't easy. I dealt with the Dean of Science who reported to a Provost, who reported to the President. We were in the Science College rather than the Engineering College. The reason was that Alan Perlis had been chairman of the Math Department, and wanted Computer Science in the same college as Mathematics. I would negotiate with the Dean of Science for positions, and there would be a bitter battle to get a single new position. It looks, in retrospect, as if it were inevitable that Carnegie would become a great department, a huge department, an impregnable department. It didn't look that way in the early 1970's. We were very small, and I wanted to build. I managed to fill the open positions rapidly. But it wasn't the case that the administration supported us. People have actually said to me, "Well, it was easy at Carnegie, since you had the support of the administration." That was not true in those days. For each position there was a major battle, and for each raise there was a major battle. One year, the raises were so tiny, around 3%, I said, "The most important thing is to keep the current faculty happy; they're great." I took a position, and didn't fill it so that I could use that money to give people the proper raises. It was very hard going those first three or four years, and it wasn't the case that we were being showered with money.

Aspray: I can understand the University's position on having to guarantee tenured faculty slots. If ARPA money were to have folded at some point, they would have been stuck with a large faculty budget.

Traub: That's true, although these were simply assistant professor positions. We had a philosophy, which in fact I have at Columbia also, of almost always hiring people with fresh Ph.D.'s. That is, there were so few top senior people in computer science, and it was so hard to move them to Pittsburgh—at least in those days, and again, the department was very different in the early 1970's from the way it is now. Now, in fact, the department has made a couple of senior appointments, but we never brought in a senior person during the time I was at Carnegie. We've always grown stars. With just two exceptions we've done the same with Columbia. It's so risky to bring someone in, unless the person is absolutely a superstar. I'm afraid to bring in tenured people, and I tend to be very conservative. So I was just asking for assistant professor positions, but Carnegie Mellon did not yet realize that its future was in Computer Science. It just wasn't clear in those days. In fact, later on, when Dean Bothnerby was replaced, Schatz was the acting dean. We used to have budget meetings over lunch and I'd say, "I wish we wouldn't have these budget meetings over lunch because I can feel it in my stomach every time we have these discussions." Carnegie Mellon was no different than any other place in that it was hard to try to increase our budget at a time when the university wasn't increasing its total budget.

Traub: The major research areas at Carnegie were artificial intelligence, with Newell, Simon, and Reddy as the leaders, and architecture and software. We built a multiprocessor machine which, though it may not have been the first multiprocessor machine, was certainly the first multiprocessor machine on which papers were written and so contributed to scientific progress. It was a machine called C.mmp, which was sixteen processors connected to sixteen memories. This was work done primarily by Bill Wulf and Gordon Bell. Later there was CM*, which was a cluster machine. That is, you had very high bandwidth within the cluster, and very low bandwidth between the clusters. Architecture was very strong. We also had great distinction in the area of programming systems, with people like Bill Wulf and Nico Habermann. In the theoretical area, the focus was on computational complexity. But Carnegie's great strength and great contribution was experimental computer science. I intentionally integrated the areas: in fact, that tends to be my philosophy anyway, not to separate out theory, but to integrate it with experimental computer science. Those were the three primary areas, AI, architecture, and software systems. In each of those three areas we were certainly as good as anybody in the world.

• • •

Traub: My role at Columbia has been rather different. Not only did I come here to build the department at a university that was described to me by my peers as a desert in terms of computer science, but I've also been one of the couple of major scientists and intellectual forces of the department. I play both roles which has been rather hard. That is, Columbia has been harder than Carnegie, because at the beginning I had to do essentially everything: represent the department at the university, create a sense of self for the department, guide the department, and conduct my own research. At Carnegie I was absolutely satisfied to play primarily an institutional role. I so admired people such as Newell, Simon, Reddy, Bell, and Wulf that I was happy to have them do the science. I was active in research but I did not view my own work as central to the department. Here it's been rather different.

Just to sum up Carnegie, there really was an enormous sense of a unique departmental culture, and there was even a certain style in which we spoke, certain mannerisms. One, which I picked up from Allen Newell: "Are we there?" meaning "Are we finished?" "The rational person principle," meaning that this is what any rational person would agree to; that was often used. We had an enormous sense of loyalty to the department. One really has the sense, looking back on it now, and we had it even then, of an absolutely golden time. It was the Golden Age.

Today, Carnegie is huge. We used to say in the mid-1970's, "What if we doubled?" Allen Newell was always a great visionary, so he would say, "Why don't we suddenly double the faculty?" I should say that we grew pretty rapidly. When I got there, there were seven or eight, in addition to a couple of people whom we let go fairly shortly. That was Carnegie in 1971. When I left in 1979, there were fifty teaching and research faculty. Essentially, I tripled the department in every dimension. Then there was to be another enormous burst of growth, of at least another doubling in the next few years. Carnegie today is always described as enormous. There are faculty who hardly see each other since it is so big. There are, of course, advantages. A world expert on almost any question is down the hall.

But Carnegie in the 1970's was really a Golden Age. There were almost no meetings. Once a semester we would have a Black Friday meeting when we'd evaluate the students. Typically there might be one other meeting of the faculty the entire semester to deal with some particular problem; for instance, if ARPA cuts our budget by one third, what's our contingency plan? Maybe once a semester or once a year I would have a long-term planning meeting of the senior faculty in my home over drinks and cold cuts. It would be an open-ended meeting, perhaps six hours of long-term planning. With the way I ran the department, people knew that if they were concerned about an issue I would consult with them. People have often mentioned that to me, that they always knew they'd be consulted, and they trusted me.

In fact, if there's one reason for my success at Carnegie and Columbia, it's that the faculty trusts me. That goes a long way. It means that I can go to the administration and speak for the department, that the department will support what I say and that I really care about the department. That trust means that you don't have to have a lot of committees hammering out things. It means you don't need a lot of meetings. Now, we do meet regularly at Columbia and we're creating the culture.

One of the remarkable things about Carnegie was that it was a rather complex, powerful department whose faculty rarely met as a whole. Yet we all were extraordinarily close. Electronic mail made a difference, of course, but mainly it was trust. I would convene a group of three or four, and we'd make a decision. There was a management committee of the main entrepreneurs on the faculty, and we would meet on a more regular basis.

Why did I leave paradise? My mother recently said that my father once described a book to her, in which the author said memories are the only paradise from which we can never be pushed out. Memories are the only Eden from which we can never be evicted. I'm trying to translate it from the German. Why did I leave Carnegie? I was very happy. It was an extraordinary place. I sometimes said I had the best job in computer science. We really worked like dogs. We really worked hard; but there was never any mickey mouse, never any tension in the department. Terrific staff, terrific people, and no tension—fighting within is so wearying. We knew we were good. The department trusted me as head, so I had a great deal of autonomy, which I didn't abuse. The senior faculty—Allen Newell, Herb Simon, Raj Reddy, Bill Wulf, and Gordon Bell—were very supportive of a strong head. They liked that; they liked somebody who could run the department, so there wasn't the distrust that there often is in academia. Also, it was a permanent position. That is, you served as head as long as the faculty were happy with you.

Why did I leave paradise? The primary reason is that my wife Pamela was really unhappy in Pittsburgh. The original arrangement was that we would stay there at least five years. As five years stretched to six, and seven, Pamela became increasingly unhappy. I had my department, but she really did not like the city; she's a woman who'd grown up on the West Coast, in the Bay Area, and was far away from her family. She was not very happy with her job at the University of Pittsburgh. She essentially gave me an ultimatum: she said she was leaving, and would I care to join her.

I looked at places in either California or New York. New York was purely serendipitous, because just at that point, Peter Likins and I started to talk about Columbia. I gave Pamela her choice, because I had also been talking to USC about building a department there, and there was some other place I was talking to. We'd spent seven years at Carnegie, and then in the eighth year, 1978-79, we were at Berkeley. Her father was dying of leukemia, and she wanted to be out there. I took leave and I said to Pamela, "I'll go where you want to go. We spent these years where I wanted to be." She picked New York. That's one reason why we came to Columbia.

There was also a pull in that there was an extraordinary man here, and that's Peter Likins, who's really the man who got me to Columbia. Our courtship began when Peter Likins came out to Berkeley, and made arrangements to see me during that sabbatical to get my advice. As he said later, also in the hopes that it would lead to more. I gave him my picture of academic computer science, the Ivy League, and so on. We had a very pleasant couple of hours together. We had lunch together at place called the Three C's in Berkeley, a coffeehouse. We hit it off so well, I rode with him on the bus to the airport so we could keep talking. Then he left something on the bus, and I mailed it to him. I remember visiting Columbia in December, just before Christmas in 1978. I knew that Jeff Ulman, who was at Princeton and is now at Stanford, was one other candidate for the chairmanship, and I don't know who else was being seriously considered. On the first working day of that new year, January 2, 1979, Peter Likins called me. This was only about ten days after the visit. He said they had selected me, and asked if I would come to Columbia. There were several months of discussions: I prepared some lists of what I wanted for the department, what I felt I had to have, and Peter said "yes" to everything. It was already the beginning of that relationship, which in some ways was very much like those long talks with Allen Newell before I went to Carnegie.

Traub: I brought Pamela here the last week of March, 1979. I remember that week we spent here very well. We saw *Sweeney Todd* on Sunday afternoon before the Greek Independence Day parade. We met with the president of Columbia, Bill McGill, who, as I recall, had a private meeting with Pamela, which was most unusual. We met the Provost, now President Michael Sovern, and Norman Mintz, Executive Vice President, and I met some of the key other people. It was a wonderful week. At the end of the week, Pamela gave me permission to consummate the relationship. So we decided on Columbia.

• • •

There I was at Columbia. The reason I mentioned this is that I had come from Carnegie Mellon, which had its extraordinary support system, a huge administrative staff, a huge technical staff, fifty teaching and research faculty, eighty superb Ph.D. students, one of the several leading universities in the world in terms of the recognition of computer science and the computing infrastructure. I came to Columbia, where there was no computing infrastructure. There was a computer center that in those days had perhaps a couple of IBM mainframes, and I think one DEC 20. The whole engineering school had one 11/45 computer. Carnegie's Computer Science Department had fifty computers. It was a real change. What was enormously helpful was the fact that Peter Likins supported me. I had a vision of what I wanted to do at Columbia, but it was very hard at the beginning. I hired the first secretary, Norrie Brassfield. She sat in an office across the hall, a small office without a window, which she shared with a graduate student. I had to do everything by myself; there was nothing here. Not only was there no infrastructure at the university in terms of the computing, but of course there was nothing in the department. I would battle with the personnel office. I would write my ads with a certain flavor: I didn't say I wanted a good typist, but said I wanted someone smart or motivated to work in the exciting area of computer science. Those weren't the words, but that was the flavor; I was looking for smart, motivated people, and the personnel office wanted me to say how many words of typing I wanted. I would battle with the personnel office. They'd change my ads, and I'd make them run the originals. I would ask for stationery from the publications department, and they made mistakes. I spent hours with the publications department trying to get stationery and so on. That's the way it is when you start.

What had been the earlier history of computer science at Columbia? IBM's Watson Lab had been there but it had been closed down in the late 1960's, early 1970's. Maybe it was inevitable once IBM decided to open Yorktown Heights, but I think in those days nobody at Columbia cared. And there was a CS effort, as part of the Electrical Engineering and Computer Science department, and another effort within Mathematical Statistics. The two departments would fight with each other over people, and nobody could do any effective recruiting. There was a national survey done about a year or two before I got to Columbia by Conway, who did a study of seventy departments in Canada and the United States. Out of those seventy departments, Columbia's program—there was no department—was ranked sixtieth out of seventy on a par with Simon Fraser and the University of Calgary. That was how computer science at Columbia was viewed.

There was some rather bad blood between the two efforts, Electrical Engineering and Computer Science, and Mathematical Statistics. I inherited the faculty from those two departments and formed a new department. I must say here, looking ahead, that the split turned out to be very successful. Since that split, computer science has prospered, and electrical engineering has boomed. Next Wednesday, there will be an announcement that the Center for Telecommunications Research of Electrical Engineering has won a national competition for a center of excellence from the National Science Foundation. Columbia and MIT are each getting $20 million. They are the two biggest winners. That department has simply taken off, so in fact, it turned out to be best for everybody.

$$\bullet \quad \bullet \quad \bullet$$

Aspray: So what were the steps you took?

Traub: I said, "We're going to recruit, and we're going to get the best. The only way to get the best is not to keep the people who are here now." They were good people. They went to some very fine institutions. I was going to compete with the top institutions in the United States for absolutely the best fresh Ph.D.'s for our faculty—that was the only way to build the department.

Within two years, every single untenured faculty member was gone, eight of them. I just brought in a whole new faculty. Essentially new faculty. There were only three people, who were tenured, who were left from the initial faculty. There were no Ph.D. students, so we formulated an elite Ph.D. program, separate from the Masters, that today has sixty students. Today, we have a faculty of twenty-four. We get on the order of $6 million to $7 million a year in outside support. There's the money from ARPA. We've been designated the New York State Center for Computers and Information Systems. A huge gift from IBM is about to be given to us. There is a major equipment gift from Bell Labs, gifts from Hewlett-Packard, etc. In my view, after the top three, there is a group of universities that includes perhaps ten universities: Berkeley, Cornell, Yale, UCLA, Illinois, schools like that; that's not a complete list. We're in that group today. We know who we're competing with for faculty positions, and for Ph.D.'s. That's how you measure how good you are. We lose more than we win to the Big Three, and we beat almost everybody else.

. . .

Another job was to convince Columbia of the importance of computer science. I spoke to the President, the Provost, and the Dean. I was invited to talk to the Board of Trustees. I tried to convince them that this is the discipline that will, as far ahead as I can see, make the difference. It will simply revolutionize science, the humanities, and the arts. It is no coincidence that a university like Stanford has come up in the national standings. Now Carnegie, which was a fairly ordinary university in the early 1970's, almost a technical institute, is today always on the list of major universities. I believe computer science, both institutionally and intellectually made a profound difference. For instance, it's not just a matter of being able to solve certain problems posed in physics, chemistry, and biology and so on. The modeling in those fields has actually been done using computer models, computer paradigms. Some of the top physicists in the world are now using computers. Nobel laureates, like Kenneth Arrow in economics, are using computer models in their thinking. That all had to be made convincing to a university where computer science was almost unknown, and rather looked down on.

. . .

To sum it up, it was much, much harder than Carnegie. At Carnegie, I had a sense when I went there that a national treasure was being placed in my hands; I was the guardian and I had to keep it. Carnegie had lost half its faculty, was terribly vulnerable in those days, and it was hard to build. But there was enormous wisdom in the department and enormous political clout. We were certainly the most powerful department at Carnegie. Then I came to Columbia, where there was nothing, and everything had to be established: the culture of the department, the attractiveness to Ph.D. students and faculty, getting the funding, and convincing the university that this was enormously important. It's a competition. Only a couple of departments can get major resources. Almost no university these days has the resources to invest in more than a couple of departments. To convince this university that that department should be computer science was pretty hard.

I'd like to turn to the building. I was determined that there was going to be a beautiful environment. Carnegie had something called Science Hall, which is a rather ugly building from the outside, almost brutalistic, but a very comfortable place to be in. I was determined to build a good building; I felt the building was very important, and the Mudd building which houses the Engineering School leaves something to be desired. I managed to convince the university to let me pick the architect. Jim Polschek, the Dean of Architecture, gave me a list of architects that he recommended, and I looked at their work. I didn't interview them or look at slides or anything—apparently that's the way competitions are done. I just wanted to walk into their buildings and see how I felt.

• • •

Aspray: Now, shall we move to Berkeley and Stanford?

Traub: I spent a very significant semester at Stanford. I showed up there in January, and I was there until the end of July 1966. At that point, Stanford was already very well known, even though the department had only been formed in 1965. When I got out there, what was particularly striking was that the place was held together with chewing gum and string. The Computer Science Department was in a low-rise, two-story wooden structure called Polya Hall. George Forsythe, for whom I had enormous respect, was the founding chairman. He died of cancer in the early 1970's, when he was still quite a young man. What's remarkable to think is that when I went out to Stanford, George, who seemed so senior to me and for whom I had so much respect, was considerably younger than I am today. Yet he seemed like such a senior man, and of course he was. That was twenty years ago. He had extensive files on research ideas, had a stream of outstanding students, and was founding chairman. Nonetheless, he was a somewhat remote man. He was not a man into whose office you'd drop and chit-chat. But he was very much respected and admired by his colleagues. He was one of the men who started academic computer science. George is remembered in all sorts of ways with various prizes, competitions, and so forth. The other people who were there were John McCarthy, whom Forsythe had gotten fairly recently from MIT, Ed Feigenbaum, whom he had brought down from Berkeley, and Gene Golub, who had been hired as a fresh Ph.D. student. Golub was on sabbatical that year. I think those were the key people. And there was Klaus Wirth, the originator of PASCAL and Euclid.

• • •

Today Berkeley is one of the top ARPA contractors and is a major force in experimental computer science. I was carrying the Carnegie Mellon message that computer science is not just a theoretical subject, that you must do experimental computer science also, and that that generally requires major funding and large projects. That certainly happened to Berkeley, I don't know to what extent I can take credit or whether it was inevitable.

Creating the Industry's First Successful Software Products Company

John Cullinane

Introduction

When I formed Cullinane Corporation, I didn't know whether it was possible to create a company that could be good at both technology and sales, and be well managed, too. I had never worked for one. My experience to date was that technology companies were dominated by either sales or technical types. Those run by sales types drove away the good technical people. Those dominated by technicians drove away the good sales types. Cullinane Corporation would turn out to be very good technically, very good at sales, *and* be well managed. As a result, it succeeded far beyond my expectations.

My oral history focuses on the business and sales side of Cullinane Corporation, including challenges to its survival, and what was done about it, vs. the very significant technical accomplishments of the company. This introduction allows me to focus on the company's technological accomplishments because there's a connection between some earlier oral histories, such as those of Larry Roberts and Robert Kahn. Their work, without my knowledge at the time, would help Cullinane Corporation cope with an incredibly difficult survival challenge.

The foundation for our major software product line came via the acquisition of IDMS, a network database management system, from BF Goodrich Chemical Company in Cleveland, Ohio. It was a very good system, but much technical work would have to be done, including the building of various related products such as an integrated dictionary, online query, and report writer. We would be a late entry into the market and would have to compete against entrenched players such as IBM, Cincom, and Adabas, and with just 15 people on staff. This was definitely a "bet your company" decision because we just had become profitable after a long struggle for survival. IDMS had originated at GE's computer division as IDS, designed by Charlie Bachman, who would eventually become an employee of my company. He was an ACM A. M. Turing Award Winner, as well as a recent recipient of a National Medal of Technology and Innovation. A network DBMS lent itself very well to industry applications, because when a customer drew a diagram of how an application should work, it often looked like a network. IDMS would ultimately become, arguably, the best database management system ever developed. To this day, it still manages some of the most complex and largest databases in the world. Performance is key in database systems. What that means is instantaneous response when accessing the database from any device. Our timing was very good as computer users in industry, government, and academia were moving to interactive systems and we had the database software to help them do it. It was the engine of these new systems.

One of our clients was the National Security Agency (NSA). They invited us to submit a proposal to implement the first backend database machine. This was a big deal because you don't get invited to submit proposals to the NSA unless they think you are very good technically. Ironically, NSA would be funding Cullinane Corporation just as DARPA did MIT. The project required linking a database on a DEC PDP 11 computer at the University of Kansas with the users running on an IBM 370 in Virginia, something that, to my knowledge, had never been done before. This is the way cloud-based systems work today. This was purely a research effort that seemed like a good idea to me at the time. However, I heard a great deal of grumbling from some members of my technical staff about how difficult it was to do. Later, much to my surprise, Tom Nelson, our Chief Database Architect, told me that what he had learned from the project about packet switching had a huge impact on his major re-design of IDMS. It featured client/server architecture driven by an "active" data dictionary, also for the first time. The new release of IDMS would be a major technological advance in database technology and come at a critical time in the company's history. At the time, this put us way ahead of our competition, technically.

Packet switching was key. For example, we could link other incompatible computers together using satellites. We demonstrated this capability in 1983 by linking an Apple Lisa computer located at our headquarters in Westwood, Massachusetts, to an IBM computer in a huge data center located in Palo Alto, California. Steve Jobs looked on in the center and commented while I worked the Lisa mouse in Westwood. I was told it was the first time he was ever in an IBM data center. It was definitely the first time I had ever used a mouse. We also demonstrated linking an IBM PC in Denmark with an IBM mainframe and IDMS database in Westwood and downloaded data from it to a spreadsheet via satellite. We did this at a User Group meeting and it wowed the audience. This was really advanced database/data communications at the time.

Again, we were doing things technically that nobody had ever done before, including building the first online applications with data sharing for industry.

The fact is that we combined very strong technical skills with very savvy marketing, a rarity in the industry. It wasn't until I read the oral histories of Roberts and Kahn that I realized how much these computer industry pioneers would eventually impact the design of my company's database/data communications software. However, the company really survived at its most difficult time thanks to just four people: Jim Baker, a brilliant computer scientist from MIT, Tom Meurer, a natural-born entrepreneur and computer engineer from Notre Dame, Jean LaPointe, son of French Canadian immigrants and a gifted programmer despite having only six months of introductory computer programming school, and myself. Eventually, Jim Blake would join us and be outstanding in sales. The worst moment was when we had just $500 in the bank of our original $480,000 seed capital, and an $8,500 payroll due that day. A check came in that morning for, literally, $8,500—a *very* close call. How we survived is in my oral history.

Cullinane Corporation would go on to become the most successful software company in the industry at the time. I have often mused about how this all happened. What I find fascinating is that we did this with people who had never done anything like it before, including myself. They were all "home grown." For example, most of our regional vice presidents, such as Jon Nackerud, Frank Chisholm, Dr. Bill Linn, Flip Filipowski, Ray Nawara, Dave Ireland, and Peter Jargowsky, had never sold anything before. However, they were very knowledgeable systems programmers and really impressed prospects with their understanding of how our database system worked. Eventually, they, along with others such as John Burton, would become very good at sales. Internationally, we had a group of outstanding representatives as well, including Gerald Goetgeluck, Jean Harriman, and Jan Picavet in Belgium, Jurgen Schoon in Germany, Sergio Ferragut in Mexico, and Vic Morris in the United Kingdom. Sitting in a meeting with this very bright, very verbal group of individuals about what the company should be doing in the future with our database software was always a challenging experience because eventually I would have to decide who was right, what we were going to do, etc. I must say it was fun watching and listening to them go at it.

Our very small technical development group was made up of gifted people such as Bob Goldman, Ron McKinney, Don Heitzman, Nick Rini, Dave Litwack, Bill Casey, and Tom Nelson, who had never built database products before. In fact, Bill Casey and Tom Nelson weren't even experienced with IBM computers when they joined the company. They were Honeywell programmers at American Mutual Insurance Company when we hired them, thanks to Tom Meurer's initial contact with Bill who then recruited Tom. My gut feeling was that they were very smart and would be far more valuable employees if given six months to come up to speed than the other, more experienced

IBM candidates at the time. It didn't take them six months. It only took three days, and they were already ahead of the curve and producing results.

As time went by, and the company grew, it saddened me to think we weren't hiring these kind of potential superstars any more. The reason is that these candidates would never get by the 3–5 year experience requirement of a typical personnel department. This is the well-intentioned system at work. At the time, all our accomplishments didn't seem like a big deal to us; it was just the way we did things. I do know we were all impressed when Dr. Bill Linn joined us from Norfolk & Southern Railroad in Atlanta. He was a bona fide Ph.D. in computer sciences from the University of Michigan, a first for us.

Often, we needed someone to take on some new and important responsibility, and I would look around for someone in the company who just might have the potential to do it. It was very satisfying to recognize such individuals and give them major responsibilities that could often be way out of their traditional jobs, and to watch them grow in the all-important confidence factor in as little as six months. It would often be an amazing transition for they could now handle anything. For example. I once asked my assistant, Martha Burnham, to take over responsibility for the company's very important User Week when it was obvious it was in trouble and we had very little time left. She had never done anything like it before. It meant hosting 3,000 people for a week in Las Vegas, registration, etc., for 100 education courses, a business office, and much more. She made it a big success. Next, she went off to open our Singapore office. I am pleased to say she is still my assistant, as well as for my wife, Diddy, and has done many such things for us over the years. All of these employees, without exception, would say that the company was the best company that they ever worked for.

I can say from first-hand experience that it's very enjoyable when everyone in a company is on the same page, pulling together, and encouraged to do business the way they want to, which is with integrity. It's also great when your people can develop state-of-the-art technical products, and you have people that know how to sell them while being supported with great customer references for support, and sophisticated product positioning. This really puts the competition on the defensive. That's what we did better than anyone for more than ten years. They were the halcyon days, as I once explained at a somewhat puzzled employee meeting. They thought every company worked this way. However, I knew it wouldn't go on forever. I see many similarities in how we did things with how the computer industry pioneers operated. Find the best people you can, ones you can trust, give them lots of responsibilities to get things done, but support them in every way you can to help them succeed. That's how the computer industry was created. That's how my company worked.

AN INTERVIEW WITH

Photo courtesy of Sapers & Wallack, Inc.

John Cullinane

Conducted by
Jeffrey R. Yost
July 29, 2003
Boston, Massachusetts

purl.umn.edu/107237

Yost: This is Jeffrey Yost of the Charles Babbage Institute and I'm here today with John Cullinane, in his office in Boston, Massachusetts. John can you begin by giving a brief description of where you were born and where you grew up?

Cullinane: I was born a couple miles from here, in Arlington, Massachusetts. While my parents were immigrants who came here in 1929 from Ireland, I had a traditional suburban experience of any young American. With regard to computers, I first came in contact with them as a co-op student at Northeastern University when I was assigned to Arthur D. Little, Inc. (ADL), the premier industrial consulting firm of its time. Around 1955, ADL installed a Burroughs 205, one of the first commercially available computers in the United States. My office happened to be located right next to the computer so I could see all those flashing lights and buttons of an "electronic brain." It was very intriguing. I remember my boss, who was head of the finance department, having a meeting about the computer and saying everybody wouldn't get fired when the computer arrived, they just wouldn't be replaced when they left. That will give you a sense of the naiveté in the 1950's. However, when I graduated they offered me a job to run the computer, but I had to learn to do it all on the fly. That's how I learned what computers did; what holes in the punch cards meant. The computer was used to support ADL's data processing department, but also those of its operations research department members, such as George Kimball who worked upstairs.

This computer experience led to a sales trainee job in Boston with a firm called CEIR, the Corporation for Economic and Industrial Research, which was the first computer services company to have a public offering. Within a year they made me a salesman, then sales manager, then Center Director. The center featured a large-scale IBM 7090 computer plus consulting services in linear programming, PERT/CPM, electric utility applications, etc. It was very enjoyable meeting with clients and prospects, along with our experts, discussing their problems and how computers could help solve them. It was an incredible education. However, CEIR was losing $50,000 per month when I took over the Boston center. Within a year I had it making $50,000 per month profit. CEIR also provided computer time to Lincoln Lab, MIT, Harvard, and many other organizations with its IBM 7090 computer. Outside of AVCO Wilmington and GE in Lynn, it was the only one available in the Boston area. It was a batch operation at a time when they were working on timesharing systems at MIT, Lincoln Lab, and BBN. I moved the operations from a bad location in Boston to Fresh Pond Parkway in Cambridge, half way between Boston and Route 128 our two major sources of business. We were within walking distance of BBN, Arthur D. Little, and many other firms.

Then I joined a firm called Philip Hankins & Company (PHI) as a Vice President of marketing because he offered 5% equity in the company. I knew by then that equity was the only way to make significant money with a company. They did traditional consulting and programming for clients such as computer companies. It was there that I got the idea to treat software as a product. We had built a number of generalized payroll systems for banks, and we kept overrunning the contracts. We were just finishing a payroll system for $35,000 for Marine Midland Banks in Buffalo when I got a call from the First National State Bank of New Jersey. They were interested in having a generalized payroll system developed, and they had exactly the same computer system as did Marine Midland Banks, a GE 415, six tape system. The thought occurred to me, why don't we sell them the one we were just finishing for Marine Midland? Then the question arose of who owns it? You have to remember IP issues were all new. I concluded that Marine Midland owned it so I proposed to them that we could sell and support the product and pay them a royalty. They agreed. I priced the system at $20,000 dollars with a royalty for them of $4,000 dollars. The First National State Bank of New Jersey was the first buyer of the PHI payroll system. They were up and running payrolls within two weeks with just ten man days of effort on our part, and they had a much better system than they ever imagined getting, that worked, was documented, and at the low cost of $20,000. They were so pleased that they paid the invoice right away.

This sale was almost all profit with no client headaches. It made a big impact on me. This was the way to do business. I felt that there had to be a business in treating software as a product, but I wasn't prepared at that moment to form a company because I didn't have the confidence or experience to do so.

Yost: Do you remember what year this was?

Cullinane: This would have been in the 1965 time frame. Then I joined Auerbach Corporation in 1966, which was a famous consulting firm.

Yost: We actually have their records at CBI.

Cullinane: Oh do you? Auerbach was a high level computer consulting business, including database. I was recruited to open up the Boston office. We were budgeted to lose $20,000 in the first six months; we made $20,000 profit—a swing of $40,000. I was selected to receive an outstanding performance award. The award turned out to be $500, payable over three years. That's what pushed me over the line to form a company to specialize in software as a product. I raised $480,000 in November of 1968 on Wall Street to start Cullinane Corporation.

Yost: Prior to seeking the venture capital, you got non-binding letters?

Cullinane: Yes, this is critically important. To this day I've used this concept many times. I asked vice-presidents of information systems, such as George Rockwell at State Street Bank in Boston, to give me non-binding letters of intent on his corporate stationery. All he was committing to was that if software products were available from my company, he would take a look at them, nothing more. I learned that it's very, very important to test the marketplace with an idea. It's very easy in a room like this to think that an idea is great. But when you're in the marketplace there's always incredible competition, you have to test it somehow. If you can get prospects to sign these non-binding letters of intent and include them as part of the financial proposal, they can be the most important thing in the financial package. It's really all the investment bankers looked at in my proposal. It really works. I can guarantee you that I can take 80% of any letters of intent to the bank. When someone signs that letter of intent, it's a psychological going over the line. So that was just a technique that worked out, and has to this day.

· · ·

Yost: In 1969, IBM announced its unbundling decision to be implemented the following year. What impact did this have on you and your idea of the software business? How did it define or redefine opportunities for software products?

Cullinane: There's a sort of two-tier answer to that question. One, is that it legitimized the business. The message from IBM was that buying software as a product separate from hardware was a reasonable and legitimate thing to do. But, you still have to have the products to sell them.

Yost: Do you remember what year this was?

Cullinane: It might have been the fall of 1969 or 1970. I must say our timing was pretty good.

Yost: So this is a time when there's a major recession.

Cullinane: Yes, in 1969 it was similar to what happened to the e-commerce business a couple years ago. Stocks plummeted. No money. Timesharing of that era was what e-commerce was of the recent era. Investors [had] poured money into timesharing companies, and the whole thing was a disaster. So everything shut down in 1969 and there was no money available, no refunding, you're on your own, and you had to figure your way out of this thing. I can't over dramatize it, because that's the way it was. I thought we were going under in six months. So I had to cut staff from nine people to five. I ended up with five people who agreed with me that we were in business to satisfy the needs of our clients. We turned out to be more efficient with five people than our original nine—this is the theory of unanticipated result again.

However, key was the EDP Auditor version of our Culprit report generator product. I noticed that some of our customers were using Culprit for auditing purposes. But I didn't know what an audit software package did. I found a brochure from Arthur Anderson and learned that Culprit matched perfectly with what audit software should do. So I created a new version of Culprit called EDP Auditor. It was really Culprit with a different name. But we also created a library of audit routines that we wrote in Culprit, statistical sampling, verification notices, etc. I formed an EDP users group, the first ever. We provided auditors separate training geared to non-programmers. We provided them separate technical support to make them independent of data processing; this gave them integrity of the audit, which was hugely important to them. This gave us another product that we sold to banks and other financial organizations, but through a different window. So, we would sell EDP Auditor to the auditing department for $15,000 and they would produce results so impressive that the chief financial officers would be saying to the data processing people, how come these guys in auditing can do in three days what you guys say will take three months to do? What's the story? Thus, the auditors would so embarrass the data processing departments that they would buy the Culprit version. What we couldn't sell many of at $10,000 we were now selling many of at $20,000. It's really as simple as that.

• • •

Yost: How did you get involved with IDMS?

Cullinane: I was on a panel at a conference. A month or two later I was on a plane with one of the panel members, and he said that he had recommended me to BF Goodrich. By that time, I was not interested in selling other people's products; we had turned the corner with our own products. But I just like to follow up on things, so I called BF Goodrich. They said they hired a consulting firm in New York called Seligman, Von Simpson to help them decide. Since they had just recommended us to an EDP Auditor prospect, I called Naomi Seligman and, after some debate, she eventually included us in their study.

IDMS originally was developed at GE as IDS by Charlie Bachman. GE sold a computer to BF Goodrich with IDS on it, and IBM sold it a 360. BF Goodrich, as part of the deal with GE, got rights to convert IDS to IBM's computers, add whatever enhancements it wanted, and own it. So that's what they did, and they in turn named it IDMS. It wasn't like they just took this product called IDS and that was it. They were on the CODASYL (Conference on Data Systems Languages) Committee, and they added many features in the process. They also used it extensively, so it was an extremely solid system. When we got it, I think it had about 30,000 lines of code; by the time we finished, it was about 3 million. We spent millions and millions on enhancement of products. The beauty of IDMS was that it was absolutely proven, it would run for months without a bug; so that was extremely helpful. I saw it as a fundamental product that gave us a long term strategy because it all started with a database.

Now we could add different products to it, including our Culprit report generator and the EDP Auditor software. Then we had developed an online query system, and our own communications capability, IDMS/DC, our application development facility ADS ONLINE, etc. Once we had developed the applications development facility, we were able to acquire well-known batch applications and re-write them and make them state-of-the-art online. So we started out as a little $1,500 product company and, by the mid-1980's, you could buy a fully integrated product line for $3.5 million.

Yost: CODASYL came out with a database standard in the middle 1970's. Was IDMS the first product that responded to this standard, and how important was that?

Cullinane: That was very important at the time because that's how we initially sold it. We used, again, the seminar approach. We promoted IDMS as the first CODASYL compliant database management system for IBM computers. It worked well with certain prospects.

• • •

Yost: Can you describe the decision to take your firm public, and what you saw as the opportunities and risks of doing so at the time.

Cullinane: The company was founded on the premise of going public. We had investors who owned 40% of the company. An IPO was always the potential payback for them, for myself, and my employees. One of our board members, Joe McNay, was very knowledgeable in the financial arena and knew Hambrecht & Quist (H&Q) of San Francisco, the premier underwriter of high tech stocks of that era. We would be the first software company that Hambrecht & Quist ever took public. This would be in August of 1978. In 1977, I sold some personal shares to Greylock Management making my company its first software investment because these IPO's were clubs. There was great interest in the industry in it because we were the first software products company that ever went public—what we did and how we did it was going to set the tone for the others that were in the wings in the years to come. H&Q arranged a road show, which was fascinating in itself because I had never done anything like it before. I remember being in San Francisco at a large room in the Bank of America building on the 52nd story presenting to a standing room only crowd. To my right were these big plate glass windows, and I could look down over the Golden Gate Bridge and the fog, but I also could see Alcatraz.

So we went public in August of 1978 at $20 per share and it went to $28 on the first day. Then a couple months later it was down to $13. But the critical moment was in January 1979. IBM announced that they had a new computer, the 4300 Series, and IDMS didn't run on it, and that all IBM applications in the future would be based on IMS/DL-1. Therefore, every prospect, every customer, was going to be out of the mainstream of IBM application development in the future. This was a big problem, the worst of the worst. We had only been public two quarters, and they were just hitting us right between the eyes. Our fiscal year ended on April 30, and I had to move really, really fast or this was going to be big trouble. First, Bob Goldman, my Chief Technical Officer at the time, got IDMS running on the 4300 series in one day. It only required changing one instruction. Then, I went to New Jersey with Bob to meet with customers and prospects to stem the tide. It became obvious that we had to do something with IDMS and IMS/DL-1. So we committed on the spot to create an IMS escape facility. In other words, if IBM ever came along with applications based on IMS, we had an interface that would allow any company to use those applications with IDMS.

When we went to the Newark airport that night, it was pouring rain, things were locked up in Boston. I said, I'm not going to sit in this plane, Bob do you want to come with me? Bob said, no I'll stay here. So, I rented a car and drove home. I don't remember driving from Newark to New Haven, literally, I was thinking so intensely. Then it hit me in New Haven: I knew how to position IDMS vs. IMS. We had created an IDMS Active Data Dictionary in response to our customers' needs. The key was moving the competitive focus from database to the dictionary. That was the solution. The light went on.

I remember going to Fort Wayne, Indiana, with Bob shortly afterwards to meet with some prospect. On the way back we put together a slide presentation in rough form. This was Wednesday, on Thursday we gave it to our media expert, Logan Smith, by Monday he created a beautiful slide presentation of "IDMS-5—The First Active Dictionary-Driven Database Management System." I immediately sent copies to all our regional managers, telling them that they were to use this presentation. A week or two later, I called a regional manager in Chicago, Andrew "Flip" Filipowski, and he said, "Well, we're using some of it." I said, "Wait a minute, I didn't put this together so you could use some of it." Then I composed the only "Thou Shalt" memo I've ever written: "Thou shalt use this presentation exactly the way it is."

What really worked were the seminars Bob Goldman, Frank Chisholm, Vice President of Sales, and I did around the United States for customers and prospects using this slide presentation. When they saw how effective it was, all our sales people bought into it as well. That's when I first learned that selling a sales force is a lot harder than selling customers. It's very difficult to convince sales people to do things differently. As a result, we were able to turn the situation around and unlock those prospects and make our numbers by our April 30 fiscal year end, an incredible accomplishment. We continued to grow at a rate of 50% in sales and earnings. We used to lose a lot to IBM, but now with this new pitch, we went from losing four-out-of-five to winning four-out-of-five. Now we knew how to take IBM on. For example, at an executive presentation we would say to a CEO, "The difference between our software and IBM's is that ours all works together, it's all driven by the dictionary." Then we'd explain why it was so important. They would respond by saying "You mean to say that IBM's doesn't?" We would say, "Yes, just ask them when they come in." So when IBM would come in, they would ask them if their software was dictionary-driven. IBM would have to say no. You're saying your database system components don't work together? Again, no. In other words, we would give them the ammunition. It worked because it was true and they loved holding IBM's feet to the fire.

IBM just made us better by trying to kill us. We went from a nice little software company doing very well on the fringes, to now taking on IBM head-to-head, and doing it extremely well. At the same time, we were fighting wars with Cincom, Adabas, and ADR, and also doing very well. Adabas was a different product with focus on queries. IDMS is really a transaction oriented, run your business, high performance system. It was not originally designed for queries but DBMS vendors were always adding various competing capabilities.

• • •

Yost: When you were marketing this, to what level of the company were you taking it?

Cullinane: That's a very interesting question, because if you go back to our earliest days we were selling to technicians, systems analysts, etc. However, we were now getting to the point where we were submitting million dollar proposals, but the CIOs couldn't make the decision to buy. So you would see all this great interest and then, suddenly, nothing, no decisions. Then, I chanced to say to a CIO from a big Boston company, do you think the CEO of your company would be willing to come and listen to a presentation by me on "Information Strategies of the 80's and 90's" done on a CEO-to-CEO basis minus all the vernacular of the computer business? He said, yes, I think so. In fact, he brought his CEO to our headquarters, along with the other top VPs in his company. At the end of the presentation the CEO asked, how much does this software cost, anyhow? I said $1 million. It was like nothing to the CEO because the plant, etc., it was to control might cost $200 million. He was amazed that it cost so little. Also, we had interfaced a system from Computer Pictures that would present information from an IDMS database for CEOs using a touch sensitive screen accessing data from their company's annual reports. It was a very impressive example of interactive computing.

Yost: Was this with IDMS or the dictionary-driven version?

Cullinane: This was the whole system, including applications such as MRP and General Ledger. In some cases, it might be just strictly database. Each CEO would fly into an airport which was ten minutes from our offices. We would have a limo pick them up, and they'd arrive by ten. It was always the same. They wanted to have a working lunch with sandwiches in our very nice boardroom designed by my wife, Diddy, and leave by two. We always got the business.

Yost: In 1983 you were the first software products company to be listed on the New York Stock Exchange.

Cullinane: That's correct.

Yost: Can you discuss the decision to be listed and how this impacted the company?

Cullinane: That was pretty simple, it's different today, but in those days your stock couldn't be purchased by a large segment of the community, mutual funds, pension funds, if you were not listed on the New York Stock Exchange. So by being there it opened up lots of buying power for our stock; that's the rationale for that.

Yost: Was it traded over the counter previously?

Cullinane: Yes, that's correct, it was NASDAQ, but going on the NYSE was a big deal. We were located next to a rail station on Route 128; we rented a club car, got all the board members and their wives, and took them to New York. The next day we went on the floor of the New York Stock Exchange. As a new listing there's a whole thing they do. The first trade of the day is in your stock. We saw a hundred Cullinane shares bought in London go across the world to all other exchanges, so that is why it was a big deal.

Yost: Was there a need to have a far greater focus on quarterly results after the company went on the NYSE? Can you describe how that changed management of the company?

Cullinane: It does change management, they don't like to admit it, but it does. And don't forget, we had twenty-nine quarters in a row where sales and earnings were in excess of 50%—that's more than seven years, so that's a pretty long run. We did it every quarter. But the focus does get to, "Are we meeting the numbers?" You start every quarter with a clean slate in the software products business. It's not like you are in the service business and you're trying to increase sales by 10% or 5%, and you know you have a lock on a certain amount of business. In the software products business, you play this Russian roulette every quarter. Meeting those numbers becomes a way of life. Depending upon the quarters and time of year, some are easy and some you have too much business, and others you're fighting to get it up to the last day. It's a tough row to hoe and it does change the focus, as the risk gets bigger and bigger.

Yost: Was it less enjoyable for you to run the company?

Cullinane: It's an awful way to run the business; you just get through one quarter and then two weeks later . . . it's no fun.

Yost: Around this time you also changed the name of the company. You were beginning to scale back on your involvement?

Cullinane: You always have an official rationale of why you do things, and there's probably other things you never acknowledge or admit. I had been in the software business for almost 25 years, and I'd done it all. Also, I'd read that if entrepreneurs stay around too long, they run into trouble. So I made Bob Goldman President and I became Chairman of the Board. I changed the name from Cullinane to Cullinet, because I wanted to re-capture my name. I didn't want someone else in control of my name in the years to come that I didn't have any influence over. I thought, "net" because everything was going to work together in the future, I wasn't thinking "Internet" per-se. But intuitively I could see that we were linking our customers, we could do it all.

Yost: I noticed from your book a lot of individuals that were at your company went on to other companies.

Cullinane: Yes, many went on to form their own companies and become very successful. They all say Cullinane Corporation was the best company they ever worked for.

Yost: You have since devoted your energies to running a venture capital enterprise with a goal of assisting IT business development in Ireland. Can you discuss that a little bit?

Cullinane: Well, I've really done lots of different things. Investment in companies is just not really a big thing, but an important one. I've spent a lot of time creating the Boston Public Library Foundation, which was twelve years ago. It has now raised $16 million. I've spent a lot of time in promoting Irish high-tech in the United States, on a pro-bono basis. I've spent a lot of time advising Northern Ireland in how to create jobs and venture capital, with some success. Jobs definitely help the peace process. I've spent a lot of time in the last couple years using Northern Ireland as a role model for peace in the Middle East.

So if you look at what I've done in the past ten or twelve years, a lot of it is using my entrepreneurial background on community related activities. I get a great sense of satisfaction that you can really impact something such as a library, or peace in Northern Ireland. If I sound more enthusiastic about that than selling software, well, so be it. I would close by saying, when I started out a lot of people said you have to cut corners to succeed in business. It turns out, integrity in business is not a burden, it's a huge asset. Everybody likes to do business with people who treat them fairly and honestly, including when there is a problem and they need help.

Yost: Your discussion of the CEO as Chief Customer Advocate was very interesting.

Cullinane: Yes, in retrospect, that's what I was. It was a daily battle trying to get the customer what he, or she wanted, and make money at it. I remember buying my wife a piano for Christmas the first year we finally made a profit, and I gave myself my first bonus. The thought occurred to me—all I have to do is to keep focused on treating customers right and they will pay my mortgage, my car payments, my kids' tuitions, presents for my wife, etc. This seemed like a really good deal to me.

Yost: Yes, this has been terrific, I greatly appreciate you taking the time to speak with me this morning.

Cullinane: Well, thanks I'm glad that you are doing these interviews because there is so little history of the software industry.

Summary

America, like every organization, needs a way to get around the "system" of entrenched special interests at all levels if it is to prosper. It's a constant battle. But, as the saying goes, recognizing a problem is half the battle. I believe there is a message in how to navigate this "system" for our political, academic, and industry leaders, and others in the management food chain, in the experiences of the pioneers of the computer industry that led to interactive computing. These leaders proved democracy does work and can solve problems. They were entrepreneurs without even realizing it.

It's really no different today. Entrepreneurs are trying to do it again. For example, Hansjörg Wyss, a hugely successful medical devices entrepreneur, is trying to help new companies cope with "crossing the valley of death" in the healthcare industry. It's called that because it's so difficult for healthcare startups to succeed. He founded the Wyss Institute, a joint venture with Harvard, a new model that encourages cross-discipline bioengineering-inspired research that addresses specific problems from idea to successful ventures. To do so will require matching any new venture with sales opportunities at participating hospitals so it can generate sales and make money. It is still a risky way of crossing the "valley of death," but one worth the effort. To help the process, Mr. Wyss gave Harvard the largest gift in its history to underwrite it, a sort of private sector DARPA. Most importantly, he understands America's healthcare system and what's necessary to get around it. It's this new kind of thinking to which I am referring. Entrenched special interests control the system. In some cases, it's a few companies that sell billion dollar deals to hospitals. It is one powerful "system."

Getting around the communications industry was an incredibly important example of its time. This would be the Bell System, including AT&T and the Baby Bells. This was the "system." Larry Roberts makes the extent of this competition with AT&T clear in his oral history. So does Sam Wyly. Thanks to Larry Roberts, ARPA funds were available for Robert Kahn and Vinton Cerf, and others, to invent and implement packet switching. Now computers could talk to each other and ARPANET was possible, and this led to the Internet. I firmly believe that if AT&T was still in control there would be no Internet today.

Incredibly, one finds Ivan Sutherland, the father of computer graphics, along with his fellow scientist and wife, Marly Roncken, doing battle with the America computer chip industry in the same way. The industry likes synchronous chips, according to Ivan, because that's what they have always made, and besides, it's very expensive to change. Ivan and Marly are trying to do at Portland State University with their Asynchronous Research Center (ARC) what the Wyss Institute is doing at Harvard, only without the same money. They believe synchronous chips can't meet the performance requirements of the next generation of computers. They would have to break the laws of physics as expressed by Albert Einstein to do so. But at ARC they are leading a small, but very smart, group of very dedicated young people in how to create asynchronous chips to get around the chip industry so that America will not lose its leadership in computer technology.

The purpose of this book is to introduce the idea that the computer industry pioneers have much to offer America as a model for getting things done in a complex environment, and might even be able to save America's democracy in the process. It could even be a "Domestic DARPA." Having spent time as a Fellow at the since-named Mossavar-Rahmani Center for Business and Government, John F. Kennedy School of Government, Harvard University, I know how the idea system often works. I watched and listened as great economists of the School, such as Center Director John Dunlop, Ray Vernon, John Meyer, and others debated the major issues of the day, such as de-regulation, global warming, etc., and what would work and what wouldn't based on the data analysis of the respective positions. From this analysis and debates could come papers that could have enormous impact on our society, such as the de-regulation of the electric power industry. Thus, someone in academia might read this book, or listen to an interview regarding it, and become intrigued by the DARPA idea. It, in turn, might spark a research article on the subject of "Would a Domestic DARPA Work?" or some other title. The article might even catch the eye of someone running for President, or a member of his, or her, staff. This is how a domestic DARPA could become a major theme in a candidate's campaign. The candidate looks smart because he, or she, has a new and imaginative idea on how to solve America's problems. The idea gets traction and is discussed on talk shows as experts from government, academia, and industry are asked to comment on its merits. Then, if the candidate gets elected, a "Domestic DARPA" becomes a major focus of the President's administration and gets implemented. Now, our major problems are being addressed in a "new" way that has been proven to work. It's nothing new, really. This has happened many times before. Some might ask, how did this new thinking come about? Others might say it originated with an Internet search of a computer industry pioneer named Richard Bloch. I think he would like that. He thought big.

Author's Biography

John Cullinane

Photo Courtesy of Craig Bailey/
Northeastern University

John Cullinane first came in contact with computers in the 1950's as a co-op student at Arthur D. Little, Inc., the premier industrial consulting firm of its era. This led to jobs with companies such as CEIR, Inc., Philip Hankins & Co., and Auerbach Corporation. At Philip Hankins & Co., he learned the inherent potential in selling software as a product, which sparked the idea for a new venture. Eventually, he would form the first company to specialize in selling software as a product with particular focus on database software as the foundation for many interactive computer systems for industry, government, and academia. At the time industry experts said it couldn't be done, others had failed, etc. However, Cullinane Corporation would go on to become the first successful software products company in the computer industry and set the stage for other software companies to follow. In the process, it would be a major factor in creating the industry as it exists today.

John is also a social entrepreneur, having created the Boston Public Library Foundation, he was the first president of the John F. Kennedy Library Foundation, and founding Chairman of the Massachusetts Technology Leadership Council, among others.

As a graduate of Northeastern University he has also been the recipient of many awards and honorary degrees. For example, he received the first honorary degree ever awarded outside the island of Ireland by the University of Ulster for his efforts in promoting peace in Northern Ireland through jobs.

John, as a Fellow at the Center for Business and Government, John F. Kennedy School of Government, Harvard University, wrote the *Entrepreneur's Survival Guide—101 Tips for Managing in Good Times and Bad* and also *Widows and Orphans—A Walk Down Wall Street from the Perspective of a High Tech Entrepreneur.* More information regarding these publications can be found by accessing his portal at www .cullinaneentrepeneurship.com.